Global South Asia on Screen

Global South Asia on Screen

John Hutnyk

AAKAR

Global South Asia on Screen
John Hutnyk

Published by Bloomsbury Academic, 2018
First Indian Edition 2019

ISBN 978-93-5002-592-5

Published by
AAKAR BOOKS
28 E Pocket IV, Mayur Vihar Phase I
Delhi 110 091
aakarbooks@gmail.com
www.aakarbooks.com

Printed at
Sapra Brothers, Noida

To the late Biren Das Sharma.
He got me into Bengali films, and I had promised him this volume.
He is very much missed.

Contents

Acknowledgements

For this study, I read new and varied work by scholars and friends such as Abhijit Roy, Moinak Biswas, Anjali Gera Roy, Raminder Kaur, Virinder Kalra, Rajinder Dudrah, Amit Rai, Sanjay Sharma, Ravi Vasudevan, Ravi Sundaram, Amitava Kumar, Biju Mathew, Vijay Prashad, Rosie Thomas and many others. In particular, I focused upon and learnt much from the noted works of four scholars: M. Madhava Prasad, Ashish Rajadhyaksha, Tejaswini Niranjana and Arvind Rajagopal. While they are not responsible for what I write, their collective work made the old media studies look obsolete. It was their fresh look at film, television, and screen cultures in general and the political contextualization offered by these scholars in particular that hit me as an imperative. In the afterglow of their different contributions – though glossing their ideas cannot make them agree by any means – extending beyond the conventions of screen studies to encompass musicology, sociology, political economy and cultural studies made it possible to conclude that the cinema–television conjunction today is a fully articulated geopolitical medium. The faults and limitations of this assessment are of course mine. Nevertheless, Abhijit Roy has nurtured this book, much more than he knows. Also Klaus-Peter Koepping, Chandrika Parmar, Gayatri Chakravorty Spivak, Joel McKim, Aparajita De, Bhaskar Mukhopadhyay, Scott McQuire, Shiv Vishvanathan, Amitava Ganguly, Amites Mukhopadhyay, Ursula Rao, Meeta Jha, Royona Mitra, Prarthana Purkayastha, Peter Phipps, Ulki Goswami, Claire Reddleman, Lara Choksey, Allen Chun, Joanna Figiel, Theresa Mikuriya, Devina Gupta and Camille Barbagallo all made important contributions, as did the incredibly generous Dorothea Schaefter. Babu at Foreign Publishers Agency kept me supplied, as did Seagull. Paramita Brahmachari did the art with care and inspiration. Liza Thompson, Susan Krogulski, Erin Duffy and Katie Gallof at Bloomsbury had faith. The copyediting and layout is by Rohini Krishnan and Shyam Sunder. Finally, although this book is not wholly her fault, Sophie Fuggle is a great writing partner, critic and mother of even greater children, and the light of my life: her involvement is second only to that of the kids, who I go on about too much and who send me to 'do your work' only after bedtime stories about elephants and songs about billabongs.

non-synonyms in 'the non-West', or 'the periphery', or 'developing nations' has a host of flaws as well, and if there are conceptual nuances that need to be taken into account, those who use such terminology come quickly to see the limitations and the need for a work around. My work around is to insist that it is a good thing that the terms require introspection, though if that is all they provide, that too is inadequate. The introspection must also be there for the last two words of the title. These are not afterthoughts or a subtitle; they name very well the focus of the book which is to do with filmed media in any of its formats *on screen*, but that focus too is a challenge. There is an element of filtering in screening, necessary but also selective-ideological. We have to look but we are told where to look. People used to look up at the cinema screen in the hall, not always in reverence, but to some degree in awe at the very idea of the movies. Increasingly the look is lowered, moving down. With the advent of television, and even more television on the computer screen, the gaze became more or less horizontal, and with the news, more and more about those who watched, at least for the powerful and celebrity elite who liked to see themselves on screen. The television then was in the corner of the living room, and the news presenter became a family friend. Sometimes it was even used to show home movies, the handy-cam plugged in for unedited footage. Later the news became entertainment, along with 'funniest home videos' that audiences sent in. Television was by then attached to the wall or the desk via computer, and while outside we still looked up at ads, increasingly we narrowed our eyes, squinting as both movies and news were reduced to miniature on digital devices, shown on the back of a chair in a plane, and carried in pockets and by hands, governed by the algorithm. The downward gaze of supremacy hovered over the images, but a democratization of broadcast was not yet in play.

Possibilities and reparations?

This book then is also about a possibility. Global South Asia might in turn be taken as the terrain of struggle over what sorts of representations and by consequence what sort of influences might flow through media production, circulation and its economies. If the structures of ownership and control are such that corporate management, government interference and academic convention remain locked, then a form of sub-imperialism internally, and neocolonialism by way of collaboration, is regrettably assured. That there is an alternative trajectory in the anti-colonial, anti-racist and class struggle politics of the Global South remains meaningful even in these times. Fostering an embattled tradition becomes an obligation, and for this reason, making films or television programmes, engaging in media debate, researching and writing the histories of media politics and its participants are necessary parts of their own social reproduction. Adequate funding would be wonderful for such projects, but the closure of investigative journalism in the press and open-ended research in the privatizing managerialist and vocational universities means this is a sequestered domain.

A massive labour of commentary exceeds the films: the efforts of publicists and copywriters, advertisers and agents, spin doctors, image makers and propagandists handling presenter 'talent' and bumbling personality national*ist* treasures, entire teams work behind the screens/scenes, bring us all versionings of 'Asia' in real time.[1] Yet, the work here – the network, the convolutions of the apparatus and its wiring, infrastructure, logistics, coordination, structure of production and transmission – is rendered transparent in a way that is not different from game show staging, in that even when shown, it remains invisible. Rajagopal says as much when he notes thus: 'Viewers may *know* that they are gathered and sold to advertisers, but they remain capable of acting *as if* they did not know this, and *as if* they thought they were free in their viewing behaviour' (2001: 335).

The metaphor of book-burning also runs throughout this text as a warning, and a marker that invokes an alternative to pogroms and destruction, the imperatives of opposition and the critique of orientalisms that are built for the reproduction of cultures and communities of resistance. This would be resistance to the 'post-colonial trajectory' where, as Kuan-Hsing Chen has it, following Fanon, the national bourgeoisie brings unsavoury outcomes and 'decolonization is followed by recolonization or neocolonization ... [if there] ... has been no critical reflection on decolonization' (2010: 63). This reflection on Global South Asia is one that begins by looking at changes in the regime of representation of South Asia that has roots in London and Washington; then tracks how this is exhibited in film and television first from the United Kingdom before moving to feature Nepal, India, Pakistan, Bangladesh and Sri Lanka; and finally focuses closely on particular Hindi, Punjabi, Bengali, Malayalam and Telugu films, all called *Mela*.

The chapters of the book follow recent and old films, street politics and literary debates, television and news documentary, and terror squads with cameras. This introduction offers some key ideas explaining the title, main concepts and context, and some warnings about what the book is not. The first chapter sets out an analytic trajectory in three main parts. The chapter first provides a detailed example that discusses one particular film, doing so in a way that anticipates the later analyses of an exotic and colonial-ideological framing of Global South Asia. To explain why certain modes of representation dominate portrayals of South Asia both in international and subcontinental screenings, I turn to an impressive body of work by a diverse group of writers which I have gathered together into what can be called Global South Asian film and television studies. The book is an introduction and appreciation of this body of work and an argument that explains why I think it should be central to all media studies. This is followed by another example to demonstrate, in its difference from the first, the tendency towards terror and horror in screening Global South Asia, and why this wider context matters so very much. The overall point of the project is to encourage enthusiastic and critical viewing of the films, and reading of the texts, in the interest of a reconfiguration of, well, everything.

In subsequent chapters there is a less satisfactory dark and critical side to the way Global South Asia appears on screen as a doubled image of unspeakable horror and lurid violent projection. There are chapters that take on the stereotypes and then go further to show that, even underneath the stereotypes, a more nuanced prejudice prevails. Crucially, the critique of orientalism is not just an inversion of orientation, but also an elaboration of resistance and the chance to see the implications of that resistance for all. Universalization does not make everything media, or everything Asian, nor is everything the same at the level of the globe. What can be learnt from the study of how media works in South Asia, its settlements and its diasporas, is a politics beyond media, in turn offering a chance to learn something new. Or at least there is an opportunity here, through reading new material from Global South Asian film and television studies, to break with the limiting conventions about how representation is nominally understood, and push forward something more than a politics of reparation, and conviviality if all goes well. Redress would have economic consequences won only through the mobilizations presently on screen.

If the mela might present that convivial festive alternative which forces consideration of Global South Asian media's universal significance, then it becomes less plausible to speak in a contained way of national film traditions – Bollywood, Hollywood or anyother*wood*. To do so would be to remain within a frame given as if regions were prescribed only upon maps drawn up in strategy rooms and bunkers. The attitude of this book must instead consider Global South Asia as an expansive, temporary, conceptual construct for thinking about images, identity, borders and stereotypes together, in a political-historical way. Such a project would attempt at least three things:

1. a critique of the geopolitical certitudes that allow national allegory to occlude and obscure the imbrication of Global South Asian film and television as the political expression of a tectonic shift in globality, where a new contest among opportunistic comprador classes and

caring migrant transnational communities, their survival and their settlement, contends for a convivial future;

2 a challenge to the cinema of muscular Hinduism, the propaganda of Wahhabi Islamism, militant Buddhism, nativism, identitarianism and similar movements with conservative and xenophobic consequences to be met without falling for 'the enemy of my enemy is my friend' collaborations with imperialism or the American-NATO invasions of Afghanistan, arms trade support of the Pakistani state, or so-called security state initiatives of India, or Sinhalese Sri Lanka, so that;

3 a ruthless critique addresses the dynamics of terrorism and exotica in a semiotic register to sustain both subcontinental, regional and settler-diasporic communities with social reproduction strategies oriented to the possible and emergent transformation of a radically politicized Europe and America.

As the projected alternative to a catastrophic global conjuncture – chaos, war, confusion – Global South Asia might also be a progressive horizon. This is a horizon where the varieties of South Asia, its regions and its diasporas, though never congealed as a coherent or unified construct, nevertheless meet and generate the intellectual movement to both maintain reproduction of an economic and forward-thinking solution at home, anywhere, and to settle every elsewhere with that same spirit. Of course it would be a very fine thing if this were sufficient to shift the so-called post-colonial trajectory towards a future where:

> the desire and energy to reexamine the legacy of the Euro-American [colonial and imperial] expansion [proceeds] at the level of theory and methodology, and simultaneously addresses the issue of how the historical responsibility of imperialism should be shouldered. (Chen 2010: 204)

Chen is aware that this movement, desire and energy are not yet in place and that Dipesh Chakrabarty's proposals (2000) would be insufficient, since 'provincializing Europe is a process that will loosen but not change the structure' (Chen 2010: 219). It is only a symptom of the corral of academic hesitation. More robust intellectual exchange and community building between constituent parts of really existing Global South Asia promise renewed possibilities, especially through the medium of transnational, regional and diasporic constituencies, potentially forcing resolution of conflicts and steps beyond mere talk of reparation. Even structural and economic posturing, mistrust and abuse through the vehicle of mass media are challenged where film and television sutures communities together in the 'for itself' mode. The massive investment in making and writing about whole schools of screen culture too often left to the margins of media studies – tellingly designated world or regional cinema, or ethnic television – repays the effort. Shah Rukh Khan stars. Nusrut does the soundtrack. India is bigger than Nepal, but not the Dalai Lama. Sri Lanka is smaller than Pakistan, but not MIA. Pakistan is not Bangladesh, but Mithun and Qawwali are huge in both Lahore and Birmingham.

Stereotype and exclusion or creative conviviality

Global South Asia as a marker for media studies and a political variant on the Global South in Asia is in no way monolithic and could not and would not aim to be hegemonic. With the extension into media and regional difference, Global South Asia is a conceptual demographic, beyond any non-exclusive and access all areas universal, as also would be, perhaps, pan-Africanism, gender, proletarianism, or *Jedi*. As opposition to the racist and colonial dispensation, it would break with racialized, propertied, white supremacy, and seek also to undo the comprador, at best, compromise position offered to those who hide in conformity from the reality of struggles. The point is not to unquestioningly celebrate the brokers, intermediaries, opium smugglers, tour guides, coconuts, radishes or mangoes that adhere to whatever middle strata opportunities are going, but it is not to demonize the necessity of such compromises either.

It is a matter of recognizing the institutional operations that have enacted exclusions in terms of money, knowledge, opportunities and resources. It means that reparations are overdue, and these are not only financial in the way the bill should be delivered. Perhaps it is a transformation of what counts as analysis in cultural studies, film, media studies, and in a project reconfigured as a wider socio-political critique in the context of militant racism, neocolonial warmongering, economic manoeuvring and institutional opportunistic manipulation.

In terms of misrepresentation, to the extent that this is considered sufficient, there could never be enough studies that deploy the work of Edward Said and Stuart Hall to critique the blatantly orientalist and class prejudiced representations of others that permeate throughout Euro-American mass media. It is well known that the propaganda machinery of the dominant works to represent only certain kinds of South Asia, in contrast to the many and mobilized really existing South Asias that would welcome more adequate understandings of complexity among its populations. Global Asia is uneven, but in global media and communication systems, stereotypes are flat. Bangladesh appears for Islam and politics, Pakistan for army and terror – the music of both countries informs the films they love.

It may still be that a tentative yet tenacious aspirational and effective radical political and convivial Left tradition in the Global South is nurtured in cultural forms, and in Global South Asia especially in music, literature and film. Tejaswini Niranjana makes a compelling case for this in comparative South to South work in her book on Trinidadian South Asia, though her point that 'in stressing similarities we might ignore real difference between specific societies in the South' (2006: 8) cannot be stressed enough. Her examination of the 'selective disavowal of certain kinds of "Indians" in the process of fashioning the new citizen of India as well as the new Indian in the world at large' (2006: 22) is important for this project, though recognizing that another disavowal operates today in the fashioning of South Asia as more than India, its regions and its diasporas. This is also seen in not so new – renovated, crusader – constructions such as those manifest in policies to bomb or ban 'Muslims', or 'Islam', in ways that cut across India, South Asia and globality in general. Over against the geopolitics of the War on Terror, Global South Asia might also be a temporary conceptual, metaphorical, oppositional and potential space that is not limited to the cartographic borders assumed in the shorthand production of a terror-industry and arms trade-oriented commodity called South Asia. The disavowal belongs to a dominant tendency that tends too often in advance to refer only to 'Indian' ownership of the subcontinent. This is exposed if we think not only of diaspora but also of the extent to which subcontinental connections historically exceed even the ocean conventionally named 'Indian'. Other names such as *Kala Pani* in Hindi, *Ratnākara* in Sanskrit, or the 'string of gems' are now appropriated by US and UK Chatham House ideologues as a 'string of pearls' to denounce Chinese economic aspirations for the area (see Marantidou 2014). The potential of Global South Asia relies on a more nuanced 'India' that now also recognizes the operation of a geocultural and systemic exclusion.

This book then is not a communications study or a study of soft power, nor media influence as such, nor the ways in which institutions and structures of South Asian media organization are beholden in some way to elsewhere. Not only a study of the radiation emanating from the image factories of Mumbai or Kolkata, although it is saturated with that influence, this work also locates Bromley and Handsworth as sites of significance for literary and musical diasporic homelands (Kureishi 1990, Sharma, Hutnyk and Sharma.1996). It is not biographical, and while the choices are idiosyncratic due to fairly random viewing and reading patterns, it is certainly not autobiographical. Neither is the study a psychosocial nor Lacanian analysis in the manner of Žižek, nor can it offer any affective Deleuzianisms, however effective these studies have been (with fieldwork, see Rai 2009); it is also not a gripping survey of Bangladeshi sex films (but see Hoek 2014 and Mukhopadhyay 2012). Instead, the present effort seeks to learn and stretch content as an experiment in comprehension and contextualization, hoping to multiply these rather than close down possibilities. Global South Asia here does not mean an uncritical celebration of the ever-bigger agglomeration of South Asia and its diasporas, or peoples. No book can map all that anyway. Neither is this book only about media, or only about regionalism or diaspora, or only about Bollywood – though it relies on many books that appear to be, seriously and justifiably, limited to something like that. Rather, in this book Global South Asia refers at one level to the politics of the circulation of images and representations – the political avatars of both actual nations and specific diasporas settled wherever they are *and* the circulation of stories about South Asians, globally, exotic, demonized, victims or benevolent, communists, communities, bureaucrats, movie stars and authors. Thus, circulating images act as ideological repositories for identification and stereotype. Rajagopal summed it up succinctly when he said, 'The geopolitical space called South Asia is being reconfigured, from Afghanistan to Sri Lanka, with locality and region becoming more specific and distinct even as they are more deeply subject to globalising forces' (2009). Indeed, this book exists as the result of an effort to seek out resources for the study of this 'space', while combating the processes that make movement of the image sometimes complicit with what makes it move. This means a modest attempt at political evaluation of resources that break the conventions of communications study and favour in turn the fundamental and cinematic experiences of street protest, anti-racist and anti-imperialist struggle. The focus is from a 'here', that takes a view supported by the migrations of the Global South, and with this makes for something other than merely a political economy that would fit in any of the good media and communications departments that grace our universities worldwide.

Rather than the too easy routine of simple description that differs from old-school orientalism only by being more or less well informed than previously, the new Global South Asian media scholarship inherits a critical theory that owes both to the heritage of the anti-colonial Left and is the residue of its demise. To bring categories to bear that unpack the exoticist, sensationalist or even self-orientalizing projections of contemporary media appearance, to identify and celebrate the renewal and relevance of self-organizing, piratical, corner-cutting media enthusiasm, to collect examples of autonomous theoretical development as well as of colloquial and vernacular resistance to global hegemony, is this inheritance. That it is squandered in a downgraded or underdeveloped organizational framework, where the formerly militant are now reliant on funding handouts within a matrix of second order institutional enclaves always under threat, is the predicament of an embattled and institutionalized politics. Bringing this potential and compromise into greater visibility is a risk and a necessity. When South Asia or its diasporas appear on mainstreamed television or cinema a strict code is enacted – terror or exotica – this has been observed and critiqued so often and for so long that the ongoing effort to shift such tropes is forlorn, and sometimes practitioners have embraced the necessary recognition of tokenism and stereotypes that won't budge. Of course there is something seriously wrong if the complicities cannot be displaced.

1

From *Viceroy's House* to the Situation Room

This chapter is necessarily less about films as such and much more framed by the idea, however tentative, of making an analysis that holds the co-constitution of here and there together. Forced into the historical context of capital, exploitation and war – as an unavoidable backstory – the first topic that imposes itself is an originary violence so that even films that are not violent have avoidance of violence as their mission. While it would not do to think of South Asia only in terms of violence, or even violence brought from Europe to crush the romantic idyll of pre-colonial times, or the non-violent resistance to that civilizational attack, or even the promises of a successful and shining future, these are all just too handy not to be fictions. Global South Asia on screen is not only a nightmare, but when British filmmakers and US presidents share – even as they would surely deny it – a militant ideological outlook from on high, there is cause for concern. This attempt to study Europe and South Asia as an intertwined and irrevocably interconnected formation is based upon long-term research on the history of accumulation using as example the East India Company and their activities in London, Kolkata and Canton, with contemporary resonances in port regeneration and gentrification projects. Within this, examples of films or television media that profess a different perspective are initially, and maybe inevitably, attractive, yet suspect. For example, the BBC television series *Taboo* (2017, dir. Nyholm and Engström) on the East India Company, written by Stephen Knight and Christopher Hardy, is a somewhat implausible example of how a story has at least two ends. The East India Company is portrayed as run, at this period if not always, as a personal fiefdom by a ruthless governor with no scruples, in cahoots with the back-room operatives of the palace, and guilty of corruption, murder and 'worse'. In the series, of course, the protagonist, a flawed and tattooed hero will give them their comeuppance, and the moral standing of British character need not be abandoned because the East India Company was a barrel of bad apples. If this sounds at all familiar, be assured from some perspectives what will be considered a whitewash is a way of selling product.

Raj revisionist films are a genre unto themselves, and *Viceroy's House* by the acclaimed British-Asian filmmaker Gurinder Chadha (2017) is an example worth extended consideration. Chadha's previous efforts such as *I'm British But...* (1990), *Bhaji on the Beach* (1993), *Bend It Like Beckham* (2002) and *Bride and Prejudice* (2004) form an enviable record for any director. She is now able to cast actors such as the iconic Om Puri, in one of his last ever roles. Chadha had known Puri for quite some time and spoke eloquently in honour of him in London at the London Asia Film Festival in March 2017. Puri's character leant gravitas to the film in ways to be discussed further. Also now Chadha could negotiate the use of prestigious shooting spaces unparalleled in her career. Part of the *Viceroy's House* film was shot at Rashtrapati Bhavan, the Viceroy's former palace and now official residence of the president of India. Shooting spaces were also found in period hotels and palaces in Jodhpur – themselves so atmospheric that a tour company has seen the tie-in potential: Cox and Kings has set up a guided vintage car tour to the filming locations, with a bonus side-visit to the Taj Mahal for good measure.

When a filmmaker of Chadha's stature turns to history, she enters an already existing deep catalogue of images such that emphases and interpretation become issues of evaluation. And the interpretations were many; the film was not everywhere well received. In a heated review, Fatima Bhutto was concerned that the very first scene 'opens to the sight of bowing, preening and scraping Indians at work on the lawns, carpets and marble floors that are to greet the last viceroy of colonised India' (2017). The hostile tone quickly drew a response from Chadha. Her film is a personal account, she said, and she had not wanted to show the fighting that characterizes partition in so many other renderings. This is an admirable non-violent move, except it is of course carried out with violence, an elision of a very large and considerable body of sensitive visual and textual work on partition. Scholarship and research programmes abound, as do other films. There is much readily available work by researchers such as Urvashi Butalia (2000) and Gyan Pandey (2002) alongside museums and commemorations in the Red Fort, Victoria Memorial and Raj Bhavan, plus a small private memorial at the Wagah border crossing, though curiously, until the launch in August 2017 of the Arts and Cultural Heritage Trust (TAACHT) of India 'Partition Museum' in Amritsar (see Bhatia 2017), there had been no significant permanent tribute to victims either in Pakistan, India or Bangladesh, prompting questions as to why partition does not excite the same remembrance as the Jewish holocaust (see Parmar 2003). There is much in terms of cultural production, plays, short stories, novels and indeed a number of other films, ranging from those that comment profoundly on the aftermath of partition, such as Ghatak's claustrophobic trilogy

Meghe Dhaka Tara (1960), *Komal Gandhar* (1961) and *Subarnarekha* (1962) through to popular versions such as *Gandhi* (1982, dir. Attenborough) where Ben Kingsley had the lead role, and the Canadian *Partition* (2007, dir. Sarin) where again non-South Asian actors played the main South Asian roles (particular well in the case of Chinese-Dutch Canadian Kirstin Kruek as Naseem, resplendent in the Mela sequence and love interest for British/Irish-Asian Jimi Mistry, as Gian). There are of course a number of documentaries and other commentaries making up a vast archive of texts and debate, with veritable armies of students over the decades poring through the archival remains of the India Office, now held at the British Library. *Viceroy's House* is not, to be sure, a documentary, and the criteria for assessment, and interpretation, must be different for imagined history even if many of Bhutto's criticisms demand attention. Chadha nevertheless claims to have contributed important 'new' facts.

In an interview with a *Guardian* journalist, Chadha is said to have made some significant discoveries:

> Studying the archives, Chadha came across confidential government documents that support a revisionist view of the lead-up to Indian independence, which was finally declared at the stroke of midnight on 15 August 1947. The British decision to draw a line through the whole of south Asia, creating two religiously defined new nations, was not entirely forced on them by the warring communities. It was, in fact, an idea hatched by Churchill during the war to protect British strategic interests. (Thorpe 2017).

The question of whether there was a Churchill-endorsed plan to keep control of the port city of Karachi away from the Soviet-friendly and socialist Nehru needs separate confirmation, and it is to Narendra Singh Sarila's book entitled *The Shadow of the Great Game* that Chadha directs us. The discovery then already belongs to Sarila, who was in a sense on the spot as an aide to Mountbatten. In a slippery slope of connections and coincidences, Chadha reveals that while Sarila was 'working on another book with an assistant in the British Library in 1997, he found documents that prove that early plans for the shape of a future Pakistan were kept hidden' (Chadha in Thorpe 2017). The version of this discovery offered by Sarila himself is worth consulting. The book's preface reads almost word for word the same as Chadha tells it, although in this version Sarila's assistant has disappeared:

> While researching on the Oriental and Indian collection of the British Library, London, in 1997, on another matter, I came across certain documents which revealed that the partition of India in August 1947 might not have been totally unconnected with the British concern that the Great Game between them and the USSR for acquiring influence in the area between

> Turkey and India was likely to recommence with even greater gusto after the Second World War ... Under the circumstances Britain could ill afford to lose control over the entire Indian subcontinent that had served as its military base in dominating the Indian Ocean area. (Sarila 2005: 9)

In addition

> a working relationship had been established between the British authorities in India and Jinnah during the Second World War and he was willing to cooperate with Britain on defence matters if Pakistan was created. (Sarila 2005: 10).

The preface then goes on to document various other collections and library sources, Sarila's role as ADC to Mountbatten in 1948, in that role his chance to catch 'glimpses of some of the players', and finally a sudden leap to the twenty-first century, the attack on the World Trade Centre in 2001, the Taliban in Afghanistan and the author's problematic view that 'many of the roots of Islamic terrorism sweeping the world today lie buried in the partition of India' (Sarila 2005: 11). Britain's crimes and Mountbatten's negligence notwithstanding, this final commentary on terrorism is an extraordinary claim on several counts that hardly need debate – it can be rebutted that what terrorism there is in the world today is not 'Islamic', nor in fact is terrorism 'sweeping the world', though certainly in 2005, as now, the scale of Western arms sales, shipment and deployment does count as terrifying. Certainly also a kind of pantomime paranoia tends to find terrors under every left luggage or freedom petition, but ultimately, if the chain of links that bind the Taliban to Osama bin Laden to Jamaat-i-Islam to Abdul Al Mawdudi to a Sharia-inspired war on unbelievers and to the US use of the Pakistani military to counter jihadis can be taken seriously as a framing context, then to suggest this also can simply 'lie buried' in partition must seem quite a long and detailed justification for a bit of cinema entertainment.

Separate from historical fidelities, it is also important to consider Chadha's film as a polemic open to interpretation and so evaluate the critical responses. Bhutto is not the only one to call out *Viceroy's House* as an anti-Muslim film, but has a strong point when listing the numerous scripted, imagined, incidents where Muslims initiate violence, whereas when the Hindus or Sikhs attack Muslims, the sympathetic point of contact character for the audience at least survives. Indeed, where Bhutto diagnoses a prejudice there is a strange double politic. She argues that we do not ever 'witness any violence on behalf of India's foreign rulers; they are serene and encouraging, weighed down with the heavy burden of soothing these wild, intemperate people'. However, all the riots are 'caused by Muslims', even as there are some 'brushes with symmetry', such as when Aalia's house is burnt down and we fear – soundtrack effects – that her blind father has been killed. But it is a false alarm: 'Don't worry! Her father didn't die; he's just sitting at a neighbour's house. No harm, no foul' (2017). Similarly, Aalia's father acts to save her from near certain death on the night train to Lahore – Chadha is correct to defend her film from Bhutto's criticism on this point at least – and while we hear no more of Om Puri, that Jeet's love interest has survived for Bhutto provides the essential cover for the otherwise barely credible denouement where Nehru is slapped in public. The slap was perhaps an actual event, but why has Chadha not instead recreated the equally fabled story where Nehru stops his taxi to save a Muslim tailor from a mob in Chandi Chowk (see Patel 2015)? In a telling contrast, the Mountbattens are portrayed as the epitome of selfless (practical, not Gandhian) service.

Against the charge that she has told the story from an anti-Muslim point of view, Chadha insists that 'everyone sees history through their own lens; some only see what they want to see. My film is my vision of the events leading up to India's partition.' Claiming the relativist interpretive high ground, she insists that she 'took infinite care to show that responsibility for the violence lay on all sides' and that her process was to 'share the script and the film with many Muslim, Hindu and Sikh academics and historians to ensure that the scenes I depicted were a fair and reasonable representation' (Chadha 2017). It might be churlish to then complain that 'some', if not all, academics and historians also see 'history through their own lens' and 'vision' – of course they do, just as much as do British-Asians. It is a well-taken point that interpretations are contested sites, but then it becomes difficult to let the significance of the sympathetic Muslim character Ali Rahim Noor played by Om Puri pass without noting a theme; he is blind throughout the film, a violent punishment inflicted in a British jail, and in the script. It might be interpretive license to look elsewhere in the cinema archive, but it is possible to see this theme in several films in South Asian cinema traditions. Recall for example that in *Sholay* Imam S'aab Rahim Chacha, played by communist freedom fighter A. K Hangal, is also without sight. The blinding of the most sympathetic senior political Muslim character in *Viceroy's House* is an instantiation of the film's opening epigraph. There is no subtlety in the textual declaration that 'History is written by the victors' – a phrase variously sourced by historians both to Niccoli Machiavelli and to Winston Churchill. In an interview about the film for *Desiblitz* (2017), Chadha says *Viceroy's House* is told from a unique British-Asian point of view. It is hard then to square this with comments about what *really* happened and victor-written history. What is sure is only that questions of interpretation are to the fore. The epigraph invites interpretive confusion, and a challenge. The phrase is also attributed, though of course not in the film, to Walter Benjamin, who uses it in the context of a more interesting assertion about all documents of culture simultaneously expressing barbarism. In the 'Theses on the Philosophy of History' he writes: 'with whom [do] the adherents of historicism actually empathize. The answer is inevitable: with the victor' ([1940] 1968: 256). Of course biased interpretations will find other sources. Om Puri may be blind, but I imagine a grumpy Churchill picking it up from surreptitious reading of a Left Labour Party newspaper – the phrase appears in a 1944 George Orwell article in *The Tribune*, though in this example the word 'Winners' is used instead of 'Victors'. Orwell was the paper's literary editor at the time.

These historical squibs and the frisson of controversy around Bhutto's article, besides getting the film discussed in a crowded marketplace, which is of course good publicity, are also welcome if they serve to raise important issues beyond film connoisseurship. The politics of interpretation between continents with a volatile historical charge is no small matter; so it is curious to see insistence that people be cautious when treating a personal history. Except that the history is only rhetorically personal, and in every sense nevertheless prejudiced and biased, exactly in its subtlety. For example, the film hints at a flirtation between Nehru and Edwina Mountbatten, but does not further exploit that sub-plot as Chadha considered it less important and anyway 'the relationship was consummated after this period' (Chadha in Thorpe 2017). Melodrama however insists on a love story and so Chadha prefers instead the Upstairs-Downstairs side-tale of the viceroy's valet, a Punjabi Hindu, having an unrequited romance with a Muslim girl, Ali Rahim Noor's daughter Aalia, who was promised to the driver of Jinnah's official vehicle. This displacement has many of the features of an often used plot device, such as that in Mira Nair's *Monsoon Wedding* (2001). In terms of overwriting sexuality onto class politics, it is unfortunate that in a discussion of *Monsoon Wedding*, Jigna Desai does not push further insightful comments made about the working-class roles, where:

> the figure of the domestic servant Alice is an incredibly rich site of analysis and investigation in relation to the issues of gender, sexuality, and political economy. The Christian Alice is depicted in primarily romantic terms. Her sweetness and simplicity render her an idealized and remote subject in relation to the other modern women … As the urban domestic worker, the film continually presents her from the perspective of someone else; unlike the other women whose subjectivities are established through intimate conversation with other women, family members, and their partners, Alice is observed almost entirely from the voyeuristic gaze modulated through Dubey. (2004: 214)

Unless they battle their way into the action, there are few examples of domestic servants granted a significant role or personality in popular cinema. Credit is due then to the key characters in the de facto 'main' sub-plot of *Viceroy's House*, and yet in this displacement, these key relationships are almost always identified from the perspective of someone else of rather more elevated class status, from which they are rendered as romantic, as fool or as sacrifice or forsaken.

The possibility of interpreting a film by opening up the subordinate characters for critical attention is a useful strategy. Spivak does this with Bertha Mason from Charlotte Bronte's *Jane Eyre,* discussed in *Critique of Postcolonial Reason* (1999). Considering the love story of the Mountbattens' servant however is high cliché standard in this respect, and in fact offers up a chain of substitutions that are revealingly selective. Picking up an incidental or seemingly inconsequential moment as a way to unpack the whole works to help understand the interpretive investments. Offering another nuance, the somewhat unsubtle but in need of explanation inter-title near the end of the film modestly refers to the 'director', without at that moment naming her but inserting her image. The notes explain that the director of *Viceroy's House* is someone with direct family experience in the tragedy of partition, in this case through a grandmother and a murdered aunt. Powerful and heartfelt, but it is a curious intervention in the film and it works, at least for this viewer, as a kind of subvention that softens the polemical effect of other moments, and especially the reveal of Sarila's secret Oriental and Indian Office 'found' documents. These documents, central to the duplicitous diplomacy narrative that has the unpleasant Jinnah character cutting a deal to create Pakistan as a buffer state, appear as a folder slapped on the table, passed among the key figures and studied by Mountbatten as a kind of final moment of realization that he had been the unwitting patsy of it all. In the film it seems as if everyone else was in on the secret anti-Soviet plan. Sarila's archival justification is reduced to a few lines on a stage prop, but the effect of the director stepping into the narrative in person is to affirm, through escalation since her personal involvement gives the intrigue the imprimatur or truth, that centuries of great game manoeuvres over Afghanistan are the context – and of course, substitution again, that the duplicity can be explained, via Sarila, as a topical and important directorial intervention. The intrigues of the film can contribute uniquely to understanding tactical approaches to Islam, Soviet history and diplomacy *while,* as allegory, questioning things like contemporary investment in the port at Karachi with its possible transport route from China to the sea, or the Russian annexation of Crimea as an access route via the Bosporus Strait to the Mediterranean.

The point about substitution and escalation is that in Chadha's film 'partition' becomes a tool for doing other things, and this is the case with many examples of overworked and overdetermined themes. This might be all well and good if the other parts of the narrative were built upon what had already been achieved in historical research and recording. Even better if the scholarship that exists in oral history and memory studies from the 1980s onwards could have been acknowledged. Exemplified by the work of aforementioned Butalia (2000), Pandey (2002) and others, this is material that, along with the many 'high politics' studies that go beyond the popular histories of Dominique Lapierre and Larry Collins (1975, 1983), deserves serious attention. Pakistani, Bangladeshi and Indian study on partition amounts to a vast literature and although also replete with interpretive variations, it is harsh indeed to be both ignored and to endure the suggestion that there were any 'victors' of partition who could write the history. Nevertheless, in a milieu where claims for the significance and relevance of one's effort is not only a publicity anecdote, it is probably only to be expected that astute commentators, directors and actors would make associations that stress the allegorical purchase of their work. *Viceroy's House* actors were no different in this regard when in publicity interviews the couple who play the star-crossed lovers – not Nehru and Edwina, but the domestics Jeet and Aalia – channelled another current contextualization when the film was claimed as relevant to then unfolding events around the election of US President Trump and his anti-Muslim travel bans (Pape 2017).

The film is presented then as a polemic against prejudice and racism, yet all the senior South Asian 'negotiators' are unsympathetic. Nehru with his 'Cambridge debating skills' is the best of them; Gandhi, in the often repeated Churchill slur, is a 'half naked fakir', also a vegetarian enthusiast for goat's cheese and dentally challenged maverick, which might be true to type or myth but will not please either fans or critics of his role. All the English are cynical except the naïve avuncular Mountbatten – 'he could charm a vulture off a corpse' – and the worthy charitable 'righting wrongs' Edwina. The portrayal that has Jinnah, and indeed Churchill and the other British tops, playing politics over such tragedy in such a calculated, inhuman way is of course as horrific as the slaughter of the entire night train carrying Muslims from Delhi to Lahore. The documents found by Sarila are then working as a claim to scholarship that must confirm not only the assertions about Jinnah, but also all the other characterizations of this historical fiction as written by the victors. Of course while Chadha's grandmother was travelling the other way in just as grim circumstances, and while sympathy for the Indian side may have been inherited as family history it could also have come from the Lapierre and Collins's book upon which the film is also avowedly based. In *Freedom* at *Midnight*, Lapierre and Collins were self-confessedly laudatory of Mountbatten and betrayed the authors' Eurocentric and rather presumptuous approach – for example, Lapierre travelling around India in a hired Rolls Royce to conduct interviews. It is regrettable that although Lapierre and Collins released another book, *Mountbatten and the Partition of India* (1983), that includes the transcripts of interviews they did, including with Mountbatten, this is from a small subsidiary publisher and less likely to be found and therefore not so readily available for interested parties to read and evaluate. The declarations of impartiality from the director in this case do not mesh with the partiality of the sourced reference to *Freedom at Midnight*, and raise questions that could be articulated in Benjamin's terms where a historian risks 'becoming a tool of the ruling class' ([1940] 1968: 255). If the timing of an anti-Muslim and anti-Soviet story is considered, the all-too-loving fascination with the silver cutlery of the Raj must tarnish this project. Chadha has made better films, usually with songs.

Other partitions

Meanwhile in India, other contemporaneous partition dramas add to a vast archive that reaches from before *Gandhi* (1982) and beyond *Jinnah* (1998, dir. Dehlavi). In Pakistan, viewers apparently may 'prefer' to watch films from the India side of partition because 'Hindi dialogue and song is more familiar to ordinary citizens than the increasingly Islamicized official idiom of news bulletins' (Ahmad 2016: 472). A separate register would be needed to track all the possible permutations and contradictions in partition films in their various significances and details, for example that it was controversial for Christopher Lee to have played Mohammed Ali Jinnah in the 1998 biopic film. Lee was primarily famous for his role as Count Dracula, which was considered problematic not because he was European and playing the secular leader of Pakistan, but because of the association of Jinnah with the dead. Casting Lee was an impressive match in terms of bearing and looks, and the actor considered it his best ever role, but at a fundraiser for the film there had been curious comments about the lead, with Ben Kingsley also suggested as a possibility in terms of balance and prestige with the Shakespearean actor having already portrayed the Mahatma.

Why shouldn't Chadha make a partition film, since it seems almost everyone does? A pity though she did not think to unpack her effort over/against the tradition of films that broach its never exhausted significance for the subcontinent as trauma and love story, for example in *Mela* (1948, dir. Sunny) starring Nargis and Dilip Kumar as star-crossed lovers, through to *Pinjar* (2003, dir. Dwivedi) which follows the dangers, dilemmas and experience of kidnapped women across the borders. Both films are discussed in a later chapter, the latter having inspired recent additions to the ever-burgeoning partition film archive in two obvious concurrent alternatives to *Viceroy's House*: *Begum Jaan* (2017) and

Rajkahini (2015). Srijit Mukherji directs both films, and *Begum Jaan* is the Hindi adapted version of the Bengali *Rajkahini*. The repetition here is something that can be shown later in this book as having a secret significance, with much to be said about casting and character – the films tell a well-worn story of sex workers who fight the prejudices of partition chaos, with significant scenes of women wielding rifles, firebombing and killing, and triumphant survival against the odds in the end. That we may already know the plot should come as no surprise, since the literature on partition is also vast and the formula symptomatic. What is curious in this case is how the promoters have made a virtue of marketing the remake as a remake. As a marketing strategy, they have staged a debate about who is the better Begum out of the two actors Vidya Balan and Rituparna Sengupta. A smart promotional angle is extended with a series of other character match-ups, and while the trailer for *Begum Jaan* is dynamic, the one for *Rajkahini* comes, inevitably, with a Tagore song and the clip lovingly follows the studio artists making the record, interspersed with lush images from the film. While neither film comes close to the Raj-a-philia of *Viceroy's House*, the Hindi effort is focused more on action while the Bengali one asserts cultural specificity by featuring a more contemplative stance. The fireworks of both are real, and a cutthroat killing in the Bengali is not outshone by the pyromaniac skills of the stunt-person managing to impersonate a map of India in flames in the Hindi version. What is noteworthy is the duplication, with a few differences, of these stories, and of course the near contemporaneous release of Chadha's *Viceroy's House*.

What if *Viceroy's House* had been different? I mean different from Merchant Ivory-style fantasy. The film in form and style owes little to oral history or to the memory studies that dominate partition scholarship, and it does not at all reference films that break with the conventional formats of narrative realism. That Chadha includes herself at the end of the film would have been a chance to problematize perspective, especially at a generation or two beyond the events shown. Documented instances exist of referred or inherited memory among those giving testimony to oral history projects, for example – Chandrika Parma told of interviewing a man who said he had survived a train attack by hiding behind his murdered mother's sari. Only in a later interview when he repeated the story did it become clear that the man was not old enough to have been there, and was relating his father's experience as if he believed it was his own (Centre for Cultural Studies seminar, Goldsmiths College 2004). What would a film capable of taking account of this level of interpretive variance look like? The experiments with form that have addressed such variance have not always been successful, but the question of who writes history implies a much bigger conversation than any to be had about a specific film made in the United Kingdom or Bengal or Mumbai.

Popular pleasures

The burden of representation (Mercer 1990, Tagg 1984, 1988) also applies to truth, and films made from one place and time must carry a context. There is a significant body of work that can provide that context and it would surely seem strange to consider Global South Asia on screen without reference to such works. Of British South Asian films such as those of Chadha's early oeuvre, especially *Bhaji on the Beach* (see Chapter 5), Sanjay Sharma describes them as often primarily concerned with struggles over the politics of racialized representation in a particular way: 'this cinema articulates a range of "popular pleasures", rather than operating as formalist pedagogic works that explicitly employ avant-garde strategies, as found in other Intercultural or black/Third Cinema' (2009: 22). It is perhaps better to recognize a multiplicity of perspectives and tactics where protagonists do not always agree yet exist in a generally shared community of reference. Sharma's analysis is focused upon teaching in the UK 'pedagogical' context, but his points make sense for a wider questioning of the sort of things that can be said about film, including South Asian film, in general, or globally. His points about race and representation can be extended. He notes a specific burden and opportunity:

> when we turn to films marked by their ethnicity – for example, labelled as 'black', 'South Asian', 'Intercultural' or 'Third Cinema' – concerns over representation, belonging, identity and difference, and so on, frame much of the analysis. Such approaches yield significant insight, particularly in relation to the operations of racial ideologies, stereotyping and nationhood. (Sharma 2009: 22)

The question of historical veracity and who gets to write the history of the struggles against racism, stereotypes and nationhood remains a contested one. The second part of this chapter shows that this questioning is already underway, and draws inspiration especially from the ways scholars and filmmakers, in the film schools and in regional film traditions, can now think of the near and far together.

In what can be considered both a related and yet radically different approach to that of Sharma, the Warwick-based sometimes Lahori music scholar Virinder Kalra and his co-author Shalini Sharma (no relation) present an excellent genealogical survey of radicalism for the Punjab Research Group. They report on that study group's solution to the dilemma of reference in having coined the portmanteau phrase 'three Punjabs: East, West and the diaspora'. They stress the need for an approach maintaining 'a space of analysis in which the national is also held in question' (Sharma and Kalra 2013: 438).

Extrapolating the same sentiment still wider, not every resident or citizen of the named countries of Global South Asia need grasp the parameters of multiple designations when all this can be examined together without homogenizing, and still have some echo of a Global South movement. The space of analysis is a critical and sustaining one that belongs to a long and unevenly reproduced tradition. Without romanticizing community, since it can also have its reactionary sides, there is a habit of care in identification with migration. In settlement and at home, looking out for village, caste, relatives, region, state, nation, cricket team, neighbours and general outlook, entails a co-constitution of here and there. It means brothers sending cousins abroad, co-workers smoothing the way; as reciprocity is the essence of sociality, the social reproduction of community operates a wide fall-out net to support members and associates. This co-constitution as a movement is conscious by necessity, fighting compromise by context, continually subject to capture and recuperation, but still something not yet wholly subsumed under the privatization and homogenization of the globe.

Film schools and influences

Corresponding with an economic frame that will need to be specified, in the last thirty years questions about knowledge, disciplinary focus and reference have been raised. In South Asia as well a body of work has emerged, ostensibly gathered together as film studies and extended to television and other media platforms, that has transformed the possibilities for considering film material in a global context. This work can be an inspiration for thinking generously and critically about other media practices and politics, both in diaspora and in relation to other aspects of South Asia and its dispersals, or potentials. The new approach inaugurated by Madhava Prasad's magisterial *Ideology of the Hindu Film* (1998) and Ashis Nandy's *The Secret Politics of Our Desires* (1998) came around the same time that controversies over films such as *Roja* (1992, dir. Ratnam, see Gaur 2011), *Fire* (1996, dir. Mehta, see John and Niranjana 2000) and *Zakhm* (1998, dir. Bhatt) took over pages in political journals, especially the *Economic and Political Weekly* but also the *Times of India*. Both the new work and the film debates of course also traded upon significant film discussions in a longer tradition that would take varied antecedents such as the work of filmmakers Ritwik Ghatak and Mrinal Sen, the Communist Party in some forms, the Progressive Writers Association (PWA) and the Indian People's Theatre Association (IPTA), the struggle in Bangladesh for separation from Pakistan, the Tamil struggle in Sri Lanka and its musical echoes, and theatre traditions such as the work of Safdar Hashmi or even Badal Sircar (see Katyal 2015) as well as the literature of Kashmiri and Punjabi diaspora. In this discussion, a follower of the debates need not worry too much about the precision of who is in and who out of traditional disciplinary 'film studies', whether the school is a 'coherent' school, whatever that would mean, or if the authors named even recognize each other in terms of schools or suchlike affinities. Perhaps what is refreshing here is that the politics of contextualization of these works has already inspired productive controversy – there is for example by now a well worked debate over what is new screen media: does it refer to film or only handheld devices, is television a new electronic media, as yet not fully understood; what of the network ontologically? Has satellite transformed the field of operations that, for a period, presented a local – pirate? – dimension in the activity of illicit cable operators and their embedded community operations? That questions about social media, satellite and network structures, big data and language policy and so on are important should be obvious, and if not, Ravi Sundaram's *Pirate Modernity* (2009) provides explanations as to why. Shared discussion in a circuit of perspectives requires risking the effort of reading.

Rajagopal bursts the reflexive indulgence with commentary on the December 1992 Babri Masjid demolition. His book *Politics after Television: Hindu Nationalism and the Reshaping of the Public in India* accepts not only a certain newness to news, but more importantly sees that:

> new electronic media set up circuits of communication across the realms (of polity, economy, and culture) that ... allow ... Hindu nationalism to fashion a range of different rhetorics outside the political sphere proper, and to suggest a homology between forms of consumption and voting behavior, and between cultural identification and the requirements of electoral affiliation. (Rajagopal 2001: 2)

Wanting to extend Bollywood or South Asian screen cultures to a wider social technological spread, taking in more and more dimensions of labour, organization, marketing – an entire socio-economic cultural-industrial construct – the new Global South Asian media theorists seem to be driven by an underlying formation that is not hard to identify: a Marxist training is standard in the institutes and histories within which South Asian film criticism thrives. Even when making variously grounded or esoteric comments about the condition of modernity – for example Ravi Vasudevan pointing out that 'Bollywood has provided a brand name for publishers to position their product' (2011: 14) or Ravi Sundaram's diagnoses of a 'pirate modernity' (2009) as a condition without respect for origins – the traces and desire for a political impact beyond film studies or media scholarship is grounded in a foundational narrative with proper names, heritage and influences. To understand these as a heritage of Marxism is one perhaps not of the party or cadre fold, in the way that IPTA is for the origin for a certain Bengali art cinema, but identifiable nevertheless.

That a film studies or media course cannot now stick only to media or film studies seems self-evident. This is acknowledged in all programmes that ask their students to pick 'option' courses alongside their film and television 'technical' or 'theory' modules. This curriculum arrangement admits that a theory of media cannot rely upon the media alone. Courses in media and politics, media and architecture, media and anthropology or media with sociology are increasingly common where an overlap with the visual arts or cultural studies is readily assumed even as it has not yet any structural integration. Ashish Rajadhyaksha is correct to observe that 'the legacy of our cinema is far more complex' (2012a: 41). Indeed, the spillage beyond media, and beyond discipline based courses, is a limit and a possibility, with the requirement that practitioners and analysts bring experience and maturity to bear if insight is to be developed.

Ethical practices

There are often quite good intentions in those who would search out an ethical practice in learning to know what others think of themselves and relating to them in those terms; a welcome even if insufficient, and of course privileged, move. European filmmaking is no more immune from such seductions than other modes of creative benevolence. The danger here is that benevolent othering makes an exotic object of that which it uses and appropriates – a dubious return, a slippery slope on the way to commercial exploitation. A degree of vigilance must be earned alongside the institutional degrees that remain the passport to recognized participation in knowledge creation – despite the often-mentioned collapse into commercial training of the university. Spivak also talks of the 'new globalisation' of the 'Indian migrant ... class heterogeneous migrant subcultures' and notes as evidence video hire then available in thousands of stores spread across the United States, and indeed the world, now via YouTube. Here, the 'space of cosmopolitan diasporic culture' (1996: 260) gives culture mass exposure as a joke circulating the overdetermined sexual politics of patriarchy as distribution and communalism. Her modest ambition that cultural studies can alert teachers of literature and film to concerns that disciplinary historians cannot is a hope that 'decolonization of the mind' can begin without positing any too easy self-other, East-West, North-South split. Why this is important is that if the Global South is conceived as supra-geographical and includes the movement of the global proletariat into the metropolitan North, with cultural supports and video, then this decolonization is potentially in place, waiting only miraculously to be enacted.

Thus, a new effort to evaluate might be learnt from film theory comrades in Global South Asia. Trying to avoid the awful realization of being either a wannabe do-gooder, Edwina doing her British best, or merely a revolutionary tourist on the banana pancake trail, the comfort-food-quaffing Netaji lookalike that hangs about in the kitchen, just off from the action proper. Let us also recognize a subjective investment. The solidarity and collaborations required within Global South Asia are salutary lessons at the level of pan-Africanist, Bandung or South-South formulas, but in later days and still grappling with the distribution powers that want to channel networks through the metropolitan West, the effort starts with an urgent call to transcend identitarianisms, nationalisms and communalisms. Without a critical evaluation of the vernacular globalism of South Asia and its political histories, any chance of revolutionary being together would be left dormant in unlearnt possibility and missed opportunities.

Are there that many people who could, or would want to, see the world from the perspective of Global South Asia? Who would see film and television in such a way? To extrapolate from fandom of diasporic and regional film to a diagnostic and prescription for political mobilization would be presumptuous unless existing mobilizations make it possible to indicate the emergence of other significant expressions of the perspective.[1] In my interpretation the articulation of a 'citizen of the world' position by Mrinal Sen is an example of such thinking. Sen certainly is a Bengali director and most of his films are set in Kolkata – a city he has often said he loves. But the world citizen is not so because his films are screened in international festivals, nor only because of an affiliation to art cinemas or the 'quixotic' internationalist third film movement (Solanis and Getino 1969) – though Sen has been described, warmly, as quixotic and artistic in temperament (see Reinhard Hauff's film *10 Days in Kolkata* [1984]). His perspective is a human universalism extracted from a set of hermeneutic circumstances that will be variously located in the Global South and South Asia, a shorthand for which, at least in this book and perhaps only for this book, is convenient as a counter to a more general demonization.[2]

Pantomime terrors in context

The world into which this indulgence of ideas around film, television, South Asia and writing exists is one that barely bears contemplation without anguish. The scarring of generations runs from colonialism through partition as a trauma carried globally by so many, through indenture and migration and for East African South Asians, a double migration to the dubious welcome of Enoch Powell and Lord Tebbit. In our world presently atrocities are plentiful still. Hundreds of thousands of migrants die crossing deserts and seas fleeing war and poverty; governments favour conflicts because they are generative of weapons sales; camps and border walls cover the most inadequate posturing of humanity-mongers: humanitarian missions as window dressing led by Tony Blair, the Clinton Foundation or some celebrity on retainer. Environmental catastrophes and pollution multiply the woes of the global proletariat paid an ever smaller proportion of the massive value they collectively produce, expropriated by the very very few, who live without want or care. Millions live below sustenance levels, with the rest in degrees of anxiety from fear for their lives, chronic illness and high mortality through to work stress, exhaustion or listlessness in bullshit jobs entailing pointless bureaucratic toil. Children grow up with screens instead of parents, fantasies instead of hopes, instruction instead of education. The possibility of a life not geared to commodity production seems hard to imagine, the community and conviviality of human togetherness appears only in the margins, when it should be centre and front in all we do. The indulgence is to imagine this can be identified, and an opposition reproduced and extended. The news from elsewhere is that it can, if we listen.

> In recent years, South Asia has produced much noise in the global terrain of trade, development, 'terrorism', politics, tourism, human resource, war, corruption, disasters, media, show-business and many other fields, as much as in academia. The suspected anti-modern networks threatening the US dominance in global market and politics coexist here with some of the largest destinations of multinational capital. India is definitely at the centre of this increasingly expanding radar. If one broadens the spectrum to include China, Chindia would be, according to many reports, the centre of attention for the corporate world. (Roy 2012: 642–643)

The film scholar Abhijit Roy has quietly inspired many great insights, and together with colleagues such as Moinak Biswas, he has kept the important Jadavpur University *Journal of the Moving Image* afloat as a meeting point for those scholars who found more than film appreciation and promotion to be their mission. It is not then out of place to consider the political context in which journals and books 'on' film find themselves to be much more 'about' politics. And what a volatile context. For the past thirty years, the implementation of World Bank social democracy promoting 'liberalization' of markets has disciplined the Global South under the comforting mantra that

European and American experience with business cycles, recession, pollution and crisis had bought a hard earned maturity. With an authoritarian tone born of privilege, it was assumed that solutions to all the problems of capital would come by way of Keynesianism, outsourcing of industry with just-in-time delivery and the grand bureaucratic summit-derived solutions: trade deals (APEC 1989, NAFTA 1994, ASEAN), gender equality (Beijing declaration 1995, Maputo protocol 2003, Council of Europe Gender Strategy 2014) and climate agreements (Geneva, Kyoto, Copenhagen, Paris etc.). In this period the West then advised, coerced and blackmailed the Global South – using cudgels such as the IMF, debt, economic sanctions, arms deals and war – into accepting the most freewheeling modes of economic liberalization and offering, in exchange for cut-rate labour provision and unrestricted resource extraction, the chance for national elites to join their capital to global capital and its selective and fickle investment bubbles for speculative gain. National local development and industry was largely abandoned to the whims of international fashion, finance deregulation and special measures, these in turn governed by fluctuations of provision: of cheap labour and tax incentives in the unregulated special plunder zones.

After the 2008 recession, the West tried to return to this model but stalled in double recession and stagnation, failing to convince anyone that they can any longer lead. The Chinese economy was strong, and Russia buoyant, so a counter-BRICS strategy was devised in Washington, with the warrant of support from the European social democratic parties, sowing discord across the Middle East, North Africa and Eastern Europe. Various former client states in these areas were subjected to a chaos strategy where war and weapon deals, the recession-proof staples, destabilized economies and encouraged social disturbance, the exposure of long-term 'strongmen', former puppets now dictators, and cashed in yet again on the cover provided by the ever handy terror war. This meant also risking uprisings and destabilization becoming a contagion as the Arab Spring turned into Greek, Spanish and London protests and the global movement of the squares became Occupy. Only the assault on Gaddafi and the quagmire of Syria with ISIS could forestall these irruptions at home, and in return a panic over crisis refugees, and a rightwards lurch into popular fascism, was a predictable follow-on result.

With this as backstory, the possibility that Global South Asia not be a simple narration of successfully adopting a shining future as promised by economic liberalization in the IMF/World Bank rhetoric of the 1990s, now become BJP and Congress(I) policy, was strong. Pervez Musharraf and Nawaz Sharif in Pakistan, Khaleda Zia and Sheik Hasina Wazed in Bangladesh, Ranil Wickremesinghe in Sri Lanka each had conservative and often long-standing entrenchments in the corridors that matter to them. Prachanda, Pushpa Kamal

Dahal, in Nepal offered an interesting twist as an elected Maoist, having regained the prime ministerial post in 2016, and reassuring both the citizens and neighbouring states – India and China – that business would be a priority, only to resign again in 2017. For these reasons, and for reasons that matter, could anyone overlook enthusiasm for the Global South only as 'emerging' economy, rather than something possibly older, not commercial, and offering prosperity to more than the elite entrepreneur?

Differences in the Global South

It should not be considered unusual that most of those writing on film and television in South Asia and across its diasporas are writing about so much more. Rajadhyaksha writes on music and London; Abhijit Roy on 'liveness', Midnapore and the Aum Party; Moinak Biswas about the declining fortunes of the CPI(M); Madhava Prasad on sartorial styles of the revolutionary heroes; Tejeswini Naranjana on feminism and the Shiv Sena (closer to film than not); Gayatri Gopinath on desi protest marches; Amit Rai on affect theory; Sunaina Maira on hip hop; Rajinder Dudrah on queer political mobilities – all in all, divergences from the script of film studies through consumerism, queer and transnational mobilizations are very welcome and show an exciting and robust promiscuity that cannot only be said to have been prepared in the institutional turbulence of a thriving multidisciplinarity.

In Rajagopal's *Politics after Television,* one of his many footnote speculations spills out from the text proper to permit him to muse on the theme of commodity consumption. He astutely relates this to modifications in the orthodox Marxist perspective:

> Recent historical work has challenged assumptions about consumption as an activity following automatically upon the development of industrial production, or about mass consumption as having a merely emulative quality, as lower classes enacted their aspirations for the lifestyles of their economic betters. Consumption as a middle-class activity began not in the late eighteenth, or early nineteenth, or in the twentieth century, but in fact appears to antedate the rise of industrial capitalism and mass production. (Rajagopal 2001: 317)

Rajagopal argues that consumption studies gained favour in part because a new middle class emerged willing to shop. While Marxist orthodoxy in some of the more moribund party forums might not wish to consider consumer society as a viable context for intervention, within a culture industry and media perspective it becomes a necessary project to politicize cultural production.

The now burgeoning work on queer perspectives in South Asia has its own film-focused contingent, with the excellent work of Gopinath, Desai, Dudrah and others, perhaps working in a space opened up to some degree by the controversy over Mehta's film *Fire*, (1998) in which Sita is renamed Nita in Hindi after the Censorship Board's order (John and Niranjana 2000: 371). If there was any doubt that film has a wider socio-political life, then just a few words from John and Niranjana's original response to *Fire* show how convoluted and obscured things quickly become once the Board and other interest groups get involved: 'Women's organisations and especially gay and lesbian groups ... raised key issues relating to questions of obscenity, on the one hand, and gay/ lesbian rights, on the other ... however, these issues tended to get deflected if not lost in the dominant focus on the Shiv Sena attacks' (1999: 581). It is instructive to see how the political debates extend beyond the theoretical first moves of film appreciation.

Transnational studies set out to map the world differently, and in relation to such a perspective, what is important about the new Global South Asian media work is not global in the sense of how one flat earth globalization propagandists might think of the global, but that regions forge their own mutating paths of intellectual and analytic access independent from the dominant disciplinary protocols. Given the up-link from local to global, critical assessment of national or regional belonging is not necessarily more pressing as a market niche than taking the same critique to minority settlements, even as use of the term Global South Asia recognizes the geography of South Asian settlement in all parts of the world as a permanent and significantly stabilizing arrangement. 'Here to stay', the slogan goes. This means not necessarily privileging a nostalgic nationalist referent from which media might flow, diasporize or transit, but when looking to shifts and realignments also seeing how they congeal into interest-bearing or guilt-deflecting associations.

This geographical bend does not deny that the Bollywood film version of Global South Asian media is a pole of attraction. But this is an attraction that moves, as in Dudrah's book title *Bollywood Travels* (2012), the emphasis is on *travel*. Nor does enthusiasm for contemporary diasporic media mean ignoring what Gopinath calls diaspora's 'traditionally backward-looking glance' (2005: 3). By no means is everything said in the name of an expanded Global South Asia progressive. All first moves are in need of further displacement. One should track the influence of demography and sociologists blended into market research here and see their avatars in the lower level pantheon of audience studies. While recognizing that 'the spatial coordinates and geographical reach of Bollywood have changed dramatically' (Punathambekar 2013: 1), the need to map these changes in different ways calls for more than quantity. As an example of the need for ethnographic studies of media 'convergence', Punathambekar describes Sri Lankan listeners tuning into Radio Ceylon for Indian film songs (2013: 8). When Anna Morcom points out that another 'major territory of global Bollywood, in addition to South Asian diaspora populations and those in close proximity with them, is the Muslim world ... [where] ... there is significant crossover with Hindi film songs' (2011: 157), the message that Global South Asia is not homogenous despite Bollywood should already have hit home. She also draws on an economic sensibility when she notes that 'the market for Bollywood in Tibet can be seen as rooted largely in migrations and trade shaped by regional history and politics' (2011: 180). With journals proliferating and all corners of the globe subject to a *filmi*-focused attention, there is no chance to reference all the material available on the global reach of South Asian film and television. As diverse and interesting as it might be to take in Andrew Hassam's (2009) work on marketing and the global city in Indian popular cinema in Melbourne, and another article by Morcom (2009) on quite different explorations of exile, both these pieces in the inaugural issue of the new journal *South Asian Film and Media* show wider acceptance of 'the importance of culture in the contemporary integration of the world of global capital' (the editors, *South Asian Film and Media* 2009: 8). The directors of this integration, its extent, dynamics, prejudices and resistances spawn entire careers. More than Disraeli's East as a Career, the East becomes global, or South, as preferred, or demanded. In her opening to *The Magic of Bollywood*, Anjali Gera Roy (2012) notes that the love of Hindi cinema extends to Afghanistan – they will kill for it; Bangladesh – a 'fix'; Burma – 'better suited' films than from elsewhere; Nepal – both Maoists and Royals are fans; Bhutan and Sri Lanka must be included. Further into the book, Gera Roy can discuss Nigeria, Uzbekistan, China, USSR, Turkey, Malaysia, Iran, North America and more in just four pages, all with strong interest in the South Asian film product. In another essay, reports on 'fieldwork by Fair, Larkin and Vender Steene in Zanzibar, Nigeria and Senegal respectively' testify to the portability of a South Asian 'cinematic narrative that lends itself to a wide variety of appropriations from providing a grammar for romance, lifestyles, fashions and a model for values' (2010: 39). Such work invites a 'rethink on the efficacy of the national framework for analyzing practices embedded in transnational flows' (Gera Roy 2010: 43).

The reference then is complicated in multiple ways, and any use of the term 'Global South Asia', like any other category such as Global, Asian, USSR, Muslim, White, racist or academic, should never be taken as uniform, uncontested or settled. 'The logic of the aggregate' is a phrase I first heard during a discussion at a 2016 Jadavpur University Film Studies Department workshop 'Territory to Screen: The Regionalism in Indian Cinema' at which Madhava Prasad was the opening speaker. The aggregation here would suggest that Bollywood rules, and both the diasporic but also the regional are mere examples to be confirmed by the national. Then the movement of territory into screen culture becomes the subsumption and eventual monetization of difference into commercial imperative.

As ways to comprehend the current volatility of societal lives are sought, a question to ask is how much of an understanding of outside is necessary to get any perspective on the inside? Can a tone-deaf person understand music? Would a film studies that was proper not require properties from beyond film studies? What specialisms and regionalisms demand reference, or ever-more exclusive focus? Region, niche, cultural frame, diasporic fraction ... can the vernacular local be considered alongside the vernacular global? Besides an undercooked comparativism – few studies of note – what chance is there for a field that acknowledges the incommensurability of its categories? It is Madhava Prasad's contention that 'an adequate explanation for the cini-political phenomenon ... cannot really be found in the content of the relevant films' (2014a: 57). He makes this claim in *Cine-Politics: Film Stars and Political Existence in South India* (2014), at the very end of a chapter on the cinema strategies of the political party DMK (Dravida Munnetra Kazagham) in Tamil Nadu. The stakes of this assertion are, I think, huge for cinema studies in South Asia and beyond, but the question is what sort of 'outside' material must be brought to bear upon film? Ajay Gehlawat begins his *Twenty-first Century Bollywood*, paraphrasing Dwyer and Pinto (2011), by asking about the temporal and aesthetic boundaries of reference when we name Bollywood. Gehlawat then cites 'the recent theoretical paradigms put forward by three of the leading scholars of popular Hindi cinema, Ravi Vasudevan, Ashish Rajadhyaksha and Madhava Prasad' (2015: 10). In this book I often come back to these thinkers, and my only quibble here is that these three do not theorize *only* on Hindi cinema, and my extension of Desai's injunction to go *Beyond Bollywood* is to take up the transnational in a more rigorous and political way, even if I cannot discuss all the films – nor even care to remind everyone just how many are made in a year – please look it up – the field is already too big for any book to be but partial, perspectival, in process. Already in the first issue of the same aforementioned Jadavpur Film Studies journal, Biswas wrote: 'The increasing circulation/dispersal of cinema in the media field, through video, TV, digital fares of every variety demands that we develop a critical framework' (1999: 9). Believing with Desai that 'the study of the role of cultural politics of film in the production of diasporic affiliations, identities, and politics is crucial to an understanding of transnationalism and globalization' (2004: 7) this critical framework tends towards the universal, even as it is specific, regional and located-demarcated. Like travel, *beyond* is the code word here. It is not necessarily correct, nor is it an imperative that escapes structured reference. The questions to ask have to do with how these theorists frame a critical approach, and to what, with what extension. Madhava Prasad calls us to move beyond the 'political communication' model – the idea that 'cinema is used as a transparent medium to transmit messages and thereby win the hearts of spectators' is not problematic because there are no messages, but because transparency and a simple message code model does not account for 'the specificity of the cinematic institution nor the complexity of political processes' (1999: 39).

Going beyond conventions of earlier film talk, the proliferation of screens and the digital 'convergence' invokes a quiver of enthusiasm. Without dismissing innovations in the film technology field, Gehlawat's survey of the work of the aforementioned three theorists is rather curt, and it has to do with a *filmi*-focus which overlooks television and other screens, such that narrowly, in Vasudevan, only the reach of the meanings of the name Bollywood are questioned; in Rajadhyaksha we deal only with Bollywood as a 'diffuse cultural conglomeration' (2008: 20); and with Madhava Prasad we see no further than how 'the term itself seems to serve different purposes for different people' (2008: 41). The limits of these demarcations are obvious if you know these authors do of course write about Hindi film, but crucially much else besides, including the new wave art cinema from Bengal, the regional film traditions of Tamil Nadu and Andhra Pradesh, the star system, representation – *darstellen* and *vertreten* (Madhava Prasad 2014a: 147, 155, following Spivak 1988) – regionalism, nationalism, globalization, and so much more. But while a few comments should not be levitated to the status of paradigms so quickly, nor short essays be taken to stand for substantial bodies of work, Gehlawat is correct to note that the terms used in any demarcation may gather 'arguably disparate films under one umbrella' (2015: 12). This is the case, he notes for example, with Joshi's (2010) distinction between Bollywood and Bollylite, which refers to US-friendly South Asian films such as *Monsoon Wedding* (2001, dir. Nair) or, we might add, *Viceroy's House*. M. K. Ragavendra contends that 'the term "Bollywood" may have become a more acceptable label ... because it does not signify any specific national identity' (2012: 31). There is no injunction on applying demarcations for different media 'products' under reference to the digital or to the global, since here the point is that electronic capitalism comes both in pirate and corporate forms (Kumar 2013: 257). The 'public archive of the contemporary' exists as a demonic and manipulated ideological apparatus and as a niche segmented one; it is regionalism and identity in slices of time and frequency, and the universal schedule of programme planning is never innocent (Sundaram 2013: 3, 122).

Screen barricades

In *Beyond Bollywood*, Desai notes thus:

> South Asian diasporic migration into the West engendered by global capitalism has created complex and contradictory cultural productions and subjectivities. Therefore, differentiating this cultural production and circulation may present oppositional politics but at the same time may traffic in normativities and self-commodification to access production and circulation. (Desai 2004: 9)

Differentiation and commodification is a contested terrain. It is for this reason that the migration of South Asians into inevitable hardworking media involvement and as advocates of labour and intellectual engagement offers critical Global South perspective. However, this can be affirmed at the same time that the term Global South too often marks only a projected economic development. No one should begrudge the need to get paid, even as this can be to share in the erasure of the political history of Global South struggles. A substantial resource with unparalleled political capital, the International, Comintern, Pan-African, Anti-colonial, Bandung, Non-aligned and Tricontinental movements, all the way to a decolonized Occupy, anti-globalization, and the international reach of the movement of the squares, is muted because of class demarcations and internal hierarchies.

Nevertheless:

> The 'peaceful rising' of China and the economic growth of India (though deeply skewed in favour of a rich minority in both countries), coinciding with cracks within the neo-liberal model of US-led Western capitalism, are set to challenge conventional frameworks for the study of international media and communication. Their combined economic and cultural impact, aided by extensive global diasporas, is likely to create globalisation with an Asian accent. (Thussu 2014).

Thus the political context to negotiate is a Global South-oriented black (anti-)racism arraigned against comprador class allies with white supremacist attachments, coupled with an economic crisis running parallel to an austere end-game spiral of proxy military expansions, with death squads on both sides. A case in point will be the televisual execution of Osama bin Laden that was played out on screen as a part of, variously, the war on terror, the election campaign of a former US president, and the geopolitical intrigue of a far wider and much longer 'great game' than that imagined in *Viceroy's House*. Perhaps it was only one part of an endless feed of horror scenes from Afghanistan, Iraq, Libya, Syria, Yemen, Nigeria, Korea, while street violence, over-policing, co-option and corruption at home book-end, so to speak, any discussion of the issues. Digital and televisual terror runs the same-old same-old crusades generalized, where screen moments proffered audience terror and death as entertainment.

Global South Asian film and television studies document both the upper and lower specificities and detail of a new interconnectivity of politics, ideology and screen. At the local end, the cable guy, VCR copy shop, dodgy wiring and knock-off brand sets of the parallel second-hand economy of reconditioned media gear are all eloquently described by Sundaram (2009) at Delhi's Nehru Place, Lajput Rai and Palika Bazaar. This means everyone is implicated: 'We are all media practitioners now … torturers also photograph now … Abu Ghraib is the allegory of our time' (Sundaram 2011a). Showing how media politics is inextricably bound up with urbanism, modernity and technological change means working in the interstices where 'thousands of informal sites like gray-market bazaars, small video cinemas, and cable networks … are run by local operators' (Sundaram 2011b). Here, the 'shops, markets, cable, wiring, cassettes [and] distributors' are only the constitutive 'pirate' end (Sundaram 2009) of a mass commercial accumulation that reconfigures the political terrain.

At the other end, an assertive and critical approach to Global South Asian media spaces is crucial where settlement contains compromises not greater, but neither less, than the convoluted comprador Global South complicities of 'homeland' and 'foreign'. This is where Spivak hopes some might recognize themselves as 'possible agents of exploitation, not its victims' by being put on the track to noticing 'the nation-state that they now call home gives "aid" to the nation-state they still call culture, in order to consolidate the new unification for international capital' (1999: 357). In a media saturated world where fictions and fantasy as rumours of terror *and* exotica are deployed in battle, there is an abstract yet material reality of Washington-sponsored death squads on the one side, with ambitious entrepreneurs, worried governments and model minorities on that very *same* side. While across at the all-too-rarefied progressive theory circle, a spectrum of alliances and shared, if squabbling, more or less leftist-realist impulses, also making media have Global South

Asia overlapping with multicultural and cosmopolitan characterizations that are admittedly unfairly, but not wholly arbitrarily, complicit as the shooting ground of unknown unknowns.

Officially into snuff films

Cinema studies had already mapped out the parameters of ideology critique, national film genre, the gaze, voyeurism, the audience and even composing for the films. Consequently screen studies in general is put under review by an emergent Global South Asia where 'globalization isn't merely another word for Americanization' (Rajadhyaksha 2008: 17). Even if a rival 'americanization of popular culture in Asia', as critiqued by Allen Chun when he stresses the importance of how we 'perceive the concatenated entity called pop music culture in a local context' (2012: 503), should remind us that received models of the global are hardly adequate for mapping patterns of practice and use. Hollywood does not shape Bollywood, and French New Wave did not shape Bengali new wave, despite it being the case that the connectivity here is obvious to media historians. What does it matter if so-called scholarship makes connections that publics – there are always more than one – do not need? We are in a plural universe and there are plural Asias, travelling in several directions at once. It is the argument of this book that Global South Asian film and television is one burgeoning part of a wider realignment. The Global South in general recoded by transnational corporate interests moving away from other possible alternatives to the hegemony of electronic capitalism seems to take its cue from the foreclosure of alternative media forms by a 'new generation of media elites' (Kumar 2013: 257). The messy wiring of local video and cable set-ups (Sundaram 2009) is not gainsaid but is rather subsumed by satellite provision owned by Murdoch and STAR (Kumar 2013: 259). Semi-covert film club obsessive affiliations and fandoms are reterritoralized by glamour and gossip magazines at the very same time a refocusing of geographical South Asia as a theatre of war was performed primarily on film and TV as theatre.

A case in point must be the controversy surrounding the images that staged the death of bin Laden. Setting aside Seymour Hersch's journalism (2015) exposing Pakistani foreknowledge of the raid, US secret service complicity and the deep machinations of spectral power, what audiences actually saw in 2011 still leaves plenty of space for interpretation. The new geopolitical reach of television was never more evident than the in photogenic scene of 2 May 2011 showing then Secretary of State Hilary Clinton and then President Obama watching a remote closed circuit tele-feed of the Seal Team 6 raid on bin Laden's Pakistan compound. In the cramped comfort of the

White House situation room, with a large group of advisors and aides, they seem, especially Clinton, to express both astonishment and concern. Obama is reported to have exclaimed 'We got him'. However, as audiences, having delegated governance to those elected through the confluence of democracy, lobbyist influence and 'in god we trust', we do not ourselves ever get to see the television. We do not even hear the television. We do not see this literally *as* television. Yet it is all translated for the cameras. The picture we do see is a still, and mute: no static, no radio camera, no shouting, no pop pop pop shots – though we can, and are indeed implicitly asked to, imagine them. In a world of war-cam and live feed CNN, the still image is more suitable for the printed press than for television news, and yet at this moment of significance the still became global television in a new guise. Watching television as propaganda in this situation room is perhaps not your usual viewing platform, but it is connections like these, in this case a secure Ethernet network with remotely connected helmet-mounted camera feed,[3] in situations like these, which by default turn a still into a live event, and make television even when it's not *tele*vision, a cross-border, live-beam, everywhere and anywhere, medium of the political.

If we set aside conspiracy theory doubts about the faking of the killing and the 'found footage' that was also presented of bin Laden himself watching television, what we see of Global South Asia here in the officially sanctioned publicity release version is basically the leaders of the 'free world', president, advisors, aides and now us all, gathered around a screen to view a snuff film assassination video. We can be sure that in some sense this *is* watching Global South Asia, however perverse. With all the contradictions it implies, this view of South Asia says it all – we can even read the hand over mouth gesture of Clinton as muted reference to the guilty contradiction of razing Afghanistan to dust. Technically, Afghanistan was already a war-ravaged rubble after the Soviet invasion and US-sponsored Mujahedeen resistance, then years of civil war, followed by the Bush administration's 2001 'Enduring Freedom' invasion. While Hersch's allegations about Pakistani complicity were denied, in any case the US administration's story bizarrely justifies invading a sensitive ally and sovereign country uninvited, killing an old man along with one of his sons and some associates, and then showing only images of him sedately watching television, while off-screen burying the body at sea, with an obligatory – election winning, carefully rehearsed – Obama news conference, precipitates unseemly celebrations in the US streets. The double- and triple-plays of this convoluted and mediated scene offer a snapshot slice of a much wider and wilder scenario: our utterly televisual world.

The images *are* indeed revealing. Clinton and Obama are paired in silence with the bloodied bin Laden we do not see, despite a photo-shopped image circulating on some websites.[4] There are claims of the existence of at least three sets of images of the body, but the most recognizable one is apparently 'too gruesome' for the front page of a newspaper (Deshishku and Yellin 2011). Unusual qualms and sensitivities in the circumstances – the leader of the 'Free World' had just celebrated a murder and provided an image of himself and his colleagues watching it live. In the associated images found in the compound and released later it does seem curious to focus upon the image of a non-threatening figure in a blanket watching TV. The veracity of this image is also questioned. The visible and invisible alternation matches the scene with the situation room crowd watching alongside Obama and Clinton, and our acceptance of the images that we can see them seeing as they watch the raid on our behalf, the assassination that protects *us*, and the alleged burial-at-sea *for us*. To ask why we do not see all the images is not to flaunt decency or protocol, but only to note how implausible it is that the tape Clinton and Obama were watching as our proxies, or the ceremony of bin Laden being buried at sea in an Islamic funeral, were not chronicled as evidentiary record by the public relations and historical-archive conscious administration. This is the moment that won Obama a second term as President. If the images are really not available for public access, even for our cynically attenuated media jaded times, it will be difficult to imagine the level of incompetence required for the White House to fail to record every minute of the attack on some form of in-house NSA-supplied VCR, possibly a Watergate-style recording device, or that they do not have documentary footage of every minute in the situation room, from the deck of the aircraft carrier *USS Carl Vinson*, Nimitz class, and so on.

There are, among the inevitable plethora of conspiracy theories, also some irregularities that are more serious than wondering if was it really bin Laden we see sitting wrapped in an old blanket before the screen: if he was left-handed why is the remote control in his right hand; he has himself filmed watching himself but does not look at the camera; why has sound been stripped from the video – this last a strangely silent coincidence also replicated with regards to the situation room. Perhaps understandably, there was concern about the propriety of any release of the bloodied body shot, but in the absence of all these possible images, conspiracy theories cannot not thrive as if on purpose, and indeed a vast number of spoof YouTube videos can be seen recreating the events, as well as a graphic novel (Dye and Dale 2011), an animated game-show cartoon and slapstick Saturday Night Live-like comedy routines, all beaming stereotypes of Global South Asia abroad in a parallel universe with glossy fan-fiction proportions, deeply implicated in dramatic events.

The snuff film *mise-en-scène* in the situation room and its spin-off press and video images offer new genre identifications for deregulated global television.

This requires a more urgent aesthetic and socio-critical appreciation of the integrated media spectacle. Innovations in the forms of political television can also be seen in the cockpit-cam of the drone bombers zeroing in on insurgents in the Kush, or the shaky phone mp4 that records Saddam Hussein's New Year 2006 execution and shown on what surely must eventually become the ultimate satellite offer – the Hanging Channel. Later I will argue something similar in relation to NDTV 24x7's mobile phone-in poll around the trial, sentencing and judicial murder of Mohammad Afzal Guru, but there are many candidates for round the clock horror ready to be screened. There are the beheadings, torture snaps and attack drone reels, but also strange sub-genres such as the spoof Osama kill vids and what I would call grunt videos – a particular grotesque consequence of sending US teens out on patrol in Afghanistan or Iraq and leaving them later confined to barracks with free time and computer kit to produce music videos with their own night vision footage and soundtracks from AC/DC's 'Highway to Hell' – or remixed with even more chilling effect – Marilyn Manson's version of the same.[5] To this I would add, hiring a cynical programmer, perhaps Gujjar Singh, the chance to screen movies like the *Dead Man Walking* on heavy rotation, and for the political theory-heads the story of Bhubhaneswari – this of course is a reference to Spivak's 'Can the Subaltern Speak?' essay and its rewrite in her book *Critique of Postcolonial Reason,* the story of a woman who killed herself in order not to betray her revolutionary comrades but was still misspoken for by family and history (1999: 306–308). This might be serious if the channel was not already policy and if drone operators in air force facilities across Nevada were not already watching it 24/7 at their murder-death-kill consoles.

The reality TV franchise that is Global South Asia's part in the war on terror has shown so much more for less than Big Brother's or Crorepati's star-studded staged scenario productions ever could. Cheap to embed, easy to download, the military journalist is a controlled, edited, and always screen-tested ideological imaging. The camera is already trained on the weapon, the footage already beamed back to transmission HQ. Only sports and parliamentary debate offers such easy access to the action – the camera knows in advance where the game will be played, how many bowls will be bowled, and who has the hits. War footage is similar – we only see the highlights, and the camera was already set up before the action. The image of global television is not Neil Armstrong setting out on the surface of the moon, but rather the stain of screen erasure when the missile-mounted camera is destroyed à la some glorified stump-cam moment writ large. The ideal view of war television, like a bowled wicket in the IPL, is the destabilisation of the viewers' perspective. The wicket is smashed, the camera askew – all the work that contrived to produce this scene, the training, the technology, the calculation of wages, Duckworth,

IPL averages and back-room deals is obscured in the thrill of that singular ultra-real close-up. This is the metaphor for television today, unashamed alienation in a distraction regime. Only on the Hanging Channel the cheer squads chant 'USA USA'.

Role models

A cultural effort necessarily accompanies the war on terror addressed to global audiences, as Gargi Bhattacharyya so perceptively said (Bhattacharyya 2008: 113). A film, or White House photograph, that hides its edits – cut, pan, zoom, montage, time, audio, narrative – develops a symbiotic relationship with the alienated but global commodity circuit, enforced by commercial and military means. We are dealing here with something that is not only a war scene, but is also the war itself, and the multivariant versions of Global South Asia have always been screened in such narrowcast terms – a double-play of the good guys – temples, Bollywood songs and Sanjay Dutt – and the bad guys – terrorists, pogroms, Ravana, Gabbar Singh/Amjad Khan and Sanjay Dutt. Today it is moderate Muslims and unknown terror, the double-play at work again. In bygone years it was *Heat and Dust* (1983, dir. Ivory) as the cinematic version, or Art Malik coming to grief in *The Jewel in the Crown* (1984, dir. Morahan et al.), as a goonda in *City of Joy* (1992, dir. Joffé) or even more grotesquely, as a Mujahedeen fighter in the Bond film *The Living Daylights* (1987, dir. Glen) and at the bludgeoning hands of Arnie Schwarzenegger as the hapless terrorist Salim in *True Lies* (1994, dir. Cameron). Malik himself as a specialist terror example of where an actor's persona across films 'begins to communicate through other channels than the films' and even in 'parallel to the diegetic content of the narrative' (Madhava Prasad 2014a: 142). Today for Global South Asian star figures – Om Puri, Roshan Seth, Shah Rukh Khan, and I would add bin Laden in his blanket as an echo of Thakur/Sanjeev Kumar in *Sholay* – we can see by way of Madhava Prasad's analysis, a non-diegetic patterning of characterization and caricature. This is alternately exotic or demotic, which inflates rates of paranoid xenophobic scaremongering, even with the proliferation of vernacular views of the global (Mukhopadhyay 2012)[6] of home movies and camera phone newscasts uploaded directly to the satellite international of Skynet. It will be worth looking again at how often the same actors keep popping up over and over in films like *East Is East* (1999, dir. O'Donnell), *Viceroy's House,* and in re-imagined period serials like *Indian Summers* (2015, dir. Tucker, Payne and Moore). An impressive genealogy of retrospectively back-cast 'terrorist' nationalist miscreants are all fathered by Roshan Seth in *My Beautiful Laundrette* (1985, dir. Frears), *A Passage to India*

(1984, dir. Lean), *Buddha of Suburbia* (1993, dir. Mitchell) and alongside Art Malik yet again, in *Indian Summers*. Om Puri has his own families, and even Arundhati Roy and Aamir Khan get multiple starring roles in this book too. Where predictable typecasting is replaced by avoidance, for example in the darker serialization of *Taboo* on BBC (2017), is it not predictable that the East India Company is defeated by the one good honest but flawed mixed race soldier hero? In these films and serial fantasies, there is no sense in which the black and white syncopation of local and global escapes the play of mere colour illustration. Subject citizens are corralled from remote to metropole, all gathered together to work the pantomime scene: bin Laden dying, Obama watching.[7]

That a 'new generation of Desi artists [have] increasingly begun to produce hip-hop' (Maira 2008: 41) is only part of the 'negotiations and positionings of Indian diasporas and global flows of culture' (Maira 2008: 54). Alongside this is the return of violence and a difficult negotiation, having to distinguish between Hindu and Pakistani, Arab and Bengali, Muslim and NRI, Sri Lanka and Bhutan, bhangra and hip hop, cricket and corruption… while having to measure the isolated to the whole and offer classificatory reassurances to the emotive dominant that was so ready to blur everything after 11 September 2001. Heavy rotation Global South Asian cinema on late-night British TV, for example, was insufficient to disabuse the rest of the British public of its stereotypes of the violent exotic subcontinent and the threat of otherness. Even the by now standardized choices of 'contemporary' British-Asian film did little to clarify – *Bend It Like Beckham* (2002), but not *My Beautiful Laundrette* (1985); *East Is East* (1999) but not *Wild West* (1992, dir. Attwood); *Four Lions* (2010, dir. Christopher Morris), *Heat and Dust* (1983) but not *Taboo* (2017) – though the clarity of ideological whitewash is clear enough in the ways 'military savagery' trumped the critique of fetishizing exoticism on the part of 'rapacious corporations' (Maira 2008: 65). It is no longer enough to only note that critical analysis of the ways an anti-Muslim pogrom had taken hold in the wake of 2001, or July 7, 2005, did not displace that pogrom. The less safe films were on late-night rotation and box set specials,[8] as television provided cheap security service-foiled plots against airlines or sci-fi scenarios with suicide jihadists. In US space operas, 'the community' circles the wagons against an outside threat, both *Battlestar Galactica* (2004, dir. Eick) and *The 100* (2014, dir. Rothenberg) fit this scenario just as much as do the strange retrospective terror plots of Raj nostalgia soaps, Merchant Ivory and *Indian Summers* in prime time.

If television is a weapon of war by other means, what resources might be required for critically extending Global South Asian media studies in this all-seeing but blinkered world? What means are available to take the proliferation of screens and capital seriously? Is it of use to see television as an extension of the neo-liberal military-commercial agenda and can we turn this into a transformatory research project that would disarm such codings? Can film and television be redeemed, or must it be always exaggerated to be everywhere and so nothing special at all – merely the fabric of a politics and economy that lies, not so much elsewhere, but upon every surface? The Hanging Channel would offer a 24/7 war, just as it already is, with product placement. Is another television possible in Global South Asia? Not so much a non-violent television, but an anti-violent one? If we tune-in another way is there another possible world to see? What would televise differently? Which screen/scene must we see behind and beyond? Let us turn to that vision, summarized again in three themes:

1 that South Asian film and television has 'gone global' as a media form – from Bollywood to art and regional film to news and music videos. So we can speak of Global South Asia in a variety of media beyond national ascription and intimately appearing in the lives and lounge rooms of the world. Should it perpetuate violence or develop a critique of that violence and beyond? As the little screen displaces the large, can the content and purchase of images on both be democratized?

2 that South Asians have been demonized since before the partition is clear, from the East India Company to the new global crusade an anti-Asian, anti-Muslim geopolitical power play runs from the Middle East through South Asia and China, as well as on 'the word stage'. And while India has both Muslim and Maoist 'problems' at home, Pakistan, Sri Lanka, Afghanistan, Nepal and Bangladesh are not without military, how should we say, entanglements internally, in turn exacerbating the global war on terror, at home and abroad;

3 that the Global South as organizing framework and community, more than diaspora or some sort of culture-nation led 'rising', is the most viable political alliance that can confront the current geopolitical impasse that divides and elides. This means questions of social reproduction, and the support for anti-colonial, anti superpower cross-border organizing also has a place and a responsibility here. Additionally, that economistic starry-eyed pundits who applaud India or China as emerging powers – India over against China or vice versa, and a role for South East Asia as well – describe what could be better thought of in terms of reconfiguring Global South as a movement of mass solidarity. There is far bigger potential here than that promised by the Bandung non-aligned movement, or third-worldism, or pan-Africanism, or any national revolution, or even perhaps the Comintern

> for different reasons. Migration and settlement as the promise of a reconfigured world moving far from the ugly and uneasy origin in colonial plunder – the East India Company 'taboo' again.

The works of comrades as varied as Vijay Prashad and Sukant Chandan, Samir Amin and Gayatri Chakravorty Spivak, Theodor Adorno and Karl Marx – the escalation is noted – are crucial theoretical resources for such thinking. This chapter only starts to plot the coordinates of their understanding however, reliant upon an as yet unsystematized system of theory – for example, variously in Madhava Prasad, Rajagopal, Niranjana, Rajadhyaksha[9] – offering a reconfigured mediation of media studies that does not start so much from the screen image of the *Viceroy's House* as with the place where the screen starts to move – so as to reinvent media studies in the widest sense as a project to undo the violence of partition and the war on terror. In this way, a Global South Asian film and television studies that takes seriously the injunction to break with alienation, exploitation and death may be the only possible form of allegiance if we are to 'notice' how affiliations to intellectual disciplines and political identification with something called 'culture' must be radically critiqued so as to challenge the new coordinates of 'international capital' (Spivak 1999: 357). Consider what kinds of struggle are required to defeat the two-pronged attack of demonization and exoticization while building, or rebuilding, capacities. It cannot be to simply move into Rashtrapati Bhavan and turn on the cameras for colour. The history of the struggles that can variously be called non-aligned, communist or anti-globalization are not easily reconciled, but given the massive effort and assuming resources might be available, finding a format for unity among differences that are not so far apart is surely something for discussion. The work of the media theorists who have battled representational stereotypes over many years and on many corners can certainly be turned away from complicity and compromise. Perhaps this is done by way of an audience of participation – by way of not retaining the borders and walls that exclude circuits of theory and interpretation that go beyond the approved and authorized topics from the dominant centres, viceroy's houses and situation rooms. By working to learn from and further promote the non-exclusive conviviality of unities in difference, a new non-monolithic, diversified, endlessly debated forum for global solidarities – plural – where a thousand schools of thought contend with a hundred blooming flowers can thrive. If Global South Asian media studies can be the locus of that, then Global South Asia as a set of representations and identifications of and with the Global South gives the possibility that media saturation, instead of being used as alibi for war, can be retooled for the better, or at least, can be detourned so as to heal the ongoing partitions of here and there.

2

Sammy and Rosie – and Salman – Get Laid

Readers may be forgiven for thinking that the war on terror began with a – grotesque – puff of dust in downtown Manhattan in late 2001, but the negative televisual profiling of Islam has a longer history. What I would call the 'prehistory of post-9/11' does not even start with the events in England I will relate in this chapter, but telling this story in the context of work that also provides other deeper contextualizations of the propaganda war may be 'salutary'. My hope is that as readers recognize the present is understood through the pictures we construe of the past, by looking at how we forget or twist the interpretation of then through the images of now, our effort to learn to read their possible recodings may teach us much. In particular, the dominant 'freedom' narrative that relies upon fear and demonization of Islam after 9/11 might not be read backward to construe earlier book-burnings as provocative in the same ways.

Almost a lifetime ago, the writer Hanif Kureishi was widely criticized as writer for two films: *My Beautiful Laundrette* (1985, dir. Frears) and *Sammy and Rosie Get Laid* (1987, dir. Frears). Less lyrically perhaps – and only slightly less filmic – novelist Salman Rushdie's book *The Satanic Verses* (1988) was famously set on fire in Bradford early in 1989.[1] Kureishi's film work and Rushdie's *Verses* are bound together by more than temporal proximity – one of the characters in Kureishi's later novel *The Black Album* called it: 'That fatwah business' (1995: 140). As a commentary that warned against an emergent hostility that owed much to fascism and xenophobia, Kureishi's novels and film scripts plundered a cosmopolitan diasporic register drawn from a certain sonic 'London' scene, undergoing a sexualized multicultural coming of age. While this may seem somehow antiquated today, the 'anti-racist desire', street riots and book-burnings of that time can be and were taken to mark the first highly visible mobilization of a diverse and complicated Global South Asian presence in the United Kingdom.[2] There had of course been 'visible' moments of Global South Asia in the United Kingdom before this, of which The Beatles heading off on that magical mystery tour with the Maharishi in the 1960s may be the high point, in more ways than one.

The importance of Kureishi's stories for those who needed to see some alternative to the dominant in the more recent period cannot be underestimated, 'as brown bodies trespassed the spaces of colonial anthropology and history to spaces marked as the present' (Desai 2004: v). What distinguished the burning of Rushdie's book compared to earlier irruptions of South Asia in the British news cycle possibly includes the South Asian-on-South Asian protestation involved, a nuance belonging to a quite different dispensation, that since the advent of the war on terror has been simplified and even erased in the reconfiguration of the streetscape of diaspora in the years since these films and the burning of the book. Burning streets and books – not particularly good in themselves – are replaced with a more virulent racial profiling in contemporary 'post-9/11' times. Without permitting every manifestation of the past to fall into the all-consuming ideological apparatus, a careful examination of the antecedents of the current conjuncture may help comprehend contemporary anxiety about and accusations against Islam and Muslims, and by extension contextualize the ways all Global South Asian peoples are now demonized at 'home', and bombed towards 'democracy' elsewhere.

More people know of *The Satanic Verses* through television news coverage and anti-Muslim profiling than do through actually reading the book. Rushdie even seemed to anticipate trouble with some readers, provocatively opening with a sequence designed to puncture conservative stereotypes with a profile of the threatening immigrant. Rushdie as celebrity novelist presented a persona that seemed to encapsulate the trajectory of Global South Asia, winning the Booker Prize in 1981 for *Midnight's Children* and earning widespread recognition, and with the same book later winning both the Booker of Bookers in 1993, and the Booker all-time prize in 2008. The dual, even triple, character of Rushdie's celebrity arrival plays out the fortunes of political migrancy on the world scene clearly, with a battle for recognition amidst white supremacist and faux tolerant liberal context, then demonized and made to act out the good Muslim in a double-play with the global dissemination of the bad Muslim. Despite some early radical posturing, Rushdie is unable to sustain access to the Global South and seems lost, like his compromised autobiographical 'leader' in *Midnight's Children*, Saleem who is absorbed by the malignant spirit of Sanjay Gandhi and the sex addicted Jinns of his later attempts to rewrite his first novel from New York. Of course to be fair, the mockery of Mohammed anticipated this future too, but in the fall of the Asian characters Gibreel Farishta and Saladin Chamcha from an exploding plane, the terror and migration nexus is displayed in a way that is difficult not to post-date as prophetic.

It was, however, the perceived insult to the prophet that occasioned the banning of imports of the book to India, which led to protests in Pakistan, and later occasioned the Ayatollah's fatwah,[3] and the global news splash and public(ity) campaigns that followed – including a march in Leicester led by MP Keith Vaz.[4] Tragically, book-burning became synonymous in the press with the name of ex-author now-celebrity Rushdie and his personal tribulations stood duty for a wider neo-liberal security scare. His publishers, translators and booksellers were threatened, with some indeed appallingly murdered, including his Japanese translator Hitoshi Igarashi and others.[5] Kureishi's dramatization in *The Black Album* relocates the book-burning incident to London, and in comedy, but the Bradford event – which happened after the protests in Pakistan and India[6] – has been embraced by commentators as the first public mobilization of a specifically Muslim South Asian presence in the United Kingdom (see Nawaz 2009 and Malik 2009). This deserves attention precisely because of its importance to the ways in which the racialization and demonization of Islam have escaped these earlier coordinates to be framed only as 'terror' and explicitly not as legitimate street mobilizations of a politically diverse multicultural compact.

Freedom of speech

There is much scholarship on this theme and the changes it brought: Spivak long ago pointed out how 'the Rushdie affair has been coded as Freedom of Speech versus Terrorism' (1993: 237). Kureishi fictionalizes the burning in the context of a staged conflict between offended narrow-scope believers and a few arrogantly illiberal defenders of liberalism (1995: 180). With a long history, the public burning of books of course agitated the sensitivities of a great many of the commentariat, some of whom were later all in favour of the bombing of Baghdad, including, presumably the destruction of various libraries, museums and bookshops (e.g. Christopher Hitchins in the 'Religion Kills' chapter of *God Is Not Great* 2007). This is never to excuse death threats upon novelists, nor do I want to enter too far into the debates about censorship or appropriate handling of Islamic sensitivities – having the wives of the Prophet as prostitutes was always going to get Rushdie into trouble, planned or not, the offense was predictable, and warnings were conveyed to his Indian publishers, of which his UK sales publicists no doubt knew, but horribly under-evaluated. Rushdie himself insists he did not intend to offend, as will be seen. Kureishi was less subtle in mocking the liberal feminists who 'select only Black and Asian lovers now' for political reasons (1995: 190). This chapter aims to think through the reconfiguration of the Global South Asian streetscape, and the transformations of desire, diaspora and the image of terror that the Rushdie book-burning achieved. Or rather, to examine how the incendiary street politics of the late 1980s prefigures, and yet is rather different from, the street politics and fear, not desire, that prevails in a rather different and more bluntly racialized frame today. The book-burning 'stunt' has subsequently and strangely lost its innocence. That is, if it ever can have mere innocence, since book-burning is almost always linked to geopolitical aspirations, and today more than ever in the context of global militarization. Rushdie tells of Hitchens offering a citation of the famous passage from Heinrich Heine on book-burning, though Rushdie extrapolates exponentially:

> [Hitchens] quoted Heine to me. Where they burn books they will afterwards burn people. (And reminded me, with his profound sense of irony, that Heine's line, in his play Almansor, had referred to the burning of the *Qur'an*.) And on September 11, 2001, he, and all of us, understood that what began with a book-burning in Bradford, Yorkshire, had now burst upon the whole world's consciousness in the form of those tragically burning buildings. (Rushdie 2012a).

The first part of this quotation is repeated almost word for word in Rushdie's memoir on that fatwah business, the autobiographical *Joseph Anton* (Rushdie 2012b: 129). In his retelling, there is no mention of Hitchins, nor how in the *Vanity Fair* version, Bradford led inexorably to the war in Iraq. The revisionism firmly in place, as Rushdie offers some comments about remembering Nazi book-burnings and then searing character assassinations of British MPs Jack Straw and Max Madden, who had both supported the Muslim communities' right to protest. Whatever the merits of the debate then, and whether Bradford or Bolton or India or Pakistan were 'first' to protest, the book-burning is now remembered as a terrorist outrage and has a prophetic character as it reconfigures and then changes shape – as Rushdie's own characters also do – in the furnace of geopolitical intrigue. The right to protest is erased in what we might see is a morphing of an identity politics, now dated. What a change since that time – looking back at a street scene of relatively 'harmless' public protest, it seems quite some effort has been deployed to retrospectively invest those characters and issues with far darker sentiments. The opening plane explosion of *The Satanic Verses* is now played out, albeit still largely unread, as emblem of a narrowed suburban and celebrity paranoia, where urban metropolitan anxiety and geopolitical militarization dominate under cover of a race war.

With the formation of Global South Asia in mind, I think it is useful to think about these issues through the prism of the two film 'texts' from Kureishi, since they are almost contemporary to, but slightly pre-date, Rushdie's satanic versifying. The films *My Beautiful Laundrette* (1985) and *Sammy and Rosie Get Laid* (1987), both directed by Stephen Frears and published as separate screenplays by Kureishi, invoke street politics in South London – where we will see burning cars and demonstrators fighting the police, riots, tenements in flames – in almost documentary, but also prophetic scenes. An American photo-journalist in the film is already documenting street rioting in culture industry style, grafting punk poses onto background images of blacks fighting the police in another kind of prophetic anticipation – think of magazines like *Vice* and *Juxtapoz* and the ill-judged 2017 Pepsi Cola Kendall Jenner Black Lives matter parody protest spot. The street here has what turns out to be a more than suitable allegorical purchase on how we think of terror and security in present times, where terror is continually called to attention by reported 'incidents', avoided incidents – due to suitably intrepid investigations by the authorities – and anniversaries of incidents, that each in turn occasion the roll-out of stock footage of scenes of conflagration. Every anniversary the requisite presidential speech commemorating 9/11 must include cutaways to the repertoire of 'freedom' imagery, as if we must constantly be pummelled by the promise of terror, even in quiet times. This iconography ensures a persistent and everyday anxiety about alerts, threats to life and racial profiling prevails in our surveillance state.

We should remember that this ideological complex has a longer history. Where Spivak attends to a geographic and linguistic 'really existing' Asia, reaching from South East to North East (Philippines, North Korea) and North West to Middle East (Afghanistan, Palestine), that has now become the major location for the sharp end of the war on terror, we must recognize this is an Asia as if filtered through US foreign policy. Global South Asia is also plural, and conceptual beyond existing geography and divisions, and it too should not be imagined *only* as a theatre of war. Spivak's effort is to 'provide exercises for imagining pluralized Asias' (2008: 2). Alongside these Global Asias, insofar as there are several already, there can also be the multiple and varied globalized versionings that will extend possibilities and their most significant iterations, mapped out in literature and films like that of Rushdie's *Verses* and Kureishi's *Sammy and Rosie*. The trouble is that being Asian in Britain, or on the streets of other big cities, like New York, morphs over time, and in the political context of the present has lost the very plurality that some had once had fought so hard to establish – and which in other circumstances would be by now the 'normal' plurality of settlement. Instead, almost fifteen years of the war on terror has been a war 'at home' – US Homeland Security, UK Border Agency, Model Minority, Moderate Muslims and the like, – and this has managed to transmute multiplicity back into stereotype. Spivak's work is a warning to resist the ways Asia, and Asians, can become fixed in the popular imagination through ignorance and fear – through the manufacture of what I call Global South Asia as the conceptual site of a threat and danger unspecified and undocumented beyond the profiling and stereotypes that this book examines. My take on this makes it possible to read authors also 'from' the space of Global South Asia, except in critical mode, read against these stereotypes. Here I have in mind work from the United States by Biju Mathew, Vijay Prashad, Amitava Kumar, Sunaina Maira and Gayatri Gopinath as useful in a way that, I suggest, can return us to the films of Kureishi and Frears, and 'that' novel by Rushdie, with sufficient nuance to be able to reclaim and deploy the critiques of stereotyping as a necessary patient corrective to the current reaction.

Given the necessity of pluralizing South Asias, we must also talk of an expanded, reconfigured Global South Asia insofar as it is host for another non-geographical theatre of the same war of terror that codifies, and bombards, really existing South Asia as a site of crisis in the global imaginary. Global South Asia as a war zone becomes a matter of everyday low-intensity violence in some parts, and disproportionate carpet-bombing and drone assassination from the sky in others. The point is to note that urban/street conflict, in locations such as London, Manchester, Bradford, Birmingham as well as New York, Washington, Freemont and New Jersey, is part and parcel, along with Kabul, Helmand, Peshawar, Mumbai, and along with Sydney, Bali, Madrid and Istanbul – all in the same warfare across Global South Asia. Another argument of this chapter then is that as we move away in time and outlook from the difficult ambiguities of Rushdie's fatwah business and Kureishi's cinema we are in danger of losing sight of the convoluted, complicated and *unequivocally ambiguous* engagements and contestations of identity that made them interesting. This contestation was fought out on the streets alongside those texts, but this now recedes to a past Thatcher-era London in favour of a different, and still more violent, version of the neo-liberal reaction. In the new dispensation, diasporic British-Asia,[7] and the visibility of 'British-Asians', loses depth and focus, even as it is captured in the generality of the term Global South Asian. Yet with this term, its referent gains a perverse new immediate but limited visual specificity through being embodied globally in the figure of the threatening Muslim: the people of the book have become book-burners and *Jihadis*, and do duty for all Asians in a trembling popular imagination that cowers in voluntary darkness or in the shadow of the two towers.

Kureishi's films, as also, then, Rushdie's book, evoked an opposition to Thatcherite conservatism and a part of this was the new times convergence of 'we are here because you were there' anti-racist, anti-imperialist sloganeering. How the many different sentiments gathered under that multiculti pageant – as expressed in the multiplicity of the Samba and circus performance of *Sammy and Rosie* – then became *only* the antecedent of a perceived militant and fanatical Islam is the work of considerable revisionist effort. Various commentators do not seem to agree on how this came to pass or what should be the response – there are far too many suggestions that have simply escalated the crisis – but clearly there are also multiple and varied globalized versionings of so-called terror and multiple ways to resist that should be open for discussion. The specificities should not be erased just because the offerings of military-inflected propaganda, tabloid newspapers, and television have displaced the once important nuances of critical literature and cinema. Rushdie's subsequent celebrity pages' endorsement of each and every 'threat' to freedom of speech, such as his widely reported tweeted criticism of Peter Carey and other's refusal to support an American PEN award to the satirical, and racist, French publication *Charlie Hebdo*, would be a case in point (see Kay 2016, Miller 2015). That tweets serve the cause of ideological simplification should come as no surprise, just as the difficult conversations of how to combat reaction and chauvinism are not easily conveyed in headlines.

Settling scores, dirty laundry

What is there new to say about the old controversies? Seen from 'here' and 'now', *My Beautiful Laundrette* and *Sammy and Rosie Get Laid,* with their self-consciously 'post-colonial' politics, and 'Western temperament' with 'uneasy familiarity' with Bollywood born of an 'old diaspora' not yet 'fully aware of a living connection with India that [would soon be] revived in the moment of globalization' (Madhava Prasad 2008: 49). The commodification of cinema as global Bollywood had not yet extracted these filmmakers from a politics inextricably mired in an 'identity debate', which they perhaps could or should have outgrown, but which even now is rehearsed as intersectionality and compartmentalized. Like Rushdie's *Satanic Verses,* these films cannot be read without reference to the difficult politics of South Asians and Islam in Britain before the advent of Global South Asia, where an earlier white supremacist colonial racism, and its complicities, was displaced and giving way to a even more convoluted, racist certainly, but not as articulate, complicated and typecast profile. As much as some might want this not to have to colour every reading and every pronouncement on diaspora, the parameters of white supremacy in a situation of long-term economic stagnation, realignment of economic trajectories towards the Asian powers – the famed 'pivot' – and the connectivities of new modes of communications technology all had decisive impact. What changed was the ratio of racism in culture, from exoticism to accusations of harbouring a deep-seated terror and resentment, and from a paternalizing development to a client state democratic 'dividend' in exchange for business. An economic change determining a cultural change. The problem with such reading would be when attempts are made to reorder the events of these contexts in ways that ignore their political ramifications. In the recodification process witnessed since 9/11, the career of Kureishi as defender of a complicated progressive position seems at odds with the fortunes of the one who was subject to a transformative house arrest in response to the *fatwah*. Of course such 'tendencies' will be read backwards to identify them in already published antecedents, but in Rushdie's late work spin is added to emphasize and confirm subsequent postures.

Rushdie's memoir *Joseph Anton* (2012) largely disregards explicit articulation of the issues I am concerned with here in favour of a tit-for-tat point scoring more suitable for a gossip column apologist than the more engaged, and engaging, author that Rushdie was before his seclusion. Like a newly minted *Munshi*, Rushdie documents the complicities and frustrations of his kept status followed by his well-rewarded and well-publicized high society, thrice-married, coming out. Reading the book as nostalgia as well as revisionism, we could still wonder if there is a way to reach back to the sensibilities of those times, when everything Asian in Britain was up for grabs and literary – pre-*fatwah*, pre-9/11, pre-Global South Asia – an urban multicultural exuberance found its metaphoric muscle in the gymnastic lyrical punning of 'Ellowen Deeowen' (Rushdie 1988: 37). Perhaps in the to be restored archive of Global South Asian, British section, cinema,[8] these films and texts so often seen as superseded – including by Madhava Prasad (2008) – might instead be assessed as touch papers for the recent, more brutal, times, even – and perhaps exactly – where today they could seem dated. The point is to recall these early antecedents and see how the differences of *that* time are recoded *now* as a part of coding as such – the necessary reworkings of the past to suit the investments of the present war show up as convolutions and contortions. The certitudes of 'I told you so' judgements become less plausible if close attention is paid to the particularities of these texts. In an early scene in *Sammy and Rosie Get Laid*, Sammy and his father Rafi are returning home after witnessing street rioting, petrol bombings, conflagration and chaos in the inner city. Sammy turns a corner a little ahead of his father and begins to shout: 'For fucks fucking fucks sake fuck it'. His father worries about his son's language and bad education – 'that I paid through my arse to get you' – but Sammy is more concerned that the street rebels have overturned and burnt his car. Sammy's pompously knowing discourse on urban vitality is doused in personal commodity dispossession, mediated by sexual expletive. We will see more of this scene, which layers a kind of comedy over a kind of violence, and is interestingly reworked as unacknowledged cultural reference by Hugh 'fuckity-fuck' Grant at the start of the hit British rom-com film *Four Weddings and a Funeral* (1994, dir. Newell). If the character Sammy can learn from the compromised Rafi that his complicity in Thatcherite urban consumerism with a veneer of leftist credential is so easily punctured, what then for the present self-assured *Guardian*-reading sophisticate who mixes glossed narrations of fanatical Islam with touristic exoticist cultural appreciation and lament for the ravages of 'development' on pristine idylls? Both Rushdie's publicly recorded erotic conquests and the less often examined sexual charge that belongs to an opposition-fascination with Jihadis are in need of a long kitchen table discussion, as portrayed in both *Sammy and Rosie* and in *Joseph Anton*, even if in the latter the conversations around the table are with Rushdie's police detail minders.

Sex scenes

It will be no surprise to say the sexual politics of Kureishi's fiction stresses ambiguity. In her important book on queer Asian diasporic cultural production and politics, *Impossible Desires,* Gayatri Gopinath begins with the scene from Kureishi's earlier film. In *My Beautiful Laundrette,* Johnny and Omar's back-room caress 'unbuttons' an 'erotics of power'. For Johnny, 'sex with Omar is a way of tacitly acknowledging and erasing' a racist past, but for Omar, 'queer desire is precisely what allows him to remember' rather than 'succumb' and give in 'to the historical amnesia that wipes out the legacies of Britain's racist past' (Gopinath 2005: 2). Desai was able to describe the films in a breathlessly positive register, where 'transgressive sexual practices become one possible strategy of resistance that challenges dominant social mores and power structures' which of course can be welcomed. And more generally,

> Kureishi's films (and writings) made a significant impact on British and Asian British culture of the eighties and nineties. *My Beautiful Laundrette* and *Sammy and Rosie Get Laid* unabashedly portrayed life in a black Britain that was not suspended between two cultures thus trapped in some Manichean binary of East and West but that rather complexly rendered the heterogeneous and hybrid subjects of postcolonial Britain and specifically

> a global London. These films produced a space for the emerging identities of British and diasporic subjects to be articulated. They presented complex, non-essentialist, and non-transparent subjectivities that did not attempt to represent British Asian identity as singular and static. (Desai 2004: 57)

Sharma, as noted before working on pedagogy, provides a clearer description of the plot, which 'focuses on a youthful gay love affair between Johnny (Daniel Day Lewis) a white, working-class ex-fascist and the middle-class Asian male, Omar (Gordon Warnecke)'. Sharma notes that both comedy and drama in the film – and I would add the critique of aspirational Thatcherism and Left identitarianism – contest 'the limited repertoire of Asian stereotypes without being determined by a positive images discourse' (2009: 23). Yet for some in 1985 and throughout the 1990s this Omar-Johnny couplet in *Laundrette* continued to raise problems, both among the Left, as well as the homophobic Right, since some found it difficult to reconcile Kureishi's up-front – shirt-front, brown shirt, national front – provocation with recognition of the 'barely submerged' histories of colonialism and racism the film also depicts. 'We did not fuck fascists, we fucked them up' insists one activist friend, with somewhat surprising aggression. My feeling is that the sort of provocation Kureishi achieves in *Laundrette* is far less provocative today, having become completely acceptable as times and values shift – indeed, in Kureishi's novel *Something to Tell You* (2008), Omar reappears as a Blair-appointed Lord of Parliament, drunk and on his knees in the toilet of a working-class pub (more below). Of course there are always fascists caught in their own vicious contradictions who find guilty pleasures through which to articulate their incoherence, and they found willing partners in the likes of Omar, with motives and desires all too neatly beyond censure. But even if the flash point of this debate has past, the suggestion Gopinath makes about memory deserves attention: 'Queer desire does not transcend or remain peripheral to these histories [of colonialism and racism] but instead it becomes central to their telling and remembering' (2005: 2). Omar interrupts Johnny's caress to remember, remind and accuse him of his racist connections, of his having been seen marching in the street with the National Front. At this point Kureishi is also asking the question of Omar, and fucking fascists is not all that is at stake. That moment was an interruption for many – as Desai relates it, an experience of rapture and return where 'neither the savage heart eaters *of Indiana Jones* nor noble-hearted survivors of colonialism in *Gandhi* ... Laundromat owners and white boy-kissing brown boys captured some other understandings of race and culture, gender and sexuality, and identity and modernity' (2004: v). Once again note how far the nuance of Kureishi's cinema script is contemporary with Rushdie's sexual politics, and yet Rushdie is the one who has been more robustly associated with freedom of speech, while Kureishi and his questioning of Omar, including his later hypocrisy, are lost.

One problem that emerges alongside Gopinath's otherwise important arguments is that the rendering of diaspora is perhaps overplayed as a 'conservative imaginary' with a 'peculiar' and 'backward-looking' 'relation to the past' (2005: 3). The reference here is to Stuart Hall, but Hall does not tarnish all those in diaspora with the same conservative brush. It is worth adding a caution when Gopinath asserts that 'in the queer diasporic texts' she examines, 'queer desire reorients the traditionally backward-looking glance of diaspora' (2005: 3). Certainly her work evokes a useful contrast to those who present 'myths of purity and origin that seamlessly lend themselves to nationalist projects' and to those who support Hindutva and Hindu nationalism abroad, and of course it is true a complicit diaspora can articulate quite well with 'processes of transnational capitalism and globalisation' (2005: 7). The caution to introduce here would be that attributing reorientations to 'queer desire' allows a slippage that can be sustained only if the radical anti-racist anti-imperialist and communist progressive 'parts' of diaspora, historically quite important, are also gathered under the label 'queer'. I would be sympathetic to this idea (Kureishi as queer is plausible, Rushdie less so – four hetero orthodox marriages if you count the one before the *fatwah*), but complicity has a variety of forms. A further problem with an extension of the terminology of queer to include all parts of a radical diasporic sensibility would be that not all of those so gathered together would necessarily want to march, for example, in the India Day parade in New York today, or at least not without considerable debate over the idea of nation thus celebrated.

And it must be debated. To march or not to march – a politics of ambiguity of course can offer all manner of justifications and rationalizations on many sides – that is why it has political purchase. The conservative politics of model minority South Asians in the United States is a peculiarly pernicious thing – not much understood in the UK context, but perhaps emergent as we watch Asian business leaders jockey for favour in the House of Lords and so forth, and Tony Blair or David Cameron fawning over the two hundred most influential British-Asian businessmen and the like, despite Cameron being on record for dislike of 'Indian dancing' (Press Association 2012). In relation to Gopinath, I am not saying that queer Asians should not make a statement on Republic Parade day – but how much more would we like it if they did so carrying the internationalist banners of the Indian Workers Association or some other Global South Asian identifier? The solution is not always to accept only an overdue turn in the participatory democratic conversation. What Ananya Jahanara Kabir, in a rather different, yet still charged analysis of Mani Ratnam's film *Dil Se* (1998) calls the 'libidinal economy of the federal democratic framework' where unrepresented groups are urged to accept the frame of discursive representation and 'work towards a successful politics of bargaining in order to claim their rightful place within the nation' (2003: 141). Roy offers a different comment on Ratnam's film that is useful here in its iteration, and repetition of connecting with aspirational representation, such that Ratnam's cinema 'can throw significant light on how the upward mobility of the middle class in inalienably *connected* with a certain idea of *connectedness* with the global ... [which] *aspires* to reinstate itself within a national terrain of global consumerist a*spirations*' (2014: 3, italics added). I am not dismissing Gopinath's work, but only suggesting we might consider other still more militant dynamics of expression on the part of the South Asian migrant labouring classes, as explored for example in Vivek Bald's detailed study of the history of Bengali-US merchant traders in *Bengali Harlem* (2013), or by those whom Mathew writes about in his engaging book *Taxi* (2005), where he makes the point that in present day New York City the 'politics of community representation evolved out of the basic symbolic material of social justice activists'. The universalism of the civil rights struggle morphed dialectically over time into 'the particular right to mark difference' in the 'framework of multiculturalism', even as that was itself breaking down into a 'separation of communities', with 'each' producing its own institutions, priorities and campaigns (Mathew 2005: 192). This is called and 'inward-looking, self dividing politics' (Mathew 2005: 193), but the burden of Mathew's book is rather to note, or insist, that alliances across differences are still very much a part of the politics of diaspora today. The taxi workers' strike built solidarity and militancy, working with other groups for an expansive Left movement towards justice. Similarly, Bald's work on history and migration to New York would also stress a more convoluted notion of diasporic cultures, drawing on maritime, restaurant and neighbourhood block narratives to bring out 'a different set of stories' (2007: 59, 2013). Prashad's book *Everybody Was Kung Fu Fighting: Afro-Asian Connections and the Myth of Cultural Purity* adds several other transnational Left dimensions in reporting the 'council' meeting of Marcus Garvey with the Gandhian Haridas T. Mazumdar and a certain Nguyễn Ái Quốc, later known as Ho Chi Minh (Prashad 2001: 67). Prashad argues that 'polyculturalist' claims of cultural belonging offer 'solace', but implicitly acknowledge a defensive trap 'able only to garner crumbs from the racist table' (2001: 68). Instead, a broad anti-racist platform that retains the idea of cultural difference does 'not abdicate the right to adjudicate between different practices in struggle', and fights to 'dismantle and redistribute unequal resources and racist structures' (Prashad 2001: 69).

Certainly the grounds of wider, intersectional, alliance are present with Gopinath in an opposition to what she condemns as 'an imaginary homeland frozen in an idyllic moment outside history' and where the 'violences of multiple uprootings, displacements and exiles' are remembered in her focus on the queer body (2005: 4). Yet, it is important that contestation and transformation of racist and colonial histories occurs through a range of very present, diverse, but often also submerged, alternative practices of diaspora and the varieties of opposition, intervention, reorientation and resistance should not be left unacknowledged or displaced by the urgency of other necessary recognitions. As counters to the revisionism that erases complicated South Asian histories post-9/11, the works of Mathew, Bald and Prashad establish lines of inquiry that can be extended – for example, South Asian Communists in Britain also have a long and proud tradition of anti-racist, anti-imperialist struggles that are neither conservative nor backward-looking, nor can studies of these important traditions be dismissed with vague repetition of a refrain that suggests Marxist analyses inevitably 'run the risk of replicating' a totalizing framework (Gopinath 2005: 38). There is no total schema, but to use fear of one to erase Communist anti-racist histories would be an error that belongs to an early period of demonization – of the House Un-American Activities Commission, rather than Homeland Security – and to recover and extend the multiplicity of oppositional movements is always a worthwhile project, undertaken critically.

In terms of the complications of opposition, the extensively detailed study of South Asian women in Britain by the always excellent scholar Amrit Wilson is worth noting. Wilson reports that there was both 'an ever-present undercurrent of resistance from women' against patriarchal oppression within South Asian families and within the wider society, but also 'a plethora of superstitions, fears and taboos [that] served to stigmatise female sexuality' (2006: 11). She rounds upon attitudes to sexuality and staple controversies like *izzat*, arranged marriages, illicit and 'mixed' relationships, parental discipline, the hijab, work and religion to present a considered and convoluted, even dialectical, picture of the ways women in Britain are neither fully free of patriarchy, nor simply 'victims' without a strong tradition of struggle, including against the colonialism, imperialism and capitalism which has 'shaped and reshaped' (Wilson 2006) social relations. In relation to the dialogue that Wilson's sociology can have with Kureishi, and indeed Gopinath, there is space for discussion and debate. Any portrayal of Muslims in this context must acknowledge a spectrum of positions, interpretation and contestation – the very multiplicity and uncertainty that was once possible and indeed plausible in identity discussion.

This is where Gopinath's reading of the disappearance of Tania at the end of *My Beautiful Laundrette* is an insightful critique of the limits of Kureishi's 'filmic universe'. That we do not know if Tania throws herself on the tracks, or leaves on the train 'to seek a presumably freer elsewhere', provocatively suggests the potentials of moving beyond the normative female diasporic subjectivity figured as 'vanishing point' (Gopinath 2005: 4). Victimhood and flight are not the only options, as we might glean from another scene from Kureishi's late 1980s work. Two years after *Laundrette,* we find the lesbian characters Vivia and Rani performing for the male gaze of the patriarchal father, Rafi, in *Sammy and Rosie Get Laid.* It might be argued, in identitarian terms, that these two do not move very far beyond the ambiguous marking of Tania, even with their aggressive, performative, queer visibility designed to shock Sammy's father. Yet a critical leftist reading will observe that they are all-important as harbingers of Rafi's doom. Spivak notes this is 'not a subplot, their function is crucial' (1993: 249) as their researched political intervention offers a more nuanced and informed, and bilingual, characterization of Rafi's impotently faded power as returned corrupt former Pakistani Government despot. Here the ghosting of torture and terror in the post-colonial elite's betrayal of the promise of independence struggles says much more than Kureishi's (bad-) boy's-own view of black lesbian-display, even as it does not displace the cliché of the clinch. Of course a scenario like this could plausibly happen, despite denials, but that it happens in the film in just this 'controversial' way says as much about stereotypes of sexuality as it does anything necessary to the plot. Dutifully acknowledged, the plot thickens to celebrate the urban license of promiscuous multiculturalism when Rosie's sexual experiments with cross-dressing Victoria manifest alongside the colonial era romance of Rafi and Alice, and the loft-living liaison of Sammy and Anna are portrayed in the justifiably famous Bollywood-style triple-horizontal-split-screen sex shot.

The triple-fuck trick makes the vertical lie horizontal

What strikes me as strange now, watching that sequence so many years after the twin towers were flattened, is how well the horizontal frame of the screen suits the old filmic version of life lived enthusiastically despite the bludgeoning oppressive atmosphere of Thatcherite London. Flat, low-rise, oppressive London. Yet, even under the weight of the overpass that covers the community squatter-camp where Victoria lives, and which is bulldozed even flatter by the end, the film invoked the optimism of resistance. The levelling of space in the face of this oppression was also one of the framing moves of the film, where street rioting and flames decorate the opening sections. Rows of houses burning in the riot torn streets of Brixton, Peckham, Lewisham and New Cross are glossed in *Sammy and Rosie* as if they merely offered a panoramic backdrop to the entertaining explanation Sammy gives to his father about being a Londoner. Yet the film had begun with a tribute to the police or immigration squad persecution of settled Londoners and the death of a woman who had been protecting her son from arrest. Kureishi was writing after the deaths of Cherry Groce and Cynthia Jarret, killed by police – a later documentary insists on the *Injustice* (2001, dir. Fero/Mehmood) of these deaths in custody.[9] There are vigils, protests and escalating tension. The street contestation as presented in this perspective is also horizontal; the police enter from the right, while the protesters surge from the left. A fire engine is attacked, a fancy dress group of busker musicians move in colourful single file among the crowds. The riot is not a riot but a carnival, the police retreat. Choreographed street fighting is perhaps not always the first perspective that contemporary sociology would bring to bear on a city like London. While I think the presentation owes a great deal to Kureishi's sentimental, and participatory, attachment to the metropolis of his birth, many years later the riots and the Thatcherite ambience – intentionally flat, dreary and grim, stiff upper lip – looks like the repetition and farce that we are so often trained to identify and will likely repeat as tragedy in the Brexit era.

An emergent vertical view of London is prefigured by Rushdie in the opening pages of *The Satanic Verses,* where the Gibreel Farishta and Saladin Chamcha enter British airspace in an inspired performative-allegory of perceived – swamping – South Asian arrival. The British-Asian, Asian-British mixed up, muddled up, transformed and hybridized characters are always-already complicating things. Farishta and Chamcha fall from the sky after a bomb goes off in their plane. It is not insignificant that Farishta is an actor in Bollywood mythologicals, playing various Hindu deities and with a passing resemblance to Amitabh Bachchan, while Chamcha is a voiceover artist, which invokes the equivalent male version of aural immortality afforded to Lata Mangeshkar and Asha Bhosle. The plane explosion though is in itself an example then becoming forever associated with immigrant news stories, pre-figuring 9/11 with horror reports of unfortunate frozen stowaways dropped over London as the wheel-housings into which they had climbed were lowered in preparation for landing. Amitava Kumar, in his book *Bombay London New York,* links this imagery to both the Rushdie *Verses* narrative and the bodies that fell from the World Trade Centre in the hours after the planes hit, but before they collapsed – and again I notice now how the images are framed vertically, in striking contrast with Kureishi's 1980s London. Kumar describes the earlier tragedy:

> According to a July 2001 report in *The Guardian*, a body was discovered in a parking lot of a department store in West London. A workman in nearby Heathrow airport had seen a figure in jeans and a black t-shirt suddenly 'plummet from the sky like a stone' ... The report said the man who had

> fallen to earth was Mohammed Ayaz, a twenty-one year old stowaway. (Kumar 2002: 230)

Against this vertical trauma, Kureishi has Sammy and Anna, Rosie and Victoria, Rafi and Alice lying together in cross-race, but hetero-normative, embrace. This triumvirate of the missionary position was much discussed on the film's release – for many viewers the first irruption of Hindi film aesthetics into popular British cinema. Now, the major cinema chains regularly feature Bollywood screenings (see Kaur and Sinha 2005), and books on Bollywood and other South Asian cinemas are now widely available if you look – I keep mentioning them, see Madhava Prasad (1998, 2014a), Rajagopal (2001) and Rajadhyaksha (2009), but also Dudrah (2006, 2012), Rai (2009), Gera Roy (2010), Thomas (2014). But look first at the sexy screen: in his informative book on Kureishi, Bart Moore-Gilbert says the author 'anatomises the quasi-colonial attitudes, institutional structures and social hierarchies which subordinate minorities within contemporary British society' (2001: 3). It is also possible to feel that the split screen sex scene flattens what might have been a radical orientation to urban living. A racial radicalism masquerades as shock in a predictable algebraic formation, even as *Sammy and Rosie* raises the spectre of post-colonial violence alongside, or perhaps exaggerating, the only then emergent flat-out opportunism of neo-liberal Thatcherism's deindustrializing, colonial-racist, god-save-the-queen, chauvinistic-jingoistic, union-jack boot Britain.

Rafi's complicit nostalgia for Britain's colonial grandeur runs to having his toast all buttery and 'cunty fingers'. Just what this is remains obscure enough to leave at least one innocent colonial migrant in the dark. A kind of a crumpet perhaps? Rushdie has the same obsessive, almost prurient, longing for the language and promiscuity of Hobson-Jobson.[10] The point is that Rafi's England of yore is not prim and proper, but embraces Alice in a wonderland plateau of nostalgic desire. As Moore-Gilbert reminds us, 'some critics have followed Spivak's lead' in ascribing a 'multi-perspectival point of view' in the 'triple-fuck' scene to 'Kureishi's desire ... to produce a more "collective" mode of representation, in which the polyphony of narrative points of view reflect the film's pluralistic and democratic social vision' (2001: 95). I am *inclined* to agree.[11]

The American journalist Anna in *Sammy and Rosie* takes a great number of photographs during the rioting. It is with her in mind that Gopinath's queer warnings can be taken as a corrective supplement to the stark anti-Thatcherism of the film and not just a sectarian insistence that 'my issue is the main issue'. The salient point being that it might also be good to try again today – as Kureishi perhaps did in bringing *Sammy and Rosie* to a joint crisis around the issue of alliances – to reorient and dis-orient the perspectives that frame multicultural encounters in the city, across the nation and globally. Thus to remember the location of the city as only a focal part of cosmopolitan, not only as a media niche, but also as a meeting place for a diversely promiscuous anti-colonial sensibility.

Global South Asia is also in the metropolitan space, making its connections and planning new worlds, new cities of dissent and accent. This is to locate the settler in the city, already involved, even if modelled by an American wow – the solidarity of Anna with the uncertain directionless of Sammy who really should join the party but the party form has been erased. This does not mean there is no organization, but that it has not been represented. The assumption with which to break here, the complacency that needs to be challenged, is the idea that at ground level there is chaos. The photographer takes her still-shots and gets actors to pose among the rubble. Windows are smashed, there are flames in the upper stories of the houses, sirens wail, but there is a degree of intentionality, and community. And everyone knows when to run. Anna as the street photographer is as much at home among the ambiguities of the urban as any of the other characters, as any of the Londoners, and her chance to lead Sammy astray holds the promise of another transnational alliance that need not only be commercial, that indeed Kureishi critiques, and which, then at least, though sadly, perhaps no longer, showed a degree of strategic optimism.

Street writing screened into global violence

The narrative of *Sammy and Rosie* takes us through the streetscape menagerie of Sammy and Rosie's social acquaintances, some of whom are sexual partners, some of whom are more interesting and colourful. In one scene, Rosie explains her thesis study on the varieties of kissing – a kind of cod-anthropology humour on Kureishi's part, again referencing his peculiarly conflicted concerns about intimacy. Rosie was described by Spivak as 'dramatizing the confrontation between radicalism' and 'simple ethics' (1993: 247–248), as having 'no final determination' (1993: 245) but being both a kind of occluded cipher for the failure to think neocolonialism and 'the best hope' we have.[12] I agree, but...

In *Sammy and Rosie* the street riots are described, by Sammy quoting Rosie, as 'an affirmation of the human spirit'. Rafi scoffs. Rey Chow suggests we need to rethink the culture of protest and its relation to a work ethic that belongs to modern secular capitalism (2002: viii). The game of street protest as representational politics, vying for a space on the spectacular news hour, forcing a minister to comment is something like a chore or a vocation – not necessarily in the most righteous sense. Do those who protest by-the-numbers – like the two million who marched against the Blair/Bush doctrine in February 2003 – do so with the reflective critical awareness of what might be the best strategic response to the coercive and co-opting powers of capital, or is this too complicity? A to B marches over and over again and the political containment of the protesters between the marked barriers and in the park at the end for a tame rally of the same old trades union moderate media-friendly speakers. All of this scripted again, visible as part of a drama. Any deviation from the hierarchical into horizontal street protest, drifting from the agreed route, spontaneous targeting of symbolic enemies, or bloc diversified tactics is met with rapid response suppression, water cannon and Jenkels. The kind of street protests characterized as disorder in the press play as victory, or at least sustain encouragement, among the protesters – and so attract all the more hostility from the police and media, always designating uncontrolled protest as 'rioting'.

Perhaps with someone like Rosie in mind, Chow invokes speaking rights but recognizes that power relations, and the threat of violence, underpin and undermine such rights:

> As long as minorities' rights to speak and to be are derived from and vested in the enabling power of liberalism, and as long as these minorities are clearly subordinate to their white sponsors, things tend to remain unproblematic for the latter. Should the reality of this power relation be exposed and its hierarchical structure be questioned, however, violence of one kind or another usually erupts, and naked forms of white racist backlash quickly reassert themselves. (2002: ix)

Rosie is never obviously troubled by the violence on the streets. Her pathos is in the death of the old white man in his bath in the council flats. The arrival of Sammy's father Rafi, which both offers and threatens to transform Sammy's previously inconsequential existence into one that promises money and power (however corrupt), also changes the comfortable dynamic over which Rosie rules. She goes out and seduces Victoria, demanding Sammy accept their polyandrous arrangement. Sammy, at least not insisting on monogamy, still enacts a fantasy of retribution in the loft with Anna. Liberalism here is the syncopated flip side of white supremacy, as a propertied ownership of representational space. Rosie is writing a thesis, Sammy is an accountant, writing the ledgers of commerce. Liberalism implicates well-intentioned 'progressive' politics in an everyday violence that references and is fortified by racism, economic privilege and brute force. The bulldozers move the alternative squatter-musician camp from beneath the flyover – under the modernist overpass – and yet Rosie continues to be lauded as centre of her world. That there are other political options in this scenario must be seen as a matter of urgency. Those who centre the world only in their own experience are nearly always ideological participants in a much wider project towards which they seem determinedly myopic.

Thirty years after the Miners' Strikes, Thatcherism and the advent of neo-liberalism, it might now read as, sadly, normal that *Sammy and Rosie* evidences a surprising absence of Reds. No communists and not even socialists of the newspaper-wielding Trotskyite variety have any major role – at best, a glimpse of an anti-National Front poster. Rosie's 'politics' stands in blatantly for that gap, erasing much in terms of British Left history, including South Asian participation in Communist Party of Great Britain organizing – its first elected parliamentarian and the editor of its journal for three decades were both prominent South Asian figures (see Hutnyk 2005b). Yet, it would not do to retrofit the context of these almost thirty-year-old texts so as to render Kureishi and Frears as card-carrying Party members, they were not explicitly pointing to the absence of the Left in their films. It remains the case that communist histories are effectively erased even by those who remember a time when such ideas were more prominent. That the Communist South Asian heritage of Sammy is forgotten, and only rendered drunk and bedridden as Papa in *Laundrette*, is something that then permits approval of Rosie as 'the best hope'. Anticipating the narrow spectrum of Gopinath's political actors, we should understand this as a scarlet exclusion of deep significance.

Nevertheless, Spivak notes Rosie is in a 'beleaguered position' and says 'you cannot really be against Rosie ... she loves all the right people. She's a white heterosexual woman who loves lesbians, loves blacks, is in an interracial marriage, etc., etc.' This is perhaps almost what Kureishi had said, in more blunt language. But Rosie has 'no final determination' (Spivak 1993: 245). Thus, while she is the most tolerant of all characters, and her guidance is love, or at least erotic pleasure, she somehow cannot be left unresolved and unredeemed. Of course I also want to approve of her as part of the more openly sexualized multicultural of a generation now past, but I am chastened by Chow who reminds us that 'tolerance remains cathected to advantage' (2002: 13), such that the notion of 'neo-racism' (Balibar and Wallerstein 1991: 21) manifests in 'anthropological culturalism' as 'inherent' to an 'expansionist logic' and accelerating 'racial and ethnicist violence' (Chow 2002: 14). I am again reminded of how Sammy is cathected to his car as its destruction undoes his allegiance to the street protests, and cements instead his filial investment in his father's dubious wealth. On the other hand,

Rosie is something like the other-loving anthropologist who, despite the very best intentions and declarations of fidelity to, at least, ideals of diversity and equality, still manages to have her chocolate cake and eat it too. There is little good to be said for what Chow calls 'well intentioned disaffiliations from overt racist practices' if professions of concern by those who scrupulously will not 'speak for others' (e.g. by leaving post-colonial theory only to people of colour) coincide with the claims of those who would help in a charitable hidden vanguardist role. These moves 'often end up reconstituting and reinvesting racism in a different guise' (Chow 2002: 17).

The Mukti Bahini

In *Outside in the Teaching Machine* (1993), Spivak identified the post-colonial figure of Rafi as the one who betrayed anti-colonial struggles in the crucible of a new elite real-politik and neocolonial restitution of global power. This film from long ago can give us materials to think through problems and inform us of historical contexts – the role models in *Sammy and Rosie* are themselves mediators of entire socio-political networks. Rosie as white guilt, the best we can hope for; Sammy, exhibiting identitarian narcissism; Victoria, sexual ambiguity/narcissism; Anna, display as photography posture, with two W's tattooed on her buttocks; Rafi, post-colonial despot and betrayal exposed; Vivia and Rani, activist lesbian commitment and 'fact-finding' (Spivak 1993: 249), while the taxi driver as damaged Mukti Bahini guerrilla fighter subjected to torture in the Bangladesh war of succession from Pakistan makes the betrayal of progressive politics seem the key critical – and significantly ghostly, haunting – vector of the film. I do not want to lament a lost complexity, but perhaps these characters open up possibilities for discussion of political diagnostics of the present time. Sammy in particular: To his father's question as they negotiate the burning streets: 'Why do you live in a war zone?', Sammy replies, with an assertion of urban pride: 'We're not British, we are Londoners' and asserts that Leonardo Da Vinci 'would have lived in the inner city'. Spivak finds the comment on Londoners so significant that she cites it four times (1993: 250, 252), a 'last ditch precariousness' (1993: 250) that as a refrain offers something like having a dream.

Even if this is a family drama, it is an educational one. We do live in a war zone. It is the faulty father who fails to lead the anti-colonial struggle beyond its initial gains, an even worse father than drunken papa in *My Beautiful Laundrette*. The son finds solace only in an accommodation with materialism that must also fail, to be comforted in the end by a cross-race, cross-generation community, but one that is being destroyed by Thatcherism, paving the way in due course for Blair and 'New Labour'. Neo-liberal bulldozers crush both music and community. Rafi dies. The story is a painful one, the prognosis as bleak as the urban squalor of the time. Intellectual leadership fails – as it often does in films of the time, as with the faulty father in *Apocalypse Now* (1979, dir. Coppola), Colonel Kurtz/Marlon Brando, who cannot lead, despite all his learning (see below). Rosie with her thesis tends towards the sensational, and events transpire despite her efforts. This is an all too common consequence, explored by Mrinal Sen in two films. In *Ek din Pratidin* (1979, dir. Sen), the family must leave the house at the denouement – under post-colonial restitution there is no place for them, despite their high self-regard, their betrayal of the unassuming hard-working daughter just because she comes home late from office one day, deserves no reward. In a kind of 'remake' that was not exactly a remake *Ek Din Achanak* (1989, dir. Sen), it is the father, a professor, who leaves near the start of the film, never to return, with damaging consequences for the family. This can be raised again later in terms of Sen's critique of bourgeois patriarchy and self-interest, but unlike Sen's working daughter, Rosie will not go anywhere in the end. She is already free to do as she pleases, so she has no interest in moving on. This is not the case for Tania at the end of *My Beautiful Laundrette,* nor really for the working daughter in *Ek Din Pratidin,* and while we do not find out where, the fact of going is open as possibility. Rosie though has complicated domestic interests, and we suppose she will get her MA and continue on as benevolent social worker. Social 'types', as portrayed by Kureishi, disavowed by Rushdie, in some cases become parodies of the committed intellectual, hopelessly weeping and defeated at the end. No wonder many are inclined not to trust the leadership egoist pretensions of the Rosie type, but in the film we have not been in the presence of an organized Left. Hardly at fault for the decline of radical politics, Rosie was a different sort of party girl than the party capable of winning against the neo-liberal wave.

Viewing the film again today, it also looks like a rehearsal in period costume. The performance of street protests are made more poignant and have to be evaluated in the context of pressing neo-imperial crises that again evoke the co-constitution of Empire and metropole. List: the United States and Britain with the Iraq war and Afghanistan, the NATO intervention in Mali and Libya, the end of civil liberties and the Green Zone security of military governance; the street violence of the Arab Spring and its counter-revolutionary 'sting' (Chandan 2015), the limits of Occupy and the 2011 London uprising, the Indignados and the grotesque conflict in Syria – in almost each scene both here and there new racist neo-liberal horror is brought together in an intimate, almost pornographic, embrace ; this is perhaps just as Kureishi's *Sammy and Rosie* joyously foretold.

The Golden Bough

The moment when celluloid burns in the projector holds a certain fascination for media studies: *Cinema Paradiso* (1988, dir. Tornatore) and so many other films use this scene to great effect. Other great fire scenes are staple fare (e.g. the merry-go-round in *Sholay* and the curtains that burn as Rafi tries to sleep in *Sammy and Rosie*), but we could also imagine this as a direct commentary by Kureishi on a more urgent politics at that time to do with street protest – a burning book allegedly started the New Cross Fire in 1981. A potent and relevant tragic moment of terror and destruction when a phone book was forced through the front door letter slot of a three storey house, 13 dead, nothing said. Clearly it is to also have Rushdie and burning books in mind with this theme, to which we must return in next chapter.

There is much to consider here, starting with linking the atrocity of book-burning to the emotional charge that comes from book learning as enlightenment. Adorno and Horkheimer are close here, but not yet. I have in mind my favourite version of this: Somerset Maugham's (1944) novel *The Razor's Edge*, which was made into a great film starring Bill Murray, whose quest for knowledge leads him down mines and up mountains, cooking for the monks at a Tibetan monastery. We see him freezing cold in a hut where he has been sent by a holy man to contemplate; he runs out of firewood and finally burns his texts to survive – cue uplifting music and *satori*-enlightenment inducing break of the sun through clouds over the Himalayas (*The Razor's Edge* (1984, dir. Byrum)). Tyrone Power in the 1946 film of the same name (dir. Golding) is also good, though the clunky sets, the strutting peacock and the Greco-Roman columns of Shangri-La are of the time. Bill Murray's enlightenment is sublime however, and his book-burning moment throws me forward to the final sequence from *Apocalypse Now* where we see a ritualized working through of the father-son relation between Colonel Kurz and Willard (Martin Sheen), where Kurz in turn throws a book at Denis Hopper's LSD-fried photo-journalist character to shut him up. In that last scene, Kurz is reading Sir James Frazer's *The Golden Bough*. There has to be a book, according to the script, but we might wonder at the knowing conceit of choosing just that book. It was a shipping book in Conrad's original tale; the *Golden Bough* references an entire series of fire rituals. The horror, the horror...

Urban guerrilla-style struggle on the streets is something many may think belongs to the past, to the 1960s and 1970s, to the Algerian Revolution and films like Gillo Pontecorvo's *Battle of Algiers* (1966), Mrinal Sen's *Calcutta* 71 (1971) or the Red Army Faction struggles in Germany, the years of lead in Italy, and perhaps the England of the early 1980s – Brixton, Peckham, Lewisham, as above. Aside from the occasional flare up in the northern cities, how is it that people might forget the constant stream of bad news from sites in Asia and the Middle East where the contemporary relevance of such struggles does not seem only historical or theatrical, though it is for the cameras? Mogadishu, Gaza, Fallujah, Aleppo – these should have changed this myopia, but now that London, New York and Madrid sweat in the same war, it perhaps might pay off to re-examine some of the street scenes from earlier times. Notting Hill, Brixton, Toxteth, Manningham, Oldham, Bradford – one set of responses. Stop and search, custody deaths, profiling, detention – scaled up internationally on TV as live news, but with special rendition. Kidnapping and remote-controlled drone death, inserted in between the routine bureaucratic arabesques of finance, health, education, workplace and housing scandals. At the high profile ends of hypocrisy we have the pomp and circumstance of Westminster, and the bad faith of humanitarian bombing campaigns.

Of course, the burning of books has its own charged and charred history: degenerate art and texts burnt in Nazi Germany, as Rushdie of course noted in his *Joseph Anton* memoir (2012: 129); McCarthy-era removal of 'communist' books from US libraries – they were burnt (as reported in Fried 1990: 136). Umberto Eco's burning library in *The Name of the Rose* (1983), echoing of course the famous, disputed (Báez [2004] 2008: 51–52), destruction of the Alexandria library, and, as Georges Bataille recounts in *Literature and Evil,* Franz Kafka left instructions that all his books and papers be burnt upon his death. Of course he told this to 'the one friend who had already informed him that he would never do so' ([1957] 1985: 151). H. G. Wells's *A Short History of the World* (1922) burnt for disrespecting the *Qur'an* in 1938 (*Guardian,* 13 August 1938). Sir Richard Francis Burton's diaries, letters and papers, and an improved translation of the erotic Arabic text *The Perfumed Garden,* with the missing final chapter 'The Scented Garden', were torched by his wife at his death (Báez [2004] 2008: 155), and so many more. Burning books is the premise of Bradbury's *Fahrenheit 451* (1953), and there are many others. Although the Rushdie controversy starts in India, commentators keep on locating it in Bradford because that burning book image was so evocative, and the dots keep on joining up, as we too often see...

Riots?

Which probably raises the question as to why the streets of London are not burning today? They were in Manningham and Oldham in 2001 – with resultant police crackdown,[13] they burnt for three days in London in August 2011, but the next summer there was only the Olympics. What I would suggest is that the complexities of Rushdie and Kureishi's texts belong to a 'back then' and now in the present, due to the changed geopolitical dispensation, globally, all South Asians in Britain, and elsewhere, are rendered more simply as terrorists or moderates, so they cannot risk and are no longer allowed any more 'ambiguous' articulation. Rather than a 'backward looking', 'conservative imaginary' (Gopinath 2005: 53), I think we can learn something of the future present from these now somehow 'earlier' media texts. While for some, the British-Asian condition has been glossed as harmless fun through comedy shows and Bollywood fashions, many Britons of South Asian provenance have suddenly been repackaged in an unrecognizably one-dimensional stereotype and retrofitted for extra-juridical deportation or detention. The police crackdown has a photo-fit profile that is simplified but is not simply a security scare, but a systematic ideological distraction that saturates our screens with the perverse alternative of either terror reports/docu-dramas or celebrity real estate personal make-over reality TV shows. Burning the streets, overturning cars, burning books even, are for sure all a bit macho: a posturing Global South Asian who no longer has the counterpoint context of Left-leaning Rosie and her friends to affirm validity in and as political expression of resistance – 'affirmation of human spirit'. Instead, the jingoistic Olympics of anodyne sporting success, including some 'multicultural' heroes – Mo Farah, Usain Bolt – running interference for a political repression that means street struggles today lose all ambiguity and all legitimacy – to be rendered merely 'terror' in the press without critical commentary or comprehension of grievances. This rapidly became as if a scene in an old movie. Global South Asian diasporic production meant screens were quickly filled with *Goodness Gracious Me* (1998, BBC), *The Kumars at Number* 42 (2005, BBC), *Bend It Like Beckham* (2002) and *Bride and Prejudice* (2004). However edifying in terms of bright colour and happy endings, there was – in the contrast everyone felt in everyday experience – no respite from entertainment vacuity and ideological heartburn.

Those who might once have joined street demonstrations and offered a militant anti-racism that had – however difficult – a relation, and relationship, to a Left critique of capital, are now demonized. South Asian Britons who protest are cast as threatening – only moderate and cowed 'community members' are, at best, tolerated in the new security compact. What the years between Bradford/Brixton and the 'post-9/11' period have brought us is a narrowing and even erasure of political expression.

There are those who would attempt a more convoluted explanation of this impasse, of the emptied out terrain – comedy Asians on the one side, bearded terrorists on the other – and attempt a political diagnostic. Kenan Malik, for example, offers a heady amalgam of anti-racist activist history and condemnation of 'the multiculturalist' tendency in the British context, a failure of the 'Left'. Malik's anti-racist history owes much to, but does not fully acknowledge, the work of Sivanandan and the Institute of Race Relations, but on multiculturalism he only sees misguided tolerant liberalism paving a path for reaction. What happened around Rushdie's book? A celebrated, televised, burning of the book in Bradford by those who, according to Malik, acted in large part:

> because of disenchantment with the secular left, on the one hand, and the institutionalisation of multicultural policies, on the other. The disintegration of the left in the 1980s, the abandonment by leftwing organisations of the politics of universalism in favour of ethnic particularism, and the wider shift from the politics of ideology to the politics of identity, pushed many young, secular Asians towards Islamism as an alternative worldview. (2008).

The critique of ethnicity, identity and multiculturalism misfires; however, here Malik insists on universalism as if it were the only and antithetical inverse of identity and ethnicity. Caught in a complimentary logic, Malik's scorched earth policy burns his own anti-racist credentials and repeats the obvious and automatic reaction – endorsing an integration model for Britain today, at a time which also sees a resurgent ultra-Right in the British National Party and the centre-right drift of all the established parliamentary players – some could call this drift more or less a firesale or bonfire of older principles. That said, agreement with most of Malik's points is possible, and the case can be, and has been, made that 'ethnic funding' elevated culturalist 'community leaders' as a complicit 'bulwark' with which to undermine militant anti-racist alliances, but to then diagnose the problem as culture and insist on its overcoming in some naïve secular French Republic post-9/11 type model is a deeply conservative, even nationalist, error.

Who speaks for the resistance?

More interesting is Spivak's essay on *The Satanic Verses,* where she uses the occasion of Rushdie to consider other cases written out of the record. Her example of the internationalist feminist reading of the 'sati' Shahbano, made a 'figure' in a contest over votes, is exemplary (1993: 240). She reflects on the position of Southall Black Sisters in relation to the 'controversy' as crisis, to then in this context think about 'freedom of expression'-talk and the 'uses to which the spectacular rational abstractions of democracy can sometimes be put' (1993: 241). Rushdie, himself accused of complicity with the West's imperialist 'crusade' against Islam by Ayatollahs and others, surely did not know or intend the extent to which his little fiction would offend, even as he aimed to offend indeed: as he had oftentimes done – *Midnight's Children* and *Shame* both also banned. More recently of course Rushdie has been forced into many, even far too many, 'explanations' of his work of fiction: 'I never set out to insult anybody'. He says he offered 'an extremely sympathetic portrait of a Muslim, and non-Muslim South Asian, community wrestling with the consequences of transnational migration' (2009: 139). The ideal high society dinner companion would be Gibreel Farishta, the movie star. Second choice, Rushdie himself.

It is still the case, and so many years later worth remembering, that *The Satanic Verses*, as literature, went unread. Mazzarella notes that 'liberals often complain – in India, as elsewhere – that those who seek bans on books or films often have not read or watched the items to which they so vociferously object' (2013: 103). At the time, something of a 'rumour' (Spivak 1993: 228) spread that Rushdie had indulged in 'gossip' about the prophet, that he had blasphemed against the *Qur'an*. Of course it is almost bad taste now to think of Rushdie's book in terms of the theoretical interests or fashions of its time of writing: when the death of the author thematic was hip, signed under the proper names of Roland Barthes and Michel Foucault, alongside celebrations of the schizoid self, and a rampant mixture and hybridity that itself celebrated difference and punning. The rumour of promiscuity, a *tamasha* in language and more, was welcome then. But author- (and bookseller-) death did not make for easy jokes about the *fatwah*. These controversies have a different context now – one that cannot ignore the US occupation of Iraq and Afghanistan, NATO in Libya and Mali, and threatening escalations across the board. Then, Iran was central in a different way, and the Ayatollah railed against America.

Notwithstanding, there is still something to be recalled for today in the literary political analysis of before. Spivak pointed out in her 1993 essay that critics of her reading of *The Satanic Verses* could complain that she 'gives resistance no speaking part' in Rushdie's text (1993: 226). We will see later that this is not the case, if her other work is read alongside, but if the book does not enact resistance as a character, perhaps we can agree with Spivak that to 'state the problem' [of the hybrid, shape-shifting, complicit post-colonial migrant and the ossified, clerical, conservative] is not bad politics'. She continues: 'In fact, it might be poor judgement to consider academy or novel as straight blueprint for action on the street' (1993: 227). I do not find this far from Adorno's critique of an introspective protest against order that is indifferent to, and so ultimately compatible with, that order (Adorno [1970] 1997: 116). Adorno is worth quoting at length here as his commentary underpins my critique of what has happened subsequent to Rushdie/Kureishi:

> [There now is a] witch hunt against expression ... Although inwardness, even in Kant, implied a protest against the social order heteronomously imposed upon its subjects, it was from the beginning marked by an indifference to this order, a readiness to leave things as they are and obey. This accorded with the origin of inwardness in the labor process: Inwardness served to cultivate an anthropological type that would dutifully, quasi-voluntarily, perform the wage labour required by the new mode of production necessitated by the relations of production. With the growing powerlessness of the autonomous subject, inwardness consequently became completely ideological, the mirage of an inner kingdom where the silent majority are indemnified for what is denied them socially. (Adorno [1970] 1997: 116)

More directly relevant, and perhaps more succinctly: 'immediately back of the mimetic taboo stands a sexual one: Nothing should be moist; art becomes hygienic' (Adorno [1970] 1997: 116). Rushdie's book might indeed need to be defended on these grounds precisely where it explores blasphemy and ambiguity within Islam – a complication neither trenchant defenders of the Holy Book, nor those who attack Islam, and desecrate the book in prisons like Bagram, Abu Ghraib or Guantanamo, can assimilate. But the situation is different now, as Evangelist US preachers and English Defence League 'associates' burn the *Qur'an* simply to provoke (EDL 2011). A belligerent white supremacism fuelled by international weapons commerce, detention and private security army regimentation, out and out invasion and geopolitics, has emerged into the vacuum where critical thinking once prevailed. This vacuum is a consequence, if not of the burning of Rushdie's book, it at least in some sense follows on from a retreat from the politics of 'stating the problem', where the problem requires a fight against stereotypes and their vicious consequences. I do not think that burning a book today would make one iota of difference here – entire libraries have been destroyed and we see only a mild outrage in the staged statecraft of those who have responsibility for these things. The books are not sacred, of course, but to burn them misses the point.

Spivak writes of Adorno's article, badly translated in English as 'Commitment', and reports that he says Brecht's use of montage 'simply turns a political problem into a joke'. *Sammy and Rosie* is genuinely funny in parts, but Spivak likes it for different reasons:

> One hopes that Kureishi's montage technique would have satisfied Adorno. It is much more concerned with negotiating a certain kind of unease, a laughter tinged with unease and bafflement. That comes through in the

> montage particularly well as the film moves away from realism and the ghostly figure of the torture victim becomes more prominent. (Spivak 1993: 254)

Is it the case that *Sammy and Rosie* also offered a multi-perspectival and collective mode of storytelling, as Moore-Gilbert (2001), lining up alongside Spivak, would have us believe? In the three-step unfolding of these scenes, it is the figure of Rosie in the middle (well, Rosie and Victoria) that is interesting because here cultural politics and sexual play has helped occlude an older involvement that was first displaced by identity concerns, and is now overwritten with narrow şinister consequences.

What next for Sammy?

Even the identitarian mode of address seems to have been suppressed in the constant barrage of station announcements, security alerts, low-level anxiety about security and surveillance – and the suspicion that your neighbour with a beard is no longer a friend called Sammy and instead a more sinister Salman. The tropes have changed; Farishta has morphed again. This is a diagnostic of the times, or rather, can be brought forward to do different duty for our times, even as we recognize the dangerous diminution of the ways in which storytelling as a mediation of multiple points of view, and varied sexualities, identities, politics, exceeds any easy calculation or ascription of the 'proper' and correct interpretive framework (contra Gopinath). Farishta now is a monstrous hybrid realized as an allegation – the mask grown to stand in not as critique of cultural certitude, but its congealed profile form and 'bad' character in the narrow dynamic of the war of terror. What Kureishi's difficult cinema supplied in terms of a critique that complicated Global South Asian presence is lost if the public view of Asians in the metropole ignores the richness of the work of Bald, Mathew, Prashad and Kumar, let alone the 'queer' diasporas of Gopinath and the potentials of pluralizing Asians of Spivak. The complications cannot be magically but rather actively restored through repeated viewing. The *Black Album* book-burning, the '*fatwah* business' and the fascist-fucking, as well as the triple-fuck scene, was once a welcome articulation of a diverse and unsettling settlement. That it came soon after – or even hand-in-hand, with the promiscuous growth of 'weird cults, superstitious groups, new agers, strange therapists, seers, gurus' (Kureishi 2005: 54) – is the nuance that *Sammy and Rosie* tried to balance. In more congealed times, the vehicles of mediation, the pathways for making intentional illustrative juxtapositions or montaged, alliterative, associative points are now reduced to no more than a single image and the jingoistic homeland security narrative iteration of the next next next constant enemy: EurAsia, EastAsia, Oceania – any enemy will do Brother Orwell. This stacked up ambiguity was important; to lose it is to lose the game.

It is still perhaps an unresolved question – for Sammy, Rafi, Rosie and for us all in our necessary debates about the post 9/11 configuration – whether old literary and cinematic controversies can rise again as prompts for debate. At present they seem damped down under a stark reaction and the global dominant. The quietening of a critical, sexually and intellectually rampant and promiscuous radical tradition in popular culture – which both Kureishi and Rushdie once wrote for, in some sense – means that efforts to restore the politics of a 'ruthless critique of everything that exists' (Marx 1843) must be more than a shrill voice in the flames. Without Marx *and* queer, without Spivak's Rosie *and* Sammy, without rethinking how the mobilization of an alternate Global South against the demonized and demonizing forms, there is no play of perspective, no multiplicity, no community and the books become ashes we cannot read.

3

The Electronic Palanquin

If Oskar Negt is to be taken seriously, we should not then start with television at the centre, in the box, or on the screen. 'A critical theory of the media cannot have the media as its center' (1978: 63). Rather, let us look at what the box is attached to, where it sits, what are its connections. To make this more specific, however problematically, something called Global South Asia will be decentred, but perhaps re-centred as 'modernity at large' (Appadurai 1996). Global South is perhaps best thought of as an always emergent political category, but it's also necessary to tell the story and find the documentary mode to save this neologism also from barbarism – and sometimes that will mean retelling the story from a different place. The import of origin stories and contest over interpretation of, and the need for research into, the history of film can never be without agendas. History as written by the victors demands a provocative alternative response. Though it may also be the case that counter-productive evocations of Global South and Global South Asia privilege a shiny economic and corporate capital screen on which are projected much more profound aspirations which cannot in this way succeed. The spokespersons for Global South Asia are not a mere matter of casting. There are urgent reasons to rethink of the way documentary presents, and how it moves, and who with – an uncle of the old colonial frame – who carries which version of 'culture' and history into the documentary niche of travel or nostalgia (Rajadhyaksha 2008: 39). Then the films will burn again with the reinvention of television and the digital centre. Fire as a theme.

Ramayana anecdotes

My interest in the screen image in and of Global South Asia and the paraphernalia that surrounds television stems from my faulty memory of what is now probably apocryphal stories, but ones with actual and resonant correlates updated to the present. I take justification for retelling anecdotes from anthropological training, held in critical suspension. But also from the comments by Gregory Ulmer, in his book *Teletheory*, that associate television, and especially both television news and the teaching of television studies, with a specifically 'anecdotal structure' (1989: 72). Similarly influential are the readings by Sundaram (2009) and Rai (2009) who both connect film and television up to networks of external and social 'assemblages' (Rai 2009: 10) which they reveal in an ethnographic and anecdotal mode that give particular importance to discussion of events and meetings 'outside' the cinema, or at the periphery of its industry. This in turn follows Madhava Prasad who, with his discussion of subsumption, articulates a deeper analysis of ideology as a socio-cultural frame within which the varieties of cinema, and so also television, are usefully to be understood (Madhava Prasad 1998). This chapter is in part an appreciation of these authors in a co-constitutional mode to take this discussion elsewhere, and after preliminary survey of this new work, the chapter moves to a certain 'national treasure' who has quite different connections to Global South Asia that is a fantasy of comedy light-entertainment and international access-all-areas pseudo-documentary. It may seem strange to cast Michael Palin in a role alongside Madhava Prasad, but attention to the connectivities of the assemblage can be revealing.

Already much commented upon, the broadcast of the serial *Ramayana* (1987, dir. Sagar) on Doordarshan is overdetermined in several ways. The well-storied mythological origin of the 'breakthrough' moment of television and VCR into Indian homes offers at least two smaller curio-like stories that capture my attention. The first to do with trinkets: the placing of devotional artifacts upon a television set during the broadcast of *Ramayana* led to the set catching fire. Sita in flames was made all too real for one accident-prone family. The TV set manifest as shrine, where the oil burner burns a little too well and the TV was reduced to ash, charred wood and wires short-circuiting an entire *bustee* area of Kolkata. It is no surprise that television sets in the home often carry a range of objects – photos in frames, sporting trophies, souvenirs, and indeed our own has a candle atop it as I write while half-watching 24-hour international news. Is it indulgent to dwell upon the place of this piece of furniture that sits in the corner, but dominates the room, as it throws its late-night glare over all the other furniture and occasionally cries out with a shrill jingle for attention?

At the risk that these stories will overplay the mystico-religious-dramatic register, my second example concerns the Haryana broadcast of *Ramayana*, which was interrupted by an unscheduled power outage, and subsequently a protesting crowd upset at having missed the show besieged the power station. Power is electricity which is the spark that permits enlightenment, and the protest was for rights to electrification and more, or at least for storytelling in the electronic hearth that now dominates most homes. But storytelling itself concatenates cinema and the 'modern state apparatus' according to Rajadhyaksha, who sees the 'privileged presence' of film in the state machinery as a way of connecting selves to structure (2009: 11–12). Global South Asian screens provide a space of subjective identification, a 'symbolic space where that self is produced in narrative' (Rajadhyaksha 2009: 125). Today, as Rai and Sundaram also show, the parameters of screen contact spill over from this scene, and from the cinema hall, to connect up with the network of, in the one story, mythological architecture, in the other the power grid. For me, these incendiary narratives do two things: they rehearse a fantasy rural-spiritual version of Asia on the one hand, an imaginary of timeless village and temple rusticity while on the other, they link electronic media haphazardly, and precariously, to traditions of storytelling at the centre of social, familial and community space that, when the community mobilizes interests that are never so sleepy and passive, can have dire homogenizing consequences just where it might also access a Global South polity as a resource for political redress. This space is in danger, yet also resilient. The screen as a mythmaker at the centre of the social, at the centre of our lives, manifests renewed structures of social form.

Of course it is still standard to mention how many 'anecdotes abound' (Dwyer 2006: 52) about the mythological shows. *Ramayana* was followed by the still more popular *Mahabharat* (1988, dir. Chopra). My two anecdotes, apocryphal or not can no longer be remembered, belong to those now strange days of the 1980s when, in ethnography and indeed in wider anthropological discussion, it was rare to see any mention of television or film, except perhaps as a knowing guilty indulgence. The one famous cartoon most anthropologists put on their office doors was the Larson one of comedy savages hiding their electronic goods in their grass hut because they could see the approach of a canoe on the river full of safari-suited 'Anthropologists, Anthropologists!' Slowly anthropology woke up to media, and in part it was attention to Bollywood that changed the discipline. With television and mass cinema, there was a transformation even in film studies: no longer was the art cinema of Bengal the primary visual media focus – like Madhava Prasad, I heard the term Tollywood, referring to the Bengali studios at Tollygunge, before I heard the term Bollywood (Madhava Prasad 2008: 42) – and by the time Bollywood had gained media space, and Dhallywood (Dhaka) and even the first hints from Kollywood (Kathmandu), the extension of a different kind of globalizing South Asian imagery started to register, and exponentially. To some degree we are still working through this today, and it is easy enough now to find studies of the influence of South Asian screen culture almost everywhere and doing everything. Indeed, the variety of that which can be allocated to Global South Asian film and television studies is huge: in Mauritius, for example, now Bollywood allows Muslim women a 'niche' opportunity to 'consume popular culture and concurrently to access a form of modernity that is tolerated', by their community (Lallmahomed-Aumeerally 2014: 160). In Guyana, Atticus Narain cautions against any 'excited' 'homogenization' through utilizing the 'transnational cultural sphere to work as diaspora politics' when 'linguistic and national differences' are prominent (2008: 165). Or consider Rajinder Dudrah's study of 'The Unforgettable Tour' of 2008, where Bollywood stars delivered 'extravaganza' live appearances across the Americas and London (2012: 100), bringing Global South Asian audiences a taste of glitz and cheese. Bachchan family 'appearance' sessions – darshan – seem almost devotional and have become a staple, if peripherally 'live', format for the cinema publicity machine at least since the great Nargis and Raj Kapoor wowed audiences in the Soviet Union (also reported by Dudrah though he says 'former' Soviet Union when talking of the 1950s [2012: 3], which must be an unintended revisionist error-slip). In any case, the global proliferation of anecdotes about Bollywood, no matter how you land on the derivation of the term, has generated at least one shared indexical reference among the many debates (Dudrah 2012: 4, Gokulsing and Dissanayake 2013: 8). These join more substantial debates over the politics of the filmic star system (Madhava Prasad 2014a: 1), film as national allegory (adapting Frederic Jameson and Aijaz Ahmad, discussed in Chapter 5) or the famously not so secret politics of desire (Nandy 1998). There are also many excellent conferences, workshops, seminars and a veritable academic industry that thrives on discussion – for example not only the workshops at Jadavpur University that provide material for the *Journal of the Moving Image*, but also meetings in Bangalore, Delhi, London, Manchester, Sydney, Singapore, Syracuse and so on. Global South Asian film studies attest to a burgeoning sophistication that threatens to leave some commentators looking a bit like Raj-era orientalists, but this itself does not even come close to matching the passion of film fan discussion – tuning in to Mirchi Radio in India, Sunrise Radio in the United Kingdom or Polskatacja in Poland, and many others, will quickly disabuse any academic from trying to compete in terms of anecdote and gossip with the far more knowledgeable fans. Indeed, which scholar would dare risk an embarrassing appearance on a quiz show like 'Bollywood or Bust', where the obsession with detailed knowledge, or rumour, about films, stars, directors, songs, playback artists, even production houses, is a key trope. The sight of film scholars squirming to keep up with the depth of knowledge that shifts and changes shape the further it is examined, let alone can it cope with fanzine contributors, is no doubt high comedy that would put

Monty Python to shame (the quiz show candidate is not autobiographical, since wiser counsel prevailed).

Origin stories

Observing film studies' new enthusiasm for historiography within Indian film history, the boundaries of that history threaten to overlap with political, cultural and regional histories more so than any national cinema. Rajadhyaksha's (2013) questioning has him convincingly deny a national cinema category for India, preferring instead many regionalisms and calling this unique. I take this as a major justification for accessing an emerging body of challenging work, best exemplified in books by Anjali Gera Roy (2015) and Rosie Thomas (2014). They each deploy antecedal thinking in tracing film history and give less prominence to any originating Hindi mythological finding, instead of the lauded Dadasaheb Phalke, a filmed tale from the *Arabian Nights* to be their candidate for first subcontinental feature. Thomas names Bengali Hiralal Sen's 1903 'lost' two-hour fantasy *Ali Baba* as contender for first South Asian film, and displacing the 'forty-minute Hindu myth' of Phalke's *Raja Harishchandra* (1913) she significantly rewrites South Asian film history in favour of a 'culturally hybrid tale ... within an Islamic fantasy world' (2014: 9). This displaces the *Ramayana* and *Mahabharat* anecdotes – as well as, almost without needing to say so, Hollywood's routines featuring Sabu, such as *The Thief of Baghdad* (1924, dir. Walsh). The need for such a displacement becomes more visible in times where 'history is written by the winners' and particular interests make far too much of 'uncritically recycled', 'fossilised', 'assumptions' about 'certain versions of Indian cinema history' (Thomas 2014: 2). Thomas notes that some two dozen other productions had already been offered by Hiralal Sen before Phalke. And adds further reorderings: the first woman filmmaker, Fatima Begum, wrote and directed her first feature in 1926; the first talkie, by Ardeshir Irani, appeared in India in 1936, also another 'Arabian Nights' story (Thomas 2014: 9).

In *Bombay Before Bollywood,* Thomas tracks several versions of *Ali Baba* and *Aladdin* through the history of cinema, especially in the films of Homi Wadia, who was 'born into a respectable Bombay Parsi family, master shipbuilders to the East India Company' (2014: 31).[1]

> Tales and tropes from the Arabian Nights fed Indian cinema's fantasy and costume genres throughout the late 1920s and early 1930s and remained a mainstay of the subaltern cinema audience circuits until the 1960s and beyond. (Thomas 2014: 32)

The Arabian Nights theme also returns in the period of serializations, when clearly acceding to popular demand the famed Ramanand Sagar wrote and directed *Alif Laila, a* serialization of *Arabian Nights* stories screened between 1993 and 1997.

Alongside Thomas, a yet more detailed volume by Gera Roy collects the ways other writers have picked up this line, with arguments in favour of recognizing antecedents in the Parsi theatre (Hansen 2003: 403, Gera Roy 2015: 30), Urdu writers (Dwyer 2006, Gera Roy 2015: 31), ghazals (Gera Roy 2015: 44) and *dastan* (Gera Roy 2015: 85–86). She also credits the Hiralal Sen film, and her work joins other acknowledgements of the importance of Bengal in film history. Indeed a forthcoming documentary called *Aurora Bioscope* (2017, dir. Bose) tells the story of the Magical Theatre Company where both Mrinal Sen and Ritwik Ghatak got their start.[2] Summarizing Pritchett's (1985) work on the importance of Fort William College publications of the *1001 Nights*, Gera Roy argues that existing studies of film culture in India produce 'a homogenous discourse of indigeneity' while ignoring the cross influence of the 'strong Islamicate strain in Hindi films' (2015: 7) and in favour of studies of *Ramayana* and *Mahabharat*, relegating 'alternative traditions to the background' (2015: 14). Gera Roy also lends support to larger narratives of film history that would complicate any singular 'origin'. She cites here Kesavan (1994), Mishra (2002) and Lutgendorf (2006) assembling important diverse views, as well as marshalling support from William Dalrymple's travel-writerly evocation of Peshawar's 'street of the storytellers', where he notes the importance of different invasions, from Alexander through Genghis Khan to the British, in rather dubious descriptive terms – 'elongated' eyes, 'curly hair and Semitic noses' (Dalrymple 1998: 317). The storyteller's street is *Qissa Kwani*, site of a major early confrontation – a massacre by British troops upon Independence movement activists (Habib 1997: 44). What is remembered is a choice, as Dalrymple emphasizes the Kalashnikovs that can be purchased in large numbers (1998: 316). Gera Roy notes that Dilip Kumar, Shah Rukh Khan and Raj Kapoor all have direct or close family origins in Peshawar (2015: 1) and makes the more forceful point about film, that

> if the narrative conflict in Hindi film is structured by the Hindu ethic of dharma or the gaze defined by the religious practice of darshan, [then] the romance or the romantic subplot is inevitably patterned according to the conventions of the Arabic *qissa* or Persian *dastan*. (Gera Roy 2015: 4)

Whether or not this research work catches the imagination of other scholars is in part shaped by prevailing currents, which perhaps do not bode well for what is ostensibly also a critique of the Hindutva-oriented atmosphere of recent book-burnings, the calls by BJP leaders to burn Romila Thapur's works for example (Nilanjana Roy 2014). In any case, what it implies is that much more new work would be needed on history and development in the light of a comprehensive weather patterns model of the flows and pressure points of global media and politics. It would be a grand thing if researchers could be deployed to further extend our understanding of 'an alternative narration of the subaltern cosmopolitanisms through which cultural exchanges took place between ordinary folks in the process of trade and travel' (Gera Roy 2010: 46). This must have far-reaching implications which would impact conceptions of the global circulation of struggles. For Africa, for example, the reach of Global South Asia and its films

> appear to have inspired a variety of activities ... from the influence of Indian political movements on African resistance struggles, the conflict between tradition and modernity ... performative practices ... [and] civilizational rhetoric that can be effectively juxtaposed to the west. (Gera Roy 2010: 41)

What is important in Gera Roy's plan for a detailed map of Urdu influences is not this particular response to a memory lapse on the part of film commentators, but that introducing some difficulty with the terminologies that describe this media, these nations, diaspora and its countervailing influences, is to keep the shifting of categories in focus. The difficulties are well noted in Iftikhar Dadi's opening line about 'the impossibility of fully disentangling cinemas identified as "Hindi" from those designated "Urdu" ' (2016: 480), despite then going on for a half dozen pages doing just such disentangling by referring to cities of production rather than language or nation, in a very welcome study.

> The phenomenon of the border-crossing Asian transnational popular culture reflects the effect cultural products have on the imagination and processes of meaning-making, meaning-changing, and negations of meaning. (Tambunan 2012: 146)

Dudrah references 'diasporic consciousness' able to work and switch between place of origin and place of settlement (2002: 20). This conception is clear, and clearly in turn in debt to Kaur and Kalra (1996). But even further destabilizing any easy settlement of concepts is that there need not even be that many actual South Asians present for the influences of South Asian film to take root in another locality, in Russia for example, in the Pacific, Africa. Forms of belonging and national identity can of course appear to be strengthened through shared screen experience as political education, and misinformation, circulates via celluloid, video, digital and music tie-ins with great relevance for rethinking institutional powers. All this builds on the fecundity of an always-already plural tradition, or rather, a plurality of co-constituted interpretation. Global South Asia required non-commensurate co-existent perspectives usually untenable in the disciplinary certitudes of convention. Any possibility of reclaiming the space of scholarship for discussion of these dimensions requires a much greater decolonization – one that begins with hiring and firing.[3]

The rumour of Asia

Whatever the case, the media space of Global South Asia has always been one of a certain density and with a little effort there is sufficient room for a thousand, and one, contending schools of thought. In this chapter, I too want to talk about television in the context of the screen fantasy image and the circulation of Global South Asia. I do not mean this as a Nehruvian update bulletin, nor as a simple rehash of the same old argument about how places and people are misrepresented, but certainly ideological critique has not been enough to yet displace the simplicity and stereotype of images of *poverty, flooding, temples, mosques, Taj, bucolic musicians, camels, cave complexes and Al Qaida* that 'stand' for the subcontinent, its peoples and cultures in mainstream documentary. Images such as that of two rotund politicians in politically appropriate 'traditional' dress – not just kurta pyjama, shalwar kameez or khadi cloth today, but all that identified overseas as exotic garb (see Madhava Prasad 2014b) – shaking hands after some brief stage-managed regional summit on Kashmir, trade, or nuclear power (see Kaur 2013), and a commentary sound bite from some pundit about intractable age-old rivalries such as satellite newscasters as part of the apparatus of 'liveness', even when faking (see Roy 2014: 2). Sensation and stereotype, or quaint tradition, are often still the common fare of 'representative' South Asian *news* outside South Asia itself. To develop this through examples of news reportage and documentary 'about' South Asia would be straightforward, albeit primarily focused upon geography documentaries – it is possible to consider more general aspects of the televisual screen and digitization. Platform and technology proliferation makes the camera in the many hands of students, families, tourists, citizen journalists and ad hoc documentarists, including CCTV, surveillance and webcam, consolidated into a kind of potential but not yet collated global eye – media convergence on the track of reducing the texture of life to a black and white in colour TV image. Here connections are reduced to content. At the very moment the television camera focuses its factual gaze on a colourful scene – 'ethnic' apparel, tradition, nature, disaster – this colour is rendered two-dimensional and always-already scripted in a way that is too often left unchallenged.

Despite the 'visibility' of Bollywood over Dhallywood or Kollywood, and even despite the overdetermined success of some Bengali art cinema at international festivals, it is not difficult to see how the documentary image of South Asia that appears on global screens is most often as a 'realist', usually tragic, news item. Images of villages awaiting rescue from cyclone, flood, earthquakes, riot, famine. Images of high mountain military stand-off or besieged temples, mosques, cave complex and Al Qaeda training camps, and increasingly drone footage of random assassinations from afar: television is particularly well suited to containing tragedy within a box. On the small screen it is images and stereotypes or clichés that move. 'Things happen to images, not people' (Deleuze 1995: 77). But the representation of Asia, here as a war zone, indicates a corresponding nether side to the tragic image – there is also a simultaneous positive gloss that is equally ideological – namely the fascination with tradition. The tradition is the great contrast, whether it be the Taliban destroying statues of the Buddha, or young women in headscarves excluded from education – in a particular nuance of ideology mismatch, the education to bring 'civilized' values that are counter-intuitively surmised traditional symbolized by the close-ups of the hijab. Hindu on Muslim violence, Muslim on Sikh, partition tit for tat, through to nuclear stand-off. The construction of a belligerent reputation for trouble, a plot device in *Viceroy's House*, but also a prurient staple of a documentary gaze that must needs seek controversy.

Sound bite emotional containment fuels the global rumour of a mythical third world Asia that is both traditional in dress and architecture – forts, camels, rustic musicians but rendered a modern mess born of a debased modernity, that perhaps, the argument implies, only the restitution of colonialism could redeem, at least in the mind-set of the imperialist power. The trick here is to gesture towards difference and openness to interpretation only for plurality to be closed down in a pincer movement. The double visage of Global South Asia is locked into fantasy and sensation: on the one hand, digital access to the kitsch and glitz of traditional exotica in temples, rich fabrics and pantomime handlebar moustaches while on the other, digital diplomacy over disaster, war, drones and death, with pantomime handlebar moustaches.[4]

This doubled representation follows an ideological investment that eases and erases imperial guilt. From abroad, it is clear (the wish is) that the vibrancy of a traditional geographic South Asia has not been destroyed despite the (rarely or reluctantly acknowledged) the ongoing impact of 300 plus years of colonialism visited on the place. Reassured by tourist brochures that most of the temples and mosques remain, the disasters are attributed to contemporary dysfunctions: poverty, corruption, mismanagement and in

Afghanistan and Pakistan the Taliban, in India, and Nepal, the Maoists, in Sri Lanka the Tamils. Never capital. Such reasoning, sometimes explicit, affirms that Afghanistan's problems are age-old, Pakistan's problems are Pakistani corruption, India's problems are Indian through and through, Asia's problems are now Asian, and independence and self-management were perhaps premature. A self-serving ideological psychic defence, to be resolved by more guilt-deflecting 'development' aid. The UN should intervene. NATO of course has, with disastrous results.

The diversity of a continent of images is channelled into a narrow ideological repertoire repeating the same tropes. The argument to be made again here is that international televisual interest in Global South Asian culture is predicated upon two oversimplified ideological strategies – representation of good Asians and bad ones: demons and exotics. This can be seen in news reportage of disasters, nature or customs – just as it can be seen in representations of globalized Asians in Britain – bad Muslims, spicy food, Asian cool. A variety of stereotypes then, diversity. The pantomime character of this scenario is not difficult to point out; the problem is rather that once knocked down the stereotypes continue to bounce back up again. The stickiness of the repertoire is secured by the service stereotyping does in assuaging intractable consequences of ongoing plunder, covert interference and explicit commercial greed. The economic imperative joins hands with the socio-ideological representation to present Asia as an emerging market, dynamic economy, trading partner and twenty-first century superpower, if only the problems of terror, corruption and chaos could be met – with purchase of more sponsored news time and weapons deals. Rarely does a media event depart from these coordinates, but when it does, only one interpretive code prevails – exotic or demon – and anything else is contained within the terminology of transnationalism, diaspora, or the complexity and flow of the economic Global South.[5]

Fire and screens

To inflame accusations of incandescent allegory, let me try to kindle a fire in Plato's cave... There could be many associations with the screen and the flame and I risk this as a good place to start, inspired by Theresa Mikuriya's (2017) book on camera effects before cameras. In a now overdetermined well-known passage, Plato presents a primordial cave in which the cave-dwellers are offered the scene of shadows flickering on a wall. Those watching the images are incredulous when told of the sun outside the cave, which reveals a greater truth. As the story goes, the proto-television retains its viewers, who after all are chained to the scene and cannot look away. Of course we get that this is an image to be conjured with by all media commentators – a kind of ground zero of televisual ideology and product placement. We are those viewers, locked in the cave with Plato. In support of this conjecture, none other than Susan Sontag also opens her book *On Photography* with a chapter on Plato's cave, where the cave is the world and photographing it is compared to collecting, nostalgia and manipulation. Photographs 'fiddle with the scale of the world', they blow it up, cut, crop, as well as age, get traded, are 'tacked on walls' and 'served up in books', but photography is power and always ruled by conventions and ideology (Sontag 1977: 4–5). For Horkheimer and Adorno (1947), the escape from 'mass deception' is crucial, but for Adorno there can be no getting back to the cave. His understanding of the cave metaphor is one in which those sitting at the back in the cheapest seats are more aware of the fabrication of the event, wondering whether they can blow off the roof and 'reconnect stage and reality ... [and build] barricades out of the wood of the folding chairs' (Adorno cited in Buck-Morss 1979: 104).

In this worthy tradition of finding foundational moments of television in mythology – that old Plato is not mythology is hardly a valid objection – I want to link the *Ramayana* television serialization with a number of other scenes of media screen and fire – the cooking show is just one among many. Fire, as we know, is both creative and destructive. It is endlessly fascinating, more than television – 'hard to light, it is difficult to put out' – a malevolent spirit (Bachelard [1938]1987: 64). I want to experiment with looking at television through a symptomatic examination of flames on the screen. This experiment may fail, and might seem spurious – but inspired by the candles on the set, think of grainy images of the Reichstag fire, of the Hindenburg zeppelin crash, of the burning monk during the Vietnam war (Sontag 1977), and of still more late-night reruns of *Cinema Paradiso*. That partition films invoke Sita's ordeal, for example in *Pinjar* (2003) is yet another, not insignificant, Ramayana link. Think also of that image from *Begum Jaan* of a person fleeing partition violence set alight by a mob, the kerosene thrown on them busting in a ball of flame that the camera catches just as the arms akimbo victim seems to imitate the map of India. The potency of that image is too much perhaps.

More contemplatively, Plato's cave establishes the precedent of fire media talk with the shadows on the wall – television and fire are inexorably linked from the start – and so this also invokes a older mythic register as perhaps more than as metaphor, or as heuristic device. I have in mind myth as it might have been narrated in a reverie of those gathered around a campfire not unlike the one in the cave. There are any number of televisual and cinematic moments that can provide a kind of archive to enable this – it is easy enough to invite readers to come up with their own greatest moments in flames, especially those who have themselves burnt books, and so know the fascination, and trauma, of watching each page crumple as they succumb one by one to the heat. This is not only a confessional moment, and to stoke television as a burning issue under a register of fire is a kind of contrivance, no doubt, but perhaps a necessary one if it allows me again to think of television as storytelling, as a fundamental social origin myth. By extension, I mean something more than mere historical development, rather also an extension of the social, connecting the physical body with its contexts, and with the search for alternate versions of the real, the possibility of seeing the world differently than it is presented on the conventionally broadcast platforms. And if this is also about extension of vision to take account of the political perspective of the Global South, then there is so much more to be said about multichannel choices when the cave is right there in all our homes.

Himalayan comedy formats

But to resist pyromania as catharsis – and before exploring fire more closely – it might be useful to present a very particular and even spectacular kind of televisual representation of Global South Asia as an 'object' for analysis. I have in mind a flimsy example taken from my own television viewership, a kind of guilty obsession, not just for pleasure, the six-part special *Himalaya* presented on British television late in 2004 by Michael Palin. No apologies that this research is coloured by subjective viewings of the screen/world – my world-view has always been framed – but to make a critical assessment of Palin's programme has, I think, general and valid implications for other telematic presentations of Global South Asia on screen, be these television news, other modes of documentary, cinema reruns or Merchant Ivory films and all the other extensions to the merchandising of cinema that have so often been indicated (Rajadhyaksha 2009: 83). Four hours of prime-time high-demographic mainstream Palin (352 minutes on the DVD version), a tie-in book by Palin, author signings and speaking tour, a separate 200-page 'coffee table format' book of photographs by Basil Pao (2004) and advertisement trailers, posters and sundry other publicity on the web and social media. The show I take as the most extended, 'representative' and symptomatically commercial example of the 'typical' mainstream and popular format foreign television documentary from Global South Asia.

Opening scene. All the tropes are already set. From high above the clouds, Nepal is presented as a trekkers' paradise – medieval, glacial, remote and timeless. The clouds and the peak, and no expense spared by the BBC to get that glider vista of the top of the world, flying down towards twenty million people, but it's mostly Sherpas we will meet – and then not at all looking at their conditions of work as couriers for privileged white tourists and television presenters.[6] The mountains are the backdrop to a much bigger story: Palin's quest, and for the cameras, his quest is our own – with free association hunting for the Pythonesque grail at viewers own risk. We watch, our positioning before the screen as consumers of Palin travelogue, so as to know what is outside the cave. Even though anyone who has travelled, or anyone who has seen a Palin documentary, that is, everyone, already knows that there is a slippage down the mountain. Our point of view will not give it all to us, and we are obliged, more or less, to accept Palin's global eyeball, and all that he carries as baggage and freight. We know of course that *Himalaya* is not going to show us all of 'really existing' geographic South Asia – the main focus after all is only Nepal – and the slippery cascade down the mountain also shows how the entire subcontinent is too often seen through the avalanche of images of India alone, so perhaps other angles are welcome. This one, perhaps, the Palinesque version. He appeals to some, as national treasure, although not everyone will travel in that matter-of-fact, easy, casual but actually ever-so-refined BBC style he displays. There could be any number of alternative manifestations of the South Asianist fantasy he has in mind, as much as we do, but what Palin will make of the subcontinent should at least spark some interest. The audience of implied reception of course is already familiar with several versions of the scene. Perhaps even beyond the Merchant Ivory style of *Heat and Dust* (1983), but also from ITV's *Jewel in the Crown* (1984) to Channel Four's *Indian Summers* (2015) and the BBC's *Taboo* (2017) the unremittingly post-colonial forlorn gritty nostalgia of it all. Some may even anticipate a bit of expatriate knees-up in the mode of the BBC's *It Ain't Half Hot Mum* (1974–1981, dir. Croft) or the all too knowing romantic eccentric pensioner routines of *The Best Exotic Marigold Hotel* (2011, dir. Madden). Others would balk at that sort of a gauche return, but topically contingent anticipations gleaned from UK audiences might also require some comments on comedy in Chadha's film *Bride and Prejudice* (2004) as an attempt after *Bend It Like Beckham* (2002) to cash-in on Bollywood's global market position. The bend in *Bend It…* was particularly unfortunate where the problematic ambition of an Asian girl is that she wants to be just like the white male football fashion star. It is both amusingly endearing and provocatively compromised; she has to go to America to succeed. In the US market, there are similar queries to raise, for example, with a much-debated film (see Gera Roy 2012: 13) in the irony-laden Californian terror success of Karan Johar's 'feel-good' Shah Rukh Khan hit *My Name Is Khan* (2010; also see Dudrah, Mader and Fuchs 2015). It is not that comedy from Global South Asia is somehow inappropriate, but that some films are approved and applauded while less compromised examinations are not funded or made might be reason to diagnose a narrowing of scope. The many examples from late-night reruns which regurgitate and regulate vestiges of and memorials for Empire mean it is comedy-drama which interprets and teaches the British their overseas history. The 'fake news' of revisionism is reinforced in full screen schmaltz – the indulgence distraction of such Asia-tainment is its own self-regarding, self-rewarding genre.

Working with Palin

A predictable move after looking at images for a while is to ask how they were made. There has been considerable work in this regard and both Ulf Hannerz and Ursula Rao have, as anthropologists, separately examined the production of 'news' (Hannerz 2004, Rao 2005). What I hope to do is provide background reflections on the connections of television to the productive circumstances, and consumptive contexts, of populist 'documentary' of the exoticist type represented in the adventures of a British comic in the mountains. The coffee table book by Pao (2004) does include some small insights into how the BBC crew worked – forty small pictures, but these are kit shots, and I am more interested in relational dynamic. Labour is never only the labour time of the celebrity key worker, nor the tools and machinery of production. Long ago we learnt to develop a rounded dialectical analysis of the working day. If this is possible for Nepal, it should be tried.

The mode of production of both news and documentary on Asia for Britain is, at best, economical: freelance, semi-feudal, on a budget. Palin actually tells us little that is news, but his team is not unlike the stringers and crews that are responsible for more weighty versionings of the subcontinent. There is a camera crew, presenter and researcher contact person, and a series of not very well-remunerated contacts, who, through serendipity, or accident, provide the story and colour for the presenter's narrative. Contractual administration produces a blizzard of paperwork as Palin, part-silly, part-sinister world-weary traveller stumbles across the Himalayas in conservative avuncular semi-colonial mode with a team of six, and all their gear, lucky to be invited to various carefully itinerary-coordinated arcane events and able, by appointment, to visit lesser or greater local rulers, personalities and living deities. None of this should get too serious however, since in the interests of popular entertainment the discussion with the Dalai Lama ponders bowel movements.

Palin's *Himalaya* serialization is in a grand tradition of minor televisual occasions for the elaboration of ideological connections and what Paul Gilroy calls a 'postcolonial melancholia' (2004). This is perhaps not dissimilar in type to what Sontag called the nostalgia of collecting (1977). Palin holds a candle, as they say, for the good old days of the Raj. This is a Raj of nostalgic fantasy, where enemies, subjects and infuriating lackeys are now renovated and romanticized in a battered picture book of faded glories, updated for the prime-time market, beautifully bound on glossy matt. The documentary format is casual, vérité with narrative management framed by a travel itinerary. There is certainly a semblance of 'news' reportage built into the picture, but presented more by accident than by design. Episode three, for example, begins with an announcement where Palin disavows the tranquillity one might expect, and he will soon learn that 'things in Nepal are not always the way they look, as communist insurgents have been waging war against the government'. These generalities after the spectacular arrival flight, Palin lands, or so the programme makes out, first of all in Lekhani in the company of a recruiting agent for a British Gurkha regiment. The irony of 'arriving' with the military is lost on him as Raj nostalgia takes over right away – 'this has been a tradition for over 200 years' – and the 'problem' of 'the Maoists' is made manifest only when the stiff-lipped Gurkha agent Lieutenant Colonel Griffith does not return to the village in which Palin is camped. With a wish-fulfilled in an Indiana Jones, James Bond, Kipling's *Kim* nostalgia, and understanding that the Maoists have 'kidnapped' Griffith, the crew and entourage nervously depart. A place that had previously 'seemed like a rustic backwater' has become one where 'friendly villagers seem like potential kidnappers'. It is a surprise, of sorts, that Palin does not then present himself as a player in the Great Game – he might go so far. The televisual potential of Kim training his memory and various further intrigues with disguises and shady cloak and dagger jingoism in 'North Asia' – a revealing term – including disparaging the traditional Great Game enemy, Russia, as a threat to British interests, must surely have been tempting. But instead there is a rush for the main road and it is only in Pokhara that it transpires the agent was unharmed, and lives to collect and colonize another day. Even though this reassurance comes only after Palin does encounter three Israeli budget travellers who tell him that at the start of their trek they had been stopped by 'Maoists' who demanded 1000 rupees and issued them with receipts, with a red flag stamp, authorizing travel in the region. Great trinket souvenir, though Palin's budget does not extend so far that he can purchase his own. He already has the scene-setting drama his story needs and can now safely ignore the more important tale of how it came to be that Communists ruled in the very highest lands of the world.

In Kathmandu, Palin interviews the journalist Kunda Dixit, publisher of *Himal* magazine, with his more activist-oriented brother Kanak Dixit. But even taking into account Dixit's 'political' position, the exchange with Palin is simply less revealing than it might have been, and thereby disappointing. The clearly well-informed Dixit makes the relevant point that no one wins in the war scenario, but there is no chance to explore issues such as US and UK military support, and armaments supply, for the royalist Rana regime at the time, nor any chance to ponder the uncertainties of an increasingly militarized city. It is not as if Dixit was unable to contribute much more than his few seconds of local colour in the context of the ancient architectural beauty of the city.[7] *Himal* for example also operated an impressive film festival that provides an antidote to *Himalaya*:

> Film South Asia is a competitive biennial festival of documentary films on South Asian subjects that provides a quality platform to exhibit new works and to promote a sense of community among independent filmmakers. It is organized by Himal Association, a not-for-profit institution dedicated to spreading knowledge and information in Nepal and South Asia. (Himal 2010)

Palin's programming prefers to segue into a sequence on the several sadhus who congregate around the main temple complex, where, as mentioned, the impressive architectural heritage signifies exoticism and ancient traditions. We are treated to an extended discussion of the dreadlocks and callisthenic achievements of an eighty-seven-year-old Shiva baba, whom Palin pictures, but does not interview. A mildly amusing sexual innuendo, then a cut to the burning ghat and soon on to Red China with another wry irony: 'from the land of Maoists, to the land of Mao' and 'the red flag flies above the frontier'. We have not met any Maoists, although it surely would have been possible to arrange some media – I managed to meet them easily enough ten years earlier when they were rather remotely establishing another kind of base camp, but different images of the exotic suit different travel narratives. That said, the exoticism of interest in the Maoists is also a left-wing romanticism which pushes up against lack of interest in corrupt security services beholden to Western intrigues and readily implementing draconian regulations unexamined by visiting journalists, or, for that matter, fellow journalists on the spot. That a conservative ideology runs alongside the Maobadi touristic fascination as its counterfoil and dark underbelly only confirms that contradictory total field in which politics is more than strategic plays on a level field and television is not well suited, at least in BBC formats, to contend. The great game was never fair. Ten years after Palin's visit, the Kathmandu temple complex is devastated by earthquake (April 2015), the monarchy had been replaced with a constituent assembly, in which Maoists had participated but after a series of convoluted manoeuvrings, with different Communist Parties taking turns at the prime ministership, a second constituent assembly elected in 2013. The Maoists did less well in the polls, and sentiment across the country remained tense, mainly because of economic concerns stemming from isolation, chronic underdevelopment, and the ongoing legacy of colonial interference, tied aid, and a paternalist client relationship with India and still to a degree Britain. In 2017, the same again, Palin was by now far away, no longer seen in these parts, his visit not even a memory.

Guides

A large gap looms in this chapter. What would repay extended study is the role of the narrator as controlling agent; despite the team that travels with Palin, his media persona as colonial character shapes the play. This is true for all storytelling in this genre no doubt, even for Valmiki who is the narrator of the *Mahabharata*, but also the media and mediating figure of the presenter who is there on a quest. With camera team two steps behind, it is he who carries the viewer into the mountains in a way wholly unlike the load bearing Sherpas who carry the kit. The Himalaya range is a fantasy image for such a quest, promising a vista of vaguely understood notions of enlightenment, *satori* and *moksha*. This is why the sadhus must displace the journalist who displaces the Maoists in the mediated sequence of Palin's narrative. The sadhus are there, in the film, to affirm a timeless devotional aesthetic, unaffected by the iniquities of contemporary politics, or inequalities and conflicts that might be rather wished away.

This is where I am reminded yet again of watching late-night television in the privacy of my own fantasy Asia. In *The Razor's Edge*, as already mentioned, Bill Murray is our shell-shocked World War I veteran hero, seeking answers to his alienation and despair. He has travelled, after reading the *Upanishads* on the recommendation of a self-taught British coalminer, to the monastery in Tibet. The head monk recognizes his problem as an attachment that must be broken. He sends Murray up the mountain to a snowbound hut for a week. Only when the firewood runs out and he is forced to burn his beloved books does he have his realization. The pages burn one by one, as they do, an elegant scene – cue uplifting raga. Murray can return home, rejoin the world and take his place in America redeemed. This narrative of self-fulfilment is a common Western projection of 'India' as a place of spirituality in which the lost soul can find redemption. What is unusual in this case is the passage through the burning book. Between first of all the chakra-branded National Socialists in Germany burning the books of degenerate Communists and Jews, in the mid -1930s, and then second, the book-burning protests of Salman Rushdie's *Satanic Verses*, in the late 1980s – the former approximately coinciding with the date Maugham wrote *The Razor's Edge*, while the latter just few years after the (re)making of the film version – these enlightening textual conflagrations confirm the phantasmatic aspect of Global South Asia.

Books with fire scenes are legion and I see them as prototypes – or pyrotypes – of Palin's film. What we have here is a rerun of the epic traveller's quest, with each day marked off one by one as ordeal, in the 'tie-in' book of the series. Palin promptly dispenses with the guides however; interviewing the Dalai Lama about his toilet habits seems more amusing that anything esoteric. No surprise that the holy leader laughs heartily through the interview up until the poignant moment when he pauses to consider seriously Palin's impending visit to Tibet, wistful that he cannot go himself. Politics raises its ugly head. The issue of Tibet is an oft-screened one, as filtered through celebrity advocates like Richard Gere and the sometimes sari-clad musician Madonna. We are spared any hint of political journalism that might raise questions about Western armaments sales to Nepal – or for that matter Indian military support to the Royal Nepal Army and then ruler King Gyanendra. Instead we are left to affirm the hegemonic pro-Lama views of the anti-China lobby. No wonder then I am surprised when my viewing is interrupted by a snippet of news that underlines the discrepancy between the example of Palin/Lama and the wider critical view of television I want to consider in this chapter. The incendiary incident that intervenes is one found at that time on the internet:

> **Nepal Maoists bomb TV station** (February 26, 2005 10: 35 IST)
>
> Heavily-armed Maoists torched and bombed a regional station of the state-run Nepal Television, causing damage worth over Rs 4 crore and disrupting the broadcast indefinitely even as the security forces gunned down 10 rebels and lost four of their own men in a clash in the west of the kingdom. The regional station of Nepal Television at Kohalpur in Banke district of mid-western Nepal was torched and bombed by hundreds of Maoists on Friday, NTV sources said. The regional broadcast of the NTV has been disrupted indefinitely after the explosion ... The Maoists also looted seven cameras and several other equipment from the station. However, no one was injured in the incident, the sources said. (PTI 2006)

This contrasts with Palin's travels. I read it also as symptomatic, and of a type as an example of what Kaur calls a 'combined media and political performance' (2003: 5). Although Palin travels through Nepal without a spiritual guide, he has both various local guides – a British military recruiter, a Sherpa, a tout, a journalist, his photographer friend Pao – and he himself is *our* guide. In both geographical and ideological terms, the presenter is a point of view characterization as emblematic performer of the refracted visitor's conception of Global South Asia. Geopolitical military intrigue is smuggled in with the scenes of the presenter mediating our orientations along an already well-trodden campaign trail. The surprises on the way, like the eagerly anticipated 360-degree mountain views, are not so surprising after all.

Palin's narrative is intentionally and aesthetically low budget at the level of content. Anything actually newsworthy is minimized or made into fun – the Dalai Lama, the military recruiting Gurkhas who do not have repatriation rights in the United Kingdom – cue Joanna Lumley, OBE, miscast here as a Posh Rosie, she had been campaigning for Gurkha recognition – and the Nepal-wide Maoist insurgency all in narrative off-screen colour. Glimpses of events, parts of longer interviews, and plenty of the presenter sitting on a rock resting after a long march provide more than circumstantial evidence that the great game continues. The briefest of meetings with the tourist trekkers, who had proudly displayed their permit to trek, is followed soon after by a scene in which Palin rests his weary feet in the waters of a mountain stream. This low-fi home movie feel is a strange contrast to the massive marketing of the series for British television. The book tie-in that is a pre-Christmas bestseller; the DVD available for the January sales, Palin interviewed on numerous morning radio shows – all extend television into the public domain with fanfare.

A different and much older film, *The Guide* (1965, dir. Anand) is worth thinking of here. In an insightful discussion of R. K. Narayan's book of the same name, Spivak turns at the end of her essay on 'How to Teach a "Culturally Different" Book' to issues that might have been informative for Palin as our guide to Nepal. Narayan's novel is from the other end of the subcontinent, although in the film version, which Narayan disliked, the original context is erased. Spivak notes that the film is based loosely on Narayan's Tamil *Guide,* yet this figure comes to 'speak for India', as indeed so often happens with 'Anglo-Indian fiction' (1996: 255). This should be the most obvious point to make about Palin's narrative, that his micro-lite overview of Nepal comes to speak for a whole subcontinent, perhaps just as Kureishi's Sammy and Rushdie's Farishta speak for a certain Global South Asian identity at one point, and terror the next. Spivak makes a more powerful point however, which also links up with *The Satanic Verses* indirectly since, as she points out, 'unity in diversity means citing *Shri 420*' (1996: 256). This is a reference to a Raj Kapoor and Nargis starrer also known as *Shree 420* (1955 dir. Kapoor) – more on Nargis in Chapter 5 – in which Kapoor performs the famous 'Mera Joota Hai Japani' song, playback singing by Mukesh: 'My shoes are Japanese, these trousers are English, the cap on my head is Russian, but still my heart is Indian.' This song is sung by Farishta on his arrival in England, in English. It was also cited by Mahasweta Devi in her acceptance speech at the Frankfurt Book Fair in 2006, but in *Shree 420* it is something like the celebration of the early multiculturalist Global South of

Nehruvian cosmopolitanism, though in evident denial of import substitution policies. It will also appear for those keen to spot such things, as the number plate on the truck in the film *Mela* (2000, dir. Darshan). The *Guide* presents the pluralism of India, encapsulated in the diverse ingredients of the pan-sellers concoction and the fraud where the hustler 'Raju' is transformed into the 'real thing' when the scam he perpetrates by the temple to pilfer donations turns out to work miracles. The number 420 is the police jargon for civil code section 420, 1860, which covers offences related to cheating. What the film version of Narayan's novel presents as plurality is like *The Satanic Verses,* perhaps, and certainly like Palin's exoticist interview with the Dalai Lama and even Kunda Dixit, the deception of mistaking the 'progressive bourgeois for primitive' where, in a commodification process for export, 'classical dance traditions of India and multiple folk forms are put into a hopper and swirled around with free-form musical structuring to produce a global India' (Spivak 1996: 258). Caution about 'distinctions such as First World-Third World, self-other and the like' (Spivak 1996: 242) should indicate the problematic character of Global South Asia here as well, even as the co-star of *The Guide* is also a 'Rosie' and in a small class fraction referentiality, Kureishi's book *The Last Word* (2014) is a disguised biography of V. S. Naipaul, suitably refracted through the tribulations of biographical authorship as regards an in turn globally renowned Indian author living in exile. Spivak's essay skewers just those problems well before this return however, when 'swiftly changing global cosmopolitan ... diversified diasporas ... upwardly mobile ... reterritorialised ... metropolitan ... writers' might translate vernacular into the scrabble – my misreading, sorry – scramble of standard English' (1996: 240).

Separate then from the 'intellectual ferment of modern India' (unsourced attributed to Chakrabarty in *EPW*, quoted in Spivak 1996: 262n) the diaspora is now much more than migration and exile; it is also global industry and aspiration. The poverty of slumdogs erased alongside linguistic specificity and urbanization over rural only shows the cracks in the home territories where jihadists and Maoists roam threateningly. As Spivak takes the opportunity to inspire in the viewer of *The Guide* an interest in the actual conditions of Devadasi temple dancers, and importantly points out that Tamil literature is 'one of the longest continuous literatures in India' (1996: 243), in another world Palin might have been equipped to investigate, meet and report on the organized Maoist presence in the Nepal he was visiting, responsibly teaching his viewers how to track the comrades. What would be required for Palin to have done something like this? It was never going to happen under the BBC watch, but what then of a book on Global South Asias, settlement, diasporas and the Global South? What is it that displaces the substitution of global bourgeois with something better organized, more promising, progressive and not 'primitive' – which entails its own anthropological exoticism – but at least more progressive as component of the necessary redistributive political project that would realign political power from the to easily and simply opposed North to South?

Telling criticisms

In this way then, attention could be focused upon the telematic circulation of images of Asia across the globe with an interest in redistributive justice. A critique of images as presented by dominant media is only the first move, important though it must be to begin with interpretation and responsibility before what we see. Who determines what we see, locally or globally, and is this a uni-directional transaction? A staple strategy of political economy of the media is to examine ownership, which is still much debated in terms of ideology, state developmentalism or private capital in its many forms. Structured managerialism clearly operates with the intent of suppressing dissent, and while audiences are not passive, the exclusion of some possible images limits choices. Entertainment has seemingly triumphed over education, probably because work is so bad, hard, stressful and unrewarding, that leisure time needs to be recuperative – with culture industry massage and mind-candy the diagnosis for soldiering on regardless. Marketing diversifies but does not negate the tendencies identified above, and new media promised much but already seems to reflect a well-ingrained pattern that chooses the images. Looking at Global South Asia from here – where? also the global – we are shown mosques turned to rubble by the saffron suited, or later by military booted; the memory-enhanced sons of Shiva are idolized in stone and drink milk before the cameras; the offspring of airline pilots and Italian beauties become preternaturally political before the fawning journalist; debonair, if aged, Bollywood icons end up as curiosity reports about local versions of game shows; on-the-set exposes of the making of *Bride and Prejudice*; and press conference outrage at Shah Rukh Khan getting held up at US customs all show more of Global South Asia than many will ever really get to know.

More professional news reportage is not all that different in terms of contact, presenter and crew. My focus on Palin should not excuse his mostly harmless antics in a diminutive mode, but let me here single out another simplistic, and symbolic, example. When the former Python travels to a school in *Himalaya* – the grouping of the six countries he visits under this single sign of his title must inevitably homogenize the diversity he finds – there is one disarmingly charming scene with kids, who are always photogenic. The bumbling performer, dishevelled and endearing, entertains them with a slapstick routine in which he keeps on losing his shoe. I wonder if this, for some, could not but evoke parallels with another contemporary mass-mediated footwear scenario in another part of the 'East': the staged slapping of Saddam Hussain's statue with slippers in Baghdad in 2003, revisited multiple times with insert-a-despot convenience since. The substitution here might evoke questions about stand-ins for stand-up, and body doubles a plenty (see Hoskins 2004: 124), though note that few question if the 'real' Saddam was captured in December that year, and hung, with mobile phone to TV coverage, on 30 December 2006 – a Cinderella and the Prince shoe fitting scene this was not, despite the effort to get ugly sister George to try it on.

What I want to suggest with these intemperate criticisms of documentary-light versions of Global South Asia is that we need to rethink ideology critique again along lines suggested by Madhava Prasad (1998). Would it be possible to see television not as a manipulated medium or even as tainted imported technology – television of national development, or as advertising vehicle for commodity culture – but rethink in a radical way that goes beyond its technical and managerial specifications? A broadcast medium bringing news from afar, yes – eyewitness news, the latest products embedded in reassuring stories about the timeless past – and ideology critique subsumed within the world brought into being through television, not as technologically determinant media, but as media and technology that worlds our world and is managed and manipulated in use with a different kind of storytelling plan. Sure, television reduces everything to an image in a box, and subsumption expands this imagery everywhere and miniaturizes with astonishing global ambition, but do we recognize this as our world, as integral part of our world? What I wonder are the prospects for other kinds of telling, ones that fill in the expectations of expected narratives with inspiration and innovation able to think with us toward other places. The aspiration of those who are maligned and sidelined could be brought back in, for example. The Maoists in Nepal, Roshan Seth playing Omar's bed-ridden drunken Communist uncle 'Papa' in *Laundrette*, and sundry other figures of whom I'd like to hear tell.

The idea of storytelling connections and schooling alternatives surrounding television might be taken metaphorically to reference and reinvigorate questions of civil society – the television news service as public forum, connected to democratic or social formations that have the potential to transform our world. Television as the 'vehicle' that brings democratization has itself a long tradition, and perhaps the Maoist, and not only the Maoist, opposition to the king in Nepal is televisual in sentiment here as well (see Karki and Seddon 2003). It is difficult to argue this case for democratic television in a place like Britain where property ladder shows are hardly democracy, or in terms of media flows, where bad soaps are sold cheaply worldwide (see Appadurai 1996). But certainly in the present conjuncture democracy and television are inextricably and perversely linked, and the effort to delink them from commercial imperative and fake versions of multicultural globality is worth the risk. And delinked, of course, negatively as well, where on-screen images of Global South Asia more often than not come with earthquakes or car bombs, refugees or detention camps, drones and body counts. Militarism is directly implicated here with the reputation of even the landlocked Hindu kingdom of Nepal constructed through violence – one interruption on the same spectrum was the more brutal than usual death of King Birendra and family at the hands of Prince Dipendra on the night of June 1, 2001. Terror and intrigue turned the palace into a twisted noire movie set and the royal family into a tragedy of proportions that might have moved Shakespeare to call for restraint. Gun toting, alcohol – and perhaps drug – fuelled resentment; a son shoots the main members of his family, including his father-king and mother-queen, effectively ending a dynasty. Of course there are conspiracy theories of CIA involvement or palace intrigue, and finally the overthrow of the monarchy was achieved in 2008, but in 2001 and through 2005 when Palin visits, the storyline of a violent archaism is all too readily available. None can say the massacre was deserved, but the actual details are certainly contested. Portrayals of the incident had very soon fallen into the predictable patterns where no one is sure what is going on, foregrounding Nepal as timeless wonderland, subject to weirdness, the distortion and destruction of an ancient culture by means of a confrontation with partial modernity, psychosis, amphetamines and whiskey, provokes a death craze, followed by repressive military crackdown and despotic rule. Armaments sales from the West were again overlooked in support of counter-insurgency against the Maoists. On the one hand the spiritual kingdom, and on the other the militarization of the mountains – the razor's edge is sharp indeed. Palin looks the other way. This was evident especially in the scene where Palin emphasized Nepal as the home of the plucky Gurkha, though, he notably kept the discussion limited to the cultural level of age-old traditions of militarism, fostered by that same, benevolently gifted, British pluck, rather than the far more brutal and exploitative aspects of colonialism, right up to the present. Well, we gave them trains – though not in Nepal. Is it surprising to link the supply of guns to the handling of cameras? The camera is a Cyclops, a one-eyed thug. Having one eye is of course a mark of lesser power compared to two eyes, or even the three eyes of the deity. Yet the simplicity of the one-eyed perspective has come to be associated with documentary truth when exactly the multiple eyes of the television system that links many views together might have suggested a democracy to come. The Maoists challenged this as they both burnt the station and stole the cameras – as radical democracy this is the cathexis of insurgency.

So, instead of Palin's documentary, and in the absence of a Global South Asia media platform for the Maoists in Nepal, what chance an education programme that would redirect diaspora to the erased Left history of the world, the Global South itself, the revolutionary story of M. N. Roy, and Saklatvala, and Rajani Palme Dutt, all of the Communist Party, founders and globalizers also, but too often overlooked or erased from the Global South Asia of travelling Bollywood or demonic terror.[8] What I understand of Spivak's talk of the denial of hope in decolonization is that it was the Communist anti-colonial and non-aligned Global South that was crushed under the weight of neo-liberalism and 'racism in post-coloniality'. The 'popular dissemination of that denial' in the film texts and documentaries offered up as Global South Asia have 'brought us to the general scene of super-state powers versus guerrilla counter-warfare and particular scenes of confusion and violence' (Spivak 1996: 256). I think this brilliantly captures what I hope can be understood as not an alibi for telling easy stories about exotic resisting others in the mountains, but the difficult and patient task of decolonizing televisual thinking so that the erasure of other possible worlds is not perpetuated in the stories we can tell.

Fetishism and fire

Susan Sontag had a point on collecting, which makes me want to suggest a rethink of ideology critique of television that might take Marx's *Capital* as a guide. The world now appears as an immerse collection of images: single scenes, repeated over and over in a blur. The media seems to be an endless archive of representations, a monstrous global montage machine. But the image has a fetish character. I know Asia is not this picture, but...

How did images become such fetish objects? Did they creep up on us? Victor Burgin notes the 'state of distraction' that accompanies the viewing of films today: 'the distraction that typically accompanies an evening's television viewing – answering telephone calls, fixing drinks, chatting, "zapping," flipping through newspapers and magazine, and so on' (2004: 33). With Barthes, he distinguishes this from the cinema experience, but maybe Burgin would do well to get a widescreen TV, give up the booze, pay attention, and turn off the light. Television does not need to be mundane, although one of its joys is that it can be. What is wrong with a boozy day in front of the cricket? It is safe, it is not crowded, it is not the streets and it is not dark – the homoerotic charge of sports television is reliable, scheduled, and sponsored. Rai points this out in his consideration of flashbacks and motivations in film (2006: 225) but the tie-in with distraction as pacification and as a prophylactic against anger, or against doing anything about the situation, leaves little option but to be lethargic. Such might be the last hope for the Western critic assailed on all sides by an unavoidable commercialization (Rajadhyaksha 2009: 83) that includes the production of books about film. Like this one. Burn.

Rachel Moore equates watching film in the dark with the archaic, but now lost, unity of the hearth fire that was used for warmth, cooking and light (2000: 122). But a still more appropriate substitute for the disenchantment of the social space of the campfire (Moore follows Schivelbusch 1988: 220–221) is the communal television experience with its movies, DIY shows and cooking programmes. That these do not happen in a single space, but rather a time slot, is a change in the geography of unity rather than its loss. Nevertheless: 'like fire, cinema brings us alone together, and although we watch the same embers and shoots of flame, its contemplation may take us in different directions. Like fire, cinema exceeds mere function' (Moore 2000: 10). To tell stories of the past, or of those who have a place on the mantelpiece above the fire or the TV, to record the myths of open interpretation and memory that belong to a more fundamental – not fundamentalist – pluralism might be the purpose of the box of stories machine that is television. The great directors always took it as a storytelling media, but only in a reified way, at a remove from the storytelling audience who had to reassemble the films from ashes or auterism and ego. What place then for uncles and aunties' stories from the struggle, might they be enticed to relate the political commitments that made Global South Asia something that could even become global, if reified, if not always Global South?

The only trouble with this extravagant metaphorics of global storytelling is that it could lead almost anywhere, and if we free associate television with passion, fire, light, luminosity and family, we might meditate upon knowledge and vision, daylight (let there be light...), lanterns (Zarathustra...) and lamps (Aladdin...). The collective hearth can also lead to the supermarket of ideas – heaven forbid the tie-in deal with Jamie Oliver cookbooks, or even – horror of horrors – *Michael Palin's Himalayan Recipes*.[9] As if storytelling were a protected and unproblematic advance, as anti-monarchy it well may be, fire is also a weapon – literally as firepower, and in India *Agni* is the name for a ballistic missile – and as we have seen, stories may burn. Fire may cleanse and cook, but it also destroys. It is divine avenging spirit and productive furnace of hell; with Lucifer it is both the fall and purgatory. The story of May Day though is the celebration of both Beltane and workers' power, but fire produces both steam and ash, energy and residue – it is north and south. Made by friction or a spark; a smouldering beginning or a sudden crash of lightning – a peal of spring thunder, as the Peking Daily greeted the news of Naxalbari 'a single spark can start a prairie fire'. Were there prairies in Bengal? The image of Mao, god, spirit, cherubim, yet also hocus pocus, obscurantist smoke and fug, fiery, inflamed, incandescent, excited, related both to flagrant and flamboyant interpretations with the story in flames. Why then is it that so often television does not always encourage the reverie which Bachelard identified in fire – also discussed in Moore (2000: 130)? Late night TV is especially evocative of the narcoleptic campfire – flickering shadows the only light lulling us towards unconsciousness. The embers of the late late show shine with a soporific glow and contemplation need not be profound.

Let us, with Bachelard, tell the story of fire as the metaphor of metaphor ([1938] 1987: 111). I am interested in collecting stories like the one about candles on the set top showing *Ramayana*. Palin also collects. Inspired by Global South Asian media ethnography, I am interested in things that are attached to television as well as those things that escape the box in the corner. I can see how television drifts into the layout of our rooms, like smoke. Television's screen burn inexorably seeps into other parts of our world. Unlike anything else in quite the same way, the television can reach out and grab our attention – it distracts, it interrupts. But it is perhaps less like the mesmerizing quality of a campfire: before television, or even a handheld screen, a conversation can become difficult, intermittent, haphazardly unfocused. Here is another phantasmagoric quality: we have all no doubt noted at some time when someone we were talking to was found not to be listening to us because the box window on the world or screen in their hand held their attention. I think this happens less frequently with other appliances: the cooker, radiator, air-conditioning unit, or even windows – but of course not that sort of Windows. Screens are insistent, restless and demanding.

Hence, it proliferates objects from the room and beyond, leaving holes in our pockets. The remote control device, the television guide, ornaments and aerial wires, videotapes and DVDs, blu-ray and hard-drives on the shelves where books might have been – I do not want to denigrate television here, but this is an old routine of media displacement. Interactions between people turn to discussions of programmes, even as we no longer say 'there was nothing good to watch last night, was there?' Television is colonization of the imagination in a very minor key – all the more insidious for that – or it is subsumption in the real sense, of every part of our day (Madhava Prasad 1998). It is not just, if at all, a colonization by technological import, but rather the culture industrialization of every minute of our lives, measured now by ISP companies to the second. Television is invasive because it turns everything into storytelling, into a commodification of time and space that was prepared by storytelling, fellow feeling, companionship and desire, digitized. We were always getting ready for television and our televisual friends: the fetish structure is confirmed by the box.

So, to rethink this fetish of image and TV screen more systematically as a storytelling system may be to adopt a global apparatus (Rai 2009) of story as interpretation. To open another angle on this same speculation, might we think of television as a prosthesis of the social – like books which help codify and proliferate memory, like a open access digital reader of books – a means of ordering, recording, storing and investing power and persuasion in tales that are not merely packaged and sold – traveller's tales – but retellings of meaning and motivation and movement. Observations from afar, sure, and recognizing the danger in that the screen shares the structure of remote killing, it invades our space: suicide bombings and drone assassination are the camcorder versions that we have to disarm and reorient to the redistribution of value equitably and universally – to each according to their need.

TV as storytelling prosthesis – we might also call this the networked global eye. After convergence, this becomes especially important as new digital media subjectivity, and intersubjectivity, opens potentials and possibilities for television that were hitherto not yet realized (Spigel and Olsson 2004). That is, the potentials of television as digital prosthesis are only now emerging, and are still without clarity. As an apparatus, the television is a multifaceted and multiconnected social machine that irrupts into our homes and more. Toby Miller points out the obvious future: 'A TV-like screen, located in domestic and other spaces, transmitting signs from other places' (2002: 3). But the extended apparatus of television infiltrates with an enormous global architecture that comes equipped with broadcasting stations, satellite relays, cameras technology, edit suites, newsrooms, back rooms, producers of programmes as well as producers of machines for making programmes, tape and lighting stores, commentators and commentaries, schools of television and journals devoted to its discussion; study programmes, degrees, credentials, awards; conferences and journalism; books, newspapers, footnotes and indexing; promotions, advertisements, embedded correspondents and Al Jazeera; RT, CNN and Dan Rather; Palin and Chadha; scandals and weather girls, back streets with repair shops, trade in second hand; hotwiring and rewiring in the Delhi Bazaar; pirate specialists in the maintenance or the calculation of planned obsolescence; update calculators and credit facilities that buy-now and pay-later forever; credit agencies, venture capitalists; dot.com technology bubble speculators into murder and executions; mergers and acquisitions; publishing. The systematic impact of television is as global as we are – and there is no – need to go – outside.

But is all this new? If the television as campfire metaphor has been updated by television as social prosthesis, we must assume that changes in technology such as VCR, satellite, and digital innovation have scattered the embers of the incandescently gleaming box. Certainly viewing habits, and advertising strategies, have gone through some major adjustments. Who is keeping up? The hand-dialled set has been replaced by the remote control and channel surfing, streaming media is controlled by the click of an optical mouse or track pad, there is television in waiting rooms, in lifts, on buses, on huge city centre billboards and in video art museums, on my watch and in my fridge, and cameras everywhere, always citing freedom, property and Bentham. For me this suggests the social connectivity of the television network apparatus is more subsumed within our daily lives globally; or rather, our day-to-day liberties are co-constituted with the social network that is the globally dominant electronic hearth. We gather around the screen, still warmed by its radiant lustre.

The lustre of television is also a personality, or even celebrity machine we should decommission when it gets out of hand. I always fancied that one way to gauge the prosthetic effect of television would be to examine how the body image of a personality, say the national leader, is plugged into the body politic, or the nation, through the dissemination of images of that leader. The circulation of the image becomes the stand-in, or doppelganger, for the leader's corporeal self. This was something that was confirmed by the US presidential process from the time of John F. Kennedy on, but especially with Reagan. In India no one needs to be reminded of the screen presence and subsequent political stature of MGR, NT Rama Rao or Rajkumar (Madhava Prasad 2014a: 99). It might however be well to recall that this stand-in scenario of representation has always been with us as well. Marx's analysis ([1852] 2000) of representation in the *18th Brumaire* is the case in point. The extension of television to the time of Napoleon's nephew is only the recognition that the culture industry explosion has made potatoes in a sack of us all.

Epic distance

That was then, as Scott McQuire (1986) once said, there was never any reason to believe in a time when television did not exist. I take further justification for a pan-televisual view of the world by reading inversely when Kaur writes of performance:

> There is a tendency, due to the entanglements of media with technological developments, to posit that the mediated comes after performance. Such views assume that what was before technological reproduction was somehow authentic, raw, and not represented in other forms ... One is not necessarily anterior to the other. (2003: 16).

I will read television backwards into pre-formance, even if it remains the case that all of Global South Asia is not yet adequately screened, it certainly is multiply mediated. Clearly, television exhibits some very weird features. It is a time folding device. You can be in your living room and in the Punjab at the same time. It is eyewitness now, live news, and it is a second sight history-making machine. Palin's *Himalaya* is timeless in the way Johannes Fabian exposed an old colonial trope in his book *Time and the Other* (1990). But there is always an other danger in advocacy, of both the past and the now. This issue burns a hole in time and again reminds me of the burning TV that triggered my interest in the *Ramayana*. Yet a more analytical tracing of how the thematic of fire and crisis is variantly dealt might lead to a renewed interventionist scholarship, if it were not so easy to fall into the dangers of Orientalism, it could be important to intervene in film history to find Urdu and Bengali origins and not only Hindi ones. Let us risk this then to discuss *Ramayana* in contexts, proliferating (Thomas 2014, Gera Roy 2015).

It would not do to import the old tribe, village and myth categories of colonialist anthropology. Voyeuristic obsession with the caste system and all it entails should be abandoned. Nonetheless, some old wounds are opened when television burns in *Ramayana* – which of course also includes Sita's ordeal by fire, sati and its her-stories. Television is not a mysterious magical moment and this moment is not a magical mystery but a signifier of the close relation between fire and the screen. The idea of the electronic hearth is not new, and while 'hundreds of films have drawn on the Ramayana and Mahabharata for plots' (Dissanayake 2003: 205) there are also variations on the disturbing theme of cleansing fire. Mankekar notes that the retelling of the 'ancient' *Mahabharata* in the new media of television means that, like all such stories, 'its meanings acquire new valence with every telling' (1993: 469).

Repeated for a new context yet again in 2013 on STAR Plus (dir. various), the *Mahabharata* is deservedly one of the *ur* texts of Global South Asian storytelling. Some point to magical realist qualities alongside more traditional ideological dimensions. As extreme examples of bookends of pre- and postmodernity: the epic's author intervenes to impregnate a character when a crucial male bloodline is at an impasse, the doctrine of karma is inherently hierarchical and conservative, and there are multiple lines of critique. The audiences however were huge.[10]

In the scene that presents Draupadi's disrobing, nationality and sexuality overlap in the folds of a sari made endless by the defensive magical decorum of Krishna. If we are to take reception theory seriously – that is, as not just an empiricist corrective to theories of the hegemonic gaze – then we must admit that the Draupadi scene also can be read in multiple ways. Viewers might see Draupadi as wronged, as victim, as proud, a symbol, as polygamist.

There are those who think that *Mahabharat* allowed more open and multiple readings across the Global South than the *Ramayana* because it is a more complicated text (Mankekar 1993: 471) with greater ambiguities more open to interpretation – but the Ramayana's demographic audience was larger, and its geographical reach perhaps wider, though it must be asked if broadcast range qualifies as a modifier. The openness of reception theory readings must surely be limited by economies of scale, and the question of translation in storytelling is still as yet open to an under-examined politics of interpretation and circulation. What authorizes the readings of such stories? What confirms or condones perspectives and values that may be read off in what more or less direct ways? How much does ideology critique still matter? Very much indeed, despite the occasional Muslim identification with Draupadi, but what then of mixed and queer, trans and global identifications, critiques or re-imaginings? Fans of other characters and dreams of exotic identification over against the militarism of muscular Hindutva in combat on a field as storied and mythic as this, filled with former teachers and familiars, characters and friends, respected ancients and confirmed fools, monsters and monkeys.

But let me not get ahead of myself – evoking the multiplicity of even single images I should be able to avoid sectarian investments so as to sidestep a dubious Hindu chauvinism that would make too much of *Ramayana* or *Mahabharata* as metaphor even in critique. Let us reimagine television – TV as a box of life – as a magic global eye to be reclaimed even as it can reduce the colour of life to pixilated squares or can just as well transport us to places we cannot otherwise see. I want to endorse Draupadi as the emblem of that very moment when the television camera focuses in upon a 'colourful scene' – as I said: ethnic apparel, tradition, natural disaster – but also as the possibility of news from the Global South Asian sphere that would tell the stories of other possibilities, affirming those who fight for alternatives to the hierarchy and exploitation of the commercial boxing of culture as barbaric documentary. Let us hear the programmes the Maoists bring. Let us see Draupadi's version. Her multiple positionality and her polyandrous vitality challenges the paradoxical way that colour and conflict is rendered two dimensional. In comparison, Palin's version of the myth of Asia is limited television. Simplified. A cookery book. Colonialism and Communists substituted with scenic views and silent sadhus. Real relations between people are obscured in the montage of image.

Who, however, has the resources – general conceptual and educational resources, as well as the camera and studio equipment – to tell the stories that Palin glosses as tourist? Again taking *Capital* as a guide, rereading the analytical concepts of Marx in a new context with a view to transforming the world is never a monopoly of academic commentary, and indeed is perhaps its contrary case. Nevertheless, academic and political commentary does exist to document, in a mode more difficult to access, but still possible, the histories of decades of work towards liberation in a strong and sustained cultural, political and theorized framing. The Cultural Revolution of fifty years ago in China also had consequences – similar and different – in India as it did in the struggles of China under Mao. Winning national liberation in the name of communism in Nepal has a heritage of nuanced contest possibly more complicated than in some other states – factionalism, fratricidal contests, interpretation differences in strategy and ideology, fellow travellers as critics and collaborators. As in South Asia, where the Marxist Cultural Movement as a bedrock to then perhaps quixotic ultra-Maoist adventures – the university students from Presidency, Calcutta University, Jadavpur abandoning studies to go to the villages to work with the peasantry. In Nepal the Maoist movement in the countryside also co-exists with a national Marxism-Leninism parliamentary Communist path, with Adhikari and the Communist Party of Nepal United Marxist Leninist (CPN-UML) a separate tradition to the Maoist insurgency (CPN-M), and indeed Adhikari's party had briefly taken power and arraigned against the Maoists in the mid-1990s, not long before Palin was concocting the idea of his own path through Nepal. The revolutionary tourist collecting communist trinkets and passport and visa stamps from the liberated Maoist base areas are understandably enough not seeped in the factionalia of this heritage, and indeed Maoist base area and Everest base camp have a different but not necessarily unrelated surface resemblance in terms of souvenirs.

Draupadi and other divinities

Is Draupadi an alternative figure? A poster girl for the Global South? It is well to remember how the celebration of resistance has often been criticized when it comes to the people's movements described from Europe and America – I want to say from the NATO-sponsoring countries. Global South is obviously conceptually paired with Global North but the relational aspect is often silences. Palin can travel from one to another without necessary comment, indeed with adventure as his code. Others offer Global South as affirmative terminology, used not so much by the peoples of the Global South as by conscious, self-declared and even vanguardist leaders, politicians and commentators. Not to only be critical here, the consciousness in the identification and self-reference of Global South is a recognition of the historic debt of the North to the South because of historical and continuing colonial extraction. Ideologues of the North would of course wish to avoid drawing attention to the foundational violence – at best accepting talk of reparations rather than the mobilized demands that the term Global South could in general use imply. The terminology then acknowledges, by denial in the one case, by contrast in the other, the historic obligations owed by North to South, but reparations without political weight are also just television. All important here in the context of representations of Global South Asia is Madhava Prasad's formative work on ideology as a subsumption process. Madhava Prasad argues that ethnographic audience studies in the West find 'resistance' – where viewers 'never completely fit the position that the text offers' – while studies in the east find 'non-western subjects ... distinguished by being completely at home in their ideological environment, the films they see corresponding exactly to their needs' (1998: 15n). Resistance has been a long beloved theme of cultural studies and has dominated audience studies for some time. It would be not be sectarianism to suggest that there is a misplaced optimism on the part of former leftists who, instead of organizing struggles, prefer rather to find the anti-hegemonic resistance of the subordinate classes already prepared for the screen – readymade for documentary. Such documentarists of Global South issues, and never disregarding their critical acumen, nonetheless still seem strangely inadequate to the effort required to displace power and win. That this deserves more than the footnote Madhava Prasad offers is clear as it shows the persistence of a hierarchical othering that is fantasy on both sides, and that the mess of reality in film, or TV, is never so neat as much audience/ethnography analysis would contend. Here we need to go beyond the audience, with Theodor Adorno: 'sociological research that would prefer to avoid the problems of analysing production and to confine itself to questions of distribution or consumption remains imprisoned in the mechanisms of the market and hence gives its sanction to the primacy of the commodity' [1978] 1999: 6). To disregard the political content and context of calls for Global South mobilization is to blindside readers with complicity in neo-liberal ideological documentary. Here, any economic focus favours business interests and capital owners, irrespective of national conditions and often in denial of mass public mobilizations in the streets – Palin's ideological function is to render Maoist opposition as exotic curiosity.

Which is also to say, even the academic analysis is part of ideological struggle; as Madhava Prasad reminds us, films, and so also television serials, are works of ideology, not mirrors of reality (2000: 237). Let us not assume that listening to television or *Ramayana* is either a case of total interpolation – she is always Sita – or of fully dynamic resistance – I am Ravana one day, Hanuman the next, Sita another. Can I be all three? The now almost obligatorily dutiful observance that the Ramayana is 'open to various interpretations' is also made in Kaur (2003: 117) and the point surely should be to insist upon the possibility of all such interpretations. The first interpretation, as much as the last, is bound up however with production, and the reproduction of story makes a ground for decoding fixed identifications, fixity and ideology. To not fix the code in the dominant register but to multiply globalizations as the first ground of unravelling Ravana's ideological grip. The pursuit of the audience which does not open up the calculations of interpretation leaves the politics of production untouched.

In his densely argued and engaging work on television within India, Rajagopal discusses the way Doordarshan state monopoly television largely failed to translate existing televisual sensibilities into the actual mechanics of television broadcasting. Such narrowcast ignoring of audience research that indicates the popularity of entertaining storytelling – and why would it not – may have some readers of Adorno approve, but this would be to miss the ways Adorno pointedly addressed audience studies in an effort to bring out political alternatives. The suggestion that the plodding paternalism of managed state television was, for many years, the provenance of crushingly boring content is undeniable, but the conventions of audience research were hardly needed to tell us this.

> Doordarshan offered a mirror to the state's official aspect, presenting it as it wished to be seen. In practice, this meant that the political party and the leader in power at any given time were presented making speeches, cutting ribbons, presiding over parades, and deliberating at meetings. (Rajagopal 2001: 77)

Are there viewers who would not agree? Watch any film in a group and listen to the commentary and critical asides, the ongoing discussion of production that runs parallel to any interpretation of the audience – the assemblage of the co-constituted scene of screen and meaning – gives an impression that the audiences already deploy the categories of analysis given by the theorists. And all the more considering the statistical facts: Rajagopal is able to show that not so many people were actually watching those early moments of state propaganda through mythologicals. He reports there were just 3 million sets in 1983, 13 million in 1987, and so on, and in any case people preferred films and songs to the Doordarshan line. As perhaps they still do, though videos, and indeed interstate jealousies, have tried to kill the playback singers and the fratricidal narrative has not yet reached the third reel resolution. It is, however, not necessarily the case that broadcast state media was without a resonant and substantial impact in India, and Rajagopal's suggestion that the ideological charge of television and politics can be understood in terms of anthropological gift exchange (Rajagopal 2001: 5) possibly underplays the politics. Consider the how and why of Gandhi's radio broadcast successes of the 1930s. Why was

India so well prepared to hear him if not the already marked out space of the democratic sphere, or civil society, anticipated already, now mediatized – able to interpret, translate and answer the call in huge numbers? Rajadhyaksha's related comments about the connection of the state apparatus to storytelling media resonates here as well (2009: 11), with implications for transmission and the alternatives of a Global South Asian politics. In a later discussion, at a Jadavpur seminar, Rajadhyaksha could make the angular observation that the reception of Marxist ideas in India had a particular connectivity also – 'European Marxism' came with particular characteristics – it was not '"any" Europe, for example [it] ... was not Dipesh Chakrabarty's Europe ... [it was] the Europe of the Latin American Third Cinema, this was the "other" of third world radicalisation' (2012a: 62). It was also of course, as already noted above, the exchange with China and Mao – a peal of Spring thunder – that brings characteristics that must be acknowledged as differently shaping the negotiations of politicized media in Global South Asia. In this light it is possible to reassess Rajagopal's suggestion about gift exchange as a frame for understanding state television as something which clearly foregrounds connectivity over alienation, belonging over instrumentality – 'no commodity transaction is purely instrumental' (2001: 5). This formulation helps us understand the attachment of audiences to messages that may be received critically, but are received, even where Rajagopal wants to hold onto an autonomous private reflective separation, and a conception of value and meaning that owes as much to media theory as it does to the underpinnings of a Marxist formation, the language of exchange must be translated when expressed in terms such as 'reproduction', 'accumulation' and 'capital' (Rajagopal 2001: 295). That this invokes an ideological critique that sutures individual interpretation to national, regional and global belonging is also open to more vernacular interpretations.

At one level at least, 'Ramayan is basically a secular epic' that even Gandhi saw as 'an expressive metaphor to symbolize a welfare state'. So says S. S. Gill, the Minister of Information and Broadcasting who commissioned Ramanand Sagar to produce and direct the serial. This of course is contested terrain, and the institutional voice is not the carrier of alternate potential; if the state introduced *Ramayana* to television, did it do so for ideological purposes, or to satisfy an impulse to entertain? Did the invisible hand of convenience see the potential in manipulation of cultural heritage for ideological advantage? Whatever the explicit intentions, the markers were already in place and the politicization of the epic was only enhanced by the technological trickery that made 'divinity appear as merely the sum of spectacular effects' (Kaur 2003: 91). And whatever the case, the programme did have some considerable impact on the space of television and its articulation with the body politic extending beyond the actual programme to the now far more widespread discussion of the programmatic. The event of the Ramayana on television – even before the introduction of set-top viewer boxes and demographic measurement – was immeasurable because it extended beyond television. Though there were socially evident visual effects, it is less clear how television in turn – in exchange – may have changed *Ramayana* although it is *perhaps* true that the multiplicity of possible interpretation makes mythology more vulnerable and available for adoption by all manner of interests, even where the possibility of resistance is more or less carefully orchestrated, stage-managed. As Rajagopal notes:

> The difficulty in discussing the Ramayana is that we are not referring to a single literary work ... rather, it refers to an extraordinary broad range of texts and performative traditions, from devotional vaishnavite retellings, to Buddhist and Jaina variations, to political propaganda, to folkloric domestications of a high classical form, and beyond. (2001: 87)

Could we nevertheless say that *Ramayana* is the foundation of television? Perhaps this is a frivolous speculation, best ignored. *Himalaya* does plug into the same public-mythic space, and the story-quest, the book, the documentary serial and now satellite and DVD versions achieve the saturation coverage for the same. We do not hear even a fraction as much news from the Maoists.[11]

My argument is not that subcontinental television should be made in order to broadcast and showcase a better Global South Asia to the world, though certainly quality documentary and filmic production that challenges the mundane Palin model could be more widely disseminated. I recognize that production of content for global broadcast need not be the best choice for those pressed for time and resources, who might better make content that was critical, informative or entertaining for their own constituencies. Who uses media to what ends, with what success, at what cost? What if the idea that television is a foreign import, and that commentaries on television in Global South Asia already informed within a restrictive media imperative mind-set, were not taken willy-nilly at face value? Rajagopal points out the 'knowing eye' of television scholarship tends to see television as a late arrival to geographic, indeed urban, South Asia, and is then concerned only with a 'focus on direct control of software and media corporations, and [with] point[ing] to Western interests being served by institutions and images endorsing the West's eminence' (2001: 75). This is a kind of digital 'intimate enemy' argument that, Rajagopal contends, must be supplemented by noticing 'how the imagination is blunted in apprehending a transplanted technology's distinctive history' (2001: 75). What if it were the case that the serials exposed not the use of ideology to television, but the use of television to ideology and this then informed the discussions of a Global South thus mobilizing interpretations in ways uncontained by the institutional apparatus? The use of every technology for delivery in creative ways, as documented so often in the literature of Global South Asian media studies, would surely make this case.

The invention of television

The need to think differently about global television is a part of the disruption required to displace the Himalayas. No easy task, since without doubt television in geographic South Asia is determined, in its operation, by patterns and privileges within local structures and possibilities (Madhava Prasad 1998: 3), just as it is everywhere. How these local considerations then shape, distort or confirm the productive practices of documentarists from 'elsewhere' requires further study. What is needed is an assessment of the longitudinal forces at stake, the various deep conditioning factors and metaphysical strictures that a politics of television may then transduce. Ask what visitors bring and what locals give, who does the work and who profits on the back of which client relationship, consortium deal, quick access, privileged access, international prestige and awards, focused internal or external ambition. What are the many varied factors that shape the kinds of programmes that can be made, and which are not funded, distributed, or consumed? Who shapes the determinant structures and codes the interpretations even at the affective levels of accent and familiarity, of intimate enmities that confirm or condone valuations without examination, which make it possible to get away with showing something in just that way, just so? Confirming worlds in a single image, or destroying them.

It must be admitted that media ownership and control of context, market and commercial imperatives, including new media convergence, tend not, despite investments in criticism, resistance and possibility, to facilitate an alternative thinking of the business of television. The conditions of production and control – the hegemony of the televisual culture that manages the imagination – is not sufficiently challenged where thinking about television still follows the centre-periphery formal subsumption and cultural imperialist models. Images of Global and geographic South Asia circulating abroad reinforce this absent alternative; we do not escape the cave, and the 'East' remains in shadow. To imagine otherwise, to enlighten ourselves, to reorient global television might mean to invert the developmental sequences somewhat, to recast Asia as the global centre, especially in terms of the development of television. This might be to see *Ramayana* and *Mahabharata*, Urdu, qissa and dastan, Ali Baba and

Scheherazade, and real subsumption and the phantasmagoric of Bollywood or the agency of images, as a productive basis for a rather different view of television. Television as counter-hegemonic, social uplift, anti-realist, libidinous investment contra the fetishizing, trinketization that is capital. Television puts the trinkets back in the box. Curse and reprieve. Would it be possible to see television as an invention of Asia? Plato would turn in his cave, perhaps at last to see the sunrise. There is no doubt this is a risky suggestion, but the thought that representation begins with stories around a fire is not unthinkable.

To take that campfire, and *Ramayana*, and cricket, as subcontinental inventions of global television is not implausible – cricket because it is done well, the camera crew has a good idea as to where the action will be, and can set up ahead of time at Eden Gardens or similar settings. To make television global also implies a critique of television as local ideology. Hindutva is not there 'in' the *Ramayana* or *Mahabharata* just as nostalgic diasporic conservative longing is not built into the exported Bollywood film every time, but it is there in the possible interpretations and the extensions of the programming to the world. The question to ask now is what composition of forces and what critique of ideology would be required to combat right wing appropriations?

This does not erase the doubt that to make the campfire the antecedent of television is nostalgic traditionalism and anti-modern fantasy all over again. But what if it was through this dangerous thought experiment that the prohibition against thinking differently about television could be lifted? A peal of spring thunder breaks over Nepal; the lightning strike lights a fire; the Rana dynasty totters as does the cascading democratic assemblies that follow. There will always be debts to pay, but the justice of them might be contested. Prometheus steals fire as freedom for humanity – a technology that gives the naked fool a chance to survive, with warmth, light, sustenance, of cooking, and fun, of firewater, but it is hard to control, and his liver pays the price.[12]

Will it make a difference to our assessment of television if we think of television itself as an Asian form? Certainly it is produced both here and there; the old dissemination model at least is reversed/disturbed. But, more fundamentally, if the capital investment is not primarily diasporic, what consequences follow? I suspect there are many more ways to rethink South Asian television globally as the centre rather than an imported media brought by imperialism to the periphery. This is not to deny media imperialism, but rather to tamper with its guiding assumptions, to invert its logic. So as I am watching *The Razor's Edge* again and Bill Murray is looking for enlightenment again, I also am sure that the exploration of things and connections between them are occluded in the fetish character through which we are compelled to comprehend otherwise social and productive relations. Hence the need to examine those relations of production that enable events like *Himalaya* to be screened, but also the need to examine the epiphenomenal vectors of television and its connections to commoditized performance as advertising, as trinketization and as culture at war. These are themselves a fetishized index of (international) social relations, congealed or reified as connections between things and as the mediated performance of the political.

A single spark can start a prairie fire

What then, for news and documentary of Asia in the Palin type? The quest for knowledge is stalled on the mountaintop because commercial and military imperatives govern the way in which Global South Asia is known – a backdrop to the extraction of products, trinkets, icons and terror. This too is not merely ideological but relies upon an identified market segment characterized by passing interest in a natural – exotic – nostalgic subcontinent. We might call the ideological context colonial melancholia (after Gilroy, 2004) and note that the dominant tropes on the screen are of time past and of practices arcane. A kind of pseudo-popular historical programming that sells relatively cheap products on relatively expensive airtime. Palin's *Himalaya* was screened in the United Kingdom on Sundays at 9 p.m., for substantial gain through advertising revenue for 'new' products tied in with the show. The margins for Palin are neither huge, nor insignificant, and as a potential crossover audience can be assumed with divergent interpretations of Palin's antics, there is plenty of margin for the programmers themselves. Palin sells ads and books – a hugely successful Christmas hit selling 250,000 was significant for a TV sponsored stocking filler. Yet, as Rajadhyaksha points out, the hyped 'Indian Summer' of 2002 in London may have showcased film stars, food and music form the subcontinent – all things Indian at Selfridges department store – but two things were conspicuously absent: 'the political ... and the Indian state' (2004: 56). If these appeared in the later version of *Indian Summers* in its television serial form, this was also an erasure of the same order as the erasure of political content beyond a brief mention of the Maoists in Nepal and some earthy comments from the Dalai Lama in the Palin docu-tainment. Of a type with the marketing of exotica in other parts of 'subcontinental Britain' – glowing sparks, embers, cinders, as literal translations of *Sholay*. Not far away from this, the Maoist movement in India is declared by then Prime Minister Manmohan Singh as the greatest terror threat to the nation, building on the long tradition of demonization of Naxals in the press, as 'countered' by the police in extra-juridical executions (more below), but also changing that characteristic to fit with global circumstances and circulating metaphors of threat. Where once the Naxals were compared to goondas and thugs, the diminutive mode is replaced by abstract comparison with Al Qaeda and the Taliban. The escalation here belies the popular movement on the ground in Nepal and across India, by way of a global associative dominant abstract 'terror'. The contradictions of this law and order framing, itself suspect and rife with corrupt cops and counter-insurgency, now steps up to a global formatting, fabricated as having international significance, emotive in a way that cannot be contained. As a counter to this, should we seek out a documentary conflagration to light the way? We were also waiting to see what use the Nepalese Maoists made of the seven video cameras looted from Kohalpur while the television station was burning. A responsibility to educate the rest of the globe cannot be the strategic preoccupation of revolutionaries engaged in immediate life and death struggles, but again from afar, from Palin's position in the micro-lite or from the sympathetic-revolutionary touristic, romantic Left, what possibility for participating in educational videography that can challenge the demonizations deployed by the likes of Manmohan Singh? Instead, the utilization of video by political groups is undermined when mainstream corporate TV promulgates a much more disturbing vision of the camera in unregulated hands – so when a grotesque menagerie of villains, monsters, evil doers and organized crime syndicates with death squad video executions and beheadings are measured up against US military footage of 'smart' bombs and drone strikes, the video graphic of the global war on terror is seen not only as an incessant public screening of good versus evil, right versus wrong. It has effects quite different than mere reception of the news. Yet, this is also another chapter unwritten: these are not explorations but implorations of television shared with film and screen cultures in general and with Great Game consequences for the negotiated economics of the 'pivot' to the Asian hemisphere and who will best benefit from the rise of India and China; the Global South Asian investigation is a demand to begin to think the ways media – portrayal of Mao or Maoists, portrayal of all political interpretation, angles, interests, investments – are always-already lodged in our thinking and fears. I am concerned at how the camera watches our every move; the return to prominence of the great civilizational powers needs a reminder of modest critical intent – and thus I have a candle on top of the set; to remind me of the folly of the cave, and to keep me looking to the light.

4

The Hanging Channel: For Mohammad Afzal Guru

How to evaluate the rhetorical media-driven re-imagining of Asia? If by uneven extension we posit Global South Asia amidst dramatic and transforming geopolitical shifts – on the one hand economic reordering, on the other escalating 'terror' – then representations of local and global political struggles and the ways they have been reported, discussed and presented through television might be considered crucial. This chapter examines one dimension of the new discursive mode of Global South Asia through attention to what is shown on television and specifically on the 'news' in relation to Kashmir and India. Of course, if the encounter with the screen apparatus is to be approached critically, the presentation and representation of political struggles moves through various distortions and reflections and mediation of all this may paradoxically mean that an exclusive use of 'media theory' might not always be the first or best step (Negt 1978: 63). Theories of the televisual and specific local mutations of genre formats in a global and post-colonial 'milieu' can of course be problematized in several ways. A non-monolithic post-colonial/globalization model may suggest a review of the theoretical frameworks that inform media theory generally, especially in the context of national(ist) and international(ist) pressures. In this chapter, examples of 'terror incidents' are a test case: in particular, the chapter raises issues surrounding the trial in 2006–2007 and execution in 2013 of Mohammad Afzal Guru in, but also with reference to the terrible Mumbai attacks of November 2008. While tragic in multiple ways, these events are made spectacular, emotive and divisive, according to interpretation, *by* television. What remains to be considered is how the 'models' available for analysis might break down these (mere) 'case studies' in ways that offer insights more generally applicable. Television news has variously engaged in information war and controversy before our eyes, and on our screens. As such, the televisual deserves to be questioned and challenged.[1]

Kali TV (black and white life)

If I were not aware of the critiques of Indology that must be applied, I would ask if the *Horror Movie* of twenty-four-hour television news in every sitting room is not the way in which the age of destruction, *Kali-yuga*, appears to us today. We are often appalled, but perhaps also somehow numbed, by the constant barrage of images of terror on our screens. For this chapter, as an experimental and only partly serious opening mythological move, I want to suggest that the idea we are witnessing the age of *Kali-yuga* is as valid, or as arbitrary, as allegorical a frame as any other for those who approach the phenomenon of present times in a mode of resignation. The news, as it is presented to us 'live', reports a world of pain and we watch this attendant to various degrees to suffering, and, more or less, becoming acclimatized to its everyday presence. Let me insist that I do not think *Kali-yuga* is the only possible way we can think of the news. Indeed, I am keen to promote rather different frames of analysis and critique. But so as to illustrate my point that there are several possible allegories available at the same time, let me start with Kali. In making a somewhat randomly mythical and intentionally exoticist opening, I am trying to contrapuntally show that we can see the news not as realist commentary on what is going on, but as commentary within interpretive frames. Staged commentary. Maya. None other than historian Summit Sarkar, in his book *Beyond Nationalist Frames: Relocating Postmodernism, Hindutva, History* (2002), starts with *Kali-yuga*, so why not? Kali is the goddess of change and her rule is the destructive end time of the cycle of ages. Kali is death, destroyer and decay of ego. Sarkar takes his material from the *Mahabharata*, Vanaparva Sections 187–190 of the 'Markandya-Samasya' (2002: 14n) and writes:

> A few details about standard notions of Kali-yuga need to be presented here ... A recurrent and powerful format for voicing high-caste male anxieties for some two thousand years, the evils of Kali-yuga include disorders in nature, oppressive alien kings, Brahmans corrupted by too much rationalistic debate, overmighty Shudras no longer serving their caste superiors, and women choosing their own partners, disobeying and deceiving husbands, and having intercourse with menials, slaves and even animals. (2002: 13)

It is somehow appealing, at least to me, that this sounds exactly like contemporary reality television both in its horror and in fact its democratizing potentiality, however stalled. We might then be tempted to suggest that television is a Global South Asian format, accidentally invented by the British, to adapt Nandy's witticism about the provenance of cricket ([1989] 2000: 1). Although I would not want to ascribe explanatory power to Kali here, I am, however, concerned to understand how the malevolent power of television, as a system of images, as representation and network, as imaginary, permeates understanding and shapes a kind of state-sponsored or endorsed cosmology of fear and anxiety, as seen in the nation, and extending worldwide. On the other side of this, an effort of critique and campaigns of support that struggle against both commercialism and reaction. The constrained voices of reason and protest forced thus far into a format that corrals. The connections tracked here between the state, the screen, social, technological and political networks, of things and people, are the price of the ticket. Hand over fist the taxation system also includes the fanzine, the monthly internet subscription, and extortionate fees for a degree with access to a library full of book length commentaries on Global South Asian screen studies. Modes of corrupt practice that winkle rupees, pounds, dollars and sense out of pockets, too much post-rationalist debate obscures the contours of exploitation and miseries of underdevelopment.

Other commentators on Global South Asian film texts make regulation moves that attribute statecraft to media. Rajagopal, for example, notes that the serialization of the *Ramayana*, discussed in the previous chapter, trades on a myth of 'a golden age of tradition that was yet ahead of the modern era in statecraft and warfare' and which 'adroitly made appeals to diverse social groups' (2001: 15). Madhava Prasad speaks of cinema as 'an institution that is part of the continuing struggles within India over the form of the state' (1998: 9) where he identifies a spectrum with 'Hindu nationalism at one end appropriating the fragile national project in an attempt to re-establish political unity on a communal foundation' and at the other end a globalization that 'seems to be eroding the function of the state as a political restraint on a re-vitalized, rampaging capitalism' (1998: 8–9). Participation in the circuits of global commerce of course does not come without its ideological inflections too, but there is something to learn from the constant recourse of these film scholars to the state as explanatory framework. Not that other national and diasporic cinemas are described without reference to the coincidence of cinema and power: as Rajadhyaksha notes of the Philippines in a footnote (2009: 11) and also when reporting that Godard could 'startlingly propose in his *Histoire(s) du cinema: Toutes les histories* (1989), that the cinema's birth and death may well be marked as coinciding with the birth and death of the Soviet Union' (2009: 221). Gore Vidal's (2000) rendering of Hollywood might best exemplify the same argument for, and Rajadhyaksha nominates Dave Morley's *Nationwide Audience* (1980) as the key British text. Yet it is in Global South Asia film and television studies that habitual recourse to the state story seems most unavoidably evident. What can be said here of cinema also holds for television news and social media formats, though remembering that cinema and television is not the same as television news or the click-bait of online news browsing. I still take the suggestion of Kaur and Sinha seriously when they offer an analytical perspective that notes 'the interdynamic relationship between the local and the global, the national and the international ... to draw attention to the audio-visual and cultural economies ... and the flow of representational capital and technologies of production' (2005: 23). The flow today is increasingly media houses driving content through sharing devices, be they TV screens or hand held. This interdynamic offers contours of attachment to the map of Global South Asia where cultural economies are joined by a critical sensitivity born of shared experience of colonialism and colonial struggle and updated for digitization.

I think there is a mode of Global South Asian analysis that can be usefully described here as watching television in the age of *Kali-yuga*. Of course I want to do this without evoking what Jyotika Virdi calls a 'throwback' to an 'indigenous anti-western, anti-imperialist epistemology' that relies upon 'foundational myths', that sees the 'figures that appear in classic epics as archetypes of Indian cinema', thus assuming some 'kernel of pure, untouched Indian culture' behind 'the ravages of colonial dislocation' (2003: 3). Nor is it only to have recourse in outrage at the manipulation of the cheesy image of bin Laden watching TV in the Abbottabad compound hideaway that motivates critical thinking here. There is still, I think, something in Sarkar's commentary on *Kali-yuga*, quoted above, that can pierce the dry 'statecraft' of the global media and media studies with the suggestion that the televised pantheon of 'overmighty' current affairs presenters, star interviewers, celebrated talking heads, 'corrupted' pundits, experts and guests can be identified as the contemporary avatars of the local-global nexus of post-national warfare while still identifying possibilities elsewhere. An entire televisional goddery makes up this videographic spectrum, and it waits ripe and ready only for the infidels to offer their irreverent and profane dissenting views with a programme capable of winning. To do more than snipe at the sidelines requires the Global South mobilization that has a heritage but is so often eclipsed or in decline beneath the onslaught of corporate blanket coverage. Underneath the rarified air in which the micro-lites, satellites and drones scan for terrorists, a rebel force harkens to an older call...

Fascism as an elementary structure of news reportage

The critiques offered by media theory are useful and deserve attention, though it will be my *con*tention that without organizational connections with more than a 'nationwide audience' these are insufficiently heretical to challenge the sway the gods of television news have over us. Blasphemy and sacrilege it might be, I do not think a media theory is adequate as a theory of the media. I will rely upon work as varied as that by people like Sarkar (2002), Spivak (1999, 2008, 2012), Beller (2006), Bharucha (1998), Stiegler ([1996] 2009) and Vasudevan (2010). All of these authors are influential, I believe, because their work is more than media theory, yet media are necessarily their stock in trade. Spivak for example, writing of 'Indian Modernity' as 'represented in videographic news', mentions Kashmir and *Roja* as 'contextualized by the fierce near-Fascist nationalism daily shown on Indian national television' (2000: 307). Rustom Bharucha, also mentioning *Roja* and Kashmir, says we 'need to confront that dangerous border where nationalism becomes fascism by questioning our own complicities in the legitimization of violence around us' (1998: 115). This is not just something to be said so that we then move on. Although Nicholas Dirks also runs a twenty-five-page commentary on the three pages of Tejaswini Niranjana's (1994) provocative review of *Roja* in the *Economic and Political Weekly*, which had, in turn, meant 'considerable further debate' (Dirks 2001: 163) even as he found 'discomfort', 'unease' and disappointment (Dirks 2001: 163, 178) in the way critical evaluation achieved wider academic exposure through such a 'brief' review which 'begs a number of questions' and 'misses a great deal' (Dirks 2001: 175). Not wanting to endorse such weasel words or point overly much at the space restrictions of EPW reviews, I choose these varied mentions of *Roja* and Kashmir because the example I want to take up – a series of violent incidents and events presented to us on television – has its origins in part in the Kashmir question, but also because a scrupulous critical commentary on South Asian modernity relies upon the kind of contextualization these authors provide. I will not however have much to say of Kashmir directly. It is thirty years since I visited, for obvious reasons, and militarization and the crisis of curfews, confrontation and bombing has worked to transmute the tourist resort into a vale of tears. I think one of the complicities we need to attend to is that for many people Kashmir is nowadays a code word, much more than it is a place. Despite ongoing at least domestic tourism, Kashmir in the news has become a cipher for something else, a frame for discussion.

Learning from Bharucha and Spivak to situate Global South Asia in the productive apparatus of both the geopolitical dispensation and the situated interpretive practices of those who study 'these things' for reasons of more than professional obligation, I think an approach that attends to presentation, to framing, to performance and the way the news is presented as 'news', deserves consideration. This is where the commodified Bollywood content 'performs the function of representing the nation to an international (though not international[ist]) audience' (Spivak 1996: 257). Beyond Bollywood, *The Guide* or *Roja*, it is news media that draws attention through a sensational international profile and incident that plugs into the structured global apparatus. What first strikes me as self-evidently necessary, but which is often ignored in media presentation, is to look closely at just what is presented on the screen – the presentation of presentations, which conventionally the viewer must look through. In a rare example, Rai opens the discussion of media interconnectivities as a genealogy where ads layered over pirate cable feeds (2009: 87) give way over time to television merchandising and promotion, internet tie-ins and 'feedback loops of capital' themselves mutating in 'vectors of evolution' (2009: 71) that nevertheless continue the political management of 'population security' (2009: 72). Such genealogical approaches offer one way to understand station identification, presentation formats, props and styles of news and examine them for clues as to what sort of media phenomenon and what sort of reach into the self-understanding of audiences we might be talking about here. The obvious things to look for are the slogans and catch phrases of media news. One example of what I mean is the possibility of an analysis of station 'idents' and slogans such as that of NDTV's strapline 'NDTV 24x7 Experience. Truth First'. Remembering that the 1998 elections were the pretext for the creation of India's first 24-hour news channel (disputed by ZEE below) it is worth acknowledging the rapid rise of the station to national prominence and its subsequent international reach. Evolved from what was initially a content provider company for Doordarshan in the days of state monopoly, New Delhi TV (NDTV) was a private concern run by Prannoy and Radhika Roy, initially broadcasting a half-hour news programme called 'The World This Week' from November 1988 until the mid-1990s. From 'The World This Week' to 24x7 is perhaps not so huge a shift, but it is possible to say that the Roy's brought with them a considerable track record.

Thinking about the strapline, one experience carried from the weekly news segment on Doordarshan to the twenty-four-hour television format version involved a quite curious temporal delay. Television scholar and journalist Nalin Mehta identifies NDTV as the best 'place to begin the story of what was happening to television news within the larger framework of television expansion' (2008: 76) in part because the idea of 'live news' so troubled the prime minister's office (Rajiv Gandhi). Prannoy Roy describes the first day of telecast:

> On the first night when I went on air, I said, 'the time is 8 o'clock', I looked at my watch and said, 'we are coming to you live with the news'. Apparently the prime minister's office people were watching and immediately they started phoning saying, 'Is this live? You can't allow him live'. They didn't understand what live meant. They were just terrified at the thought. (Roy interviewed in Mehta 2008: 77)

NDTV's solution was to delay the live telecast by ten minutes, broadcasting at 8 p.m. a programme recorded at 7.50 p.m. The story of the multiplication of television channels through satellite in India is already well known, see Rajagopal (2001), Mankekar (1999) and Nilanjana Gupta (1998), but it is curious that the delay in live transmission of the news was still in place when NDTV moved from Doordarshan to Rupert Murdoch Star TV network to start the first twenty-four-hour dedicated news channel. If precedents are a concern, Mehta's contention that the channel was introduced to cover the 1998 general election as the first round the clock provider is disputed by Zee but this point is generally conceded to NDTV (for more see Mehta 2008: 81, 329). On the Star platform the output delay was slightly shorter, but all NDTV offices had two clocks in each room according to Roy, 'one on Indian Standard Time, and the other on "NDTV time", which was always five minutes behind' (Metha 2008: 82). Roy insists that despite receiving specific and urgent calls, for example during the Gujarat riots of 2002, including threats, the station did not stop its 'live' broadcasts. Live that is, for those in the room on NDTV time, and for everyone watching unaware outside 'live', it was happening five minutes later. This makes the NDTV slogan: 'Experience. Truth First' particularly significant when the place of the full stop directly after experience is noted. The viewer will not experience truth first, but rather the experienced news editor looks at events first and then broadcasts what they say is true.

Generally, a five-minute delay won't be sufficient to manage all ideological angles, but the principle is breached. The rhetoric of 'live' news is operative from the start and determines larger frames. What is screened shapes understanding, today as before. Biswas has made the general point that the 'resurfacing' and 'resurgence' of old cinema imagery was not just 'nostalgia', for example when video and television needed material to fill airtime (2000: 123). Similarly, we can argue that today the news is never simply present as the news, despite a reporting-as-public-service function rhetoric. Even if this is not the same structure of nostalgia, it is significant because NDTV 24x7 *melodramatically* shifts towards something that updates what some might nostalgically call national project television – Doordarshan – though with a much more glitzy and globally oriented, commercial attention-economy focus.

Speaking of NDTV's weekly debate format show 'The Big Fight', Mehta says television 'turns politics into spectacle, but politics has always been about spectacle' (2008: 255). Mehta interviews NDTV's managing editor Rajdeep Sardesai (1997–2004) who says:

> TV is now increasingly entertainment. News is entertainment. You have to create some element of entertainment ... people shouting at each other ... or some kind of conflict. It is not always about information. I am not saying in the *Big Fight* you don't try to inform but if the entertainment element was not there the programme would probably not have survived. You have to package it ... First Punch, Second Punch ... Otherwise who will see? There has to be some heat. (Sardesai interviewed in Mehta 2008: 255)

Even if NDTV is not watched by everyone all the time and not everyone is entertained by this format, it is still possible to elaborate what is presented on the channel as indicative of a certain interpretive agenda without falling for the hyperbolic justifications of management. The suggestion that the news be entertaining is all well and good, but the format of debate itself is not transparent. Just as the name NDTV makes visible but does not discuss the 'New Delhi' view of India – where New Delhi here could be code for a politically centralist nationalist and parliamentary project, so too the 'First Punch Second Punch' format of the debating chamber does not draw attention to the entertainmentalization of contested information. To do so would of course undermine any pretence to newsworthiness or relevance, foregoing a whole other kind of television. All television to some extent participates in the ideological formation of the national and the international – Game and Reality TV shows just as much as movies have often been examined in this way – but Reality TV is not (always) as horrific as the news. To turn on the television and see that it is always on, that the news never sleeps, that the most monstrous atrocities, crimes, injuries, deceits and iniquities are played over and over as *current* affairs is to confirm the most grotesque structural interpretive consequence of news as entertainment. Concern does not need to be only about the degree to which viewers are appalled or inured to bombings, death horror or terror attacks, but also how infotainment entails acquiescence to the routine hype that promotes the very State security regime which provokes attacks and manages responses. Further, accepting surveillance and constraints upon civil liberties that should deserve our contempt is reported as initiative of Government, endorsing the transparent deceptions of those who operate detention centres, extra-juridical assassinations, special renditions, black ops and in fact the whole militarized counter-intelligence terror regime for 'us'. This complicity is the staple of daily news experience and truth in uncertain geopolitical times.

Trial by media

On 13 December 2001, a little over two months after another now overdetermined date of significance in New York, five men (at least) piled out of a white ambassador car that had driven into the grounds of the parliament building in New Delhi. The winter session was on, and, as if out of the latest blockbuster movie sequel, these miscreants, with guns-blazing, attacked and killed nine people, then themselves died in a hail of bullets, failing to set off their car bomb because they had damaged their detonator in a collision with the president's parked vehicle. Military immediately deployed and the border with Pakistan sealed, terror legislation and terror threat level escalated for a year, high profile court case, and debate all through the press as consequences.

Alleged accomplices of the attackers were subsequently arrested. The Inspector of Police declaring all hands initiate a national effort, the nation appreciates the sacrifice of the police who left no stone unturned, and so on. Many commentators have said that the raid of 13 December was fairly incompetent, and the news channels reported it as such. The accomplices were presented as dupes or clichéd troublemakers, no match for the intrepid security forces; these were 'amateurs', 'miscreants', but also 'terrorists'. In *The December 13 Reader*, published in December 2006 to expose contradictions and inconsistencies in the case, Arundhati Roy questioned the swift 'case cracked' response of the police in arresting and bringing to trial four accomplices. Another volume, *Manufacturing Terrorism: Kashmiri Encounters with Media and the Law* (Geelani 2006), was published in the same year by Syed Bismillah Geelani, columnist brother of one of the four accused. That brother, Syed Abdul Rahman Geelani, was a PhD student at Delhi University when arrested on 14 December 2001, so Syed Bismillah's book gave details on Kashmir and defended the accused against a patent frame-up. Both publications raised a series of disturbing questions within the wider public debate where the 'facts of the case' became fairly common knowledge, but were also drowned somewhat in a news media circus. Of significance for the case I am making, as something that reveals the spectacular economy of news-casting in this scene, NDTV's Vikram Chandra (not the novelist) hosted a 'Big Fight' teleconference in a boxing ring set-up.

A big-money telecast sporting metaphor surely illustrates the stakes involved in the Kafkaesque boxing ring containment. The segment was particularly poorly thought out and more than anything else resembled television's idea of a show trial:

> The trial should have been an opportunity to establish the truth about the attacks, but degenerated into a media circus and ritual scapegoating. Afzal and Geelani were separately paraded before the press by Special Cell and forced to confess on camera. When asked about this in court, the police officers who had arranged the event lied under oath and denied that it had happened, even though all major television stations had broadcast the event round-the-clock. In Tihar Jail, where the accused were held, they were attacked by 'patriotic' prisoners. (Mathur 2013)

Three of the cases, including Geelani's, were eventually dismissed, only Mohammad Afzal Guru was found guilty and sentenced to hang, so as to appease what the presiding judge would call the 'collective conscience' of the nation (Supreme Court, 4 August 2005). Mohammad Afzal, also known as Afzal Guru, had been a twenty-year-old border crossing militant youth in Kashmir, but had 'surrendered' to authorities in the early 1990s and then also enrolled for university in Delhi. His experience with said authorities was of course not all pleasant as he was first tortured in the mid-1990s, but found to be 'clean' by one Davinder Singh. It was Singh who proudly announced in a television interview that he tortured 'for the nation' (as cited by Roy in *The Guardian*,15 December, 2006). Disturbingly the method of 'chilli and petrol enema' was the 'cleansing' facilitator of confession when Afzal was picked up and interrogated after the 13 December 2001 incident. Afzal's video confession implicating himself in the raid was later judged by the Supreme Court to have been illegally obtained, leaving his conviction to be based upon circumstantial evidence. The case against him revolved around three pieces of evidence: a shopkeeper seeing Afzal buying the mobile phones and explosives used in the parliament raid (the phones left in the Ambassador car); he rented rooms to the five men (or were there in fact perhaps six attackers – as CCTV footage shown immediately after the attack seemed to suggest, though this footage was later restricted); and Afzal had been in possession of the computer which was used to make the fake ID cards.

Afzal was found guilty and slated for hanging on 20 October 2006, at which point NDTV 24x7 replayed Afzal's illegally obtained video confession. They did so without mentioning that this was by then a five-year-old wholly discredited piece of footage. After the screening, a report emerged from a police inspector that this video was version three of a much rehearsed 'statement'. NDTV omitted mentioning the Supreme Court rejection of the footage, all the while allowing an on-screen SMS commentary to announce the 'collective conscience' viewpoint: that terrorists should hang, that Pakistan was behind it all, that the national institutions of law must be respected and due process must take its course. At this time, Afzal's execution was being reviewed on appeal, but an SMS poll seems to have decided his fate. The death sentence was upheld by the Supreme Court on 12 January 2007. Only a plea for clemency by his wife forestalled the hanging at that point. President A. P. J. Abdul Kalam and then President Pratibha Devisingh Patil, sitting in Rashtrapati Bhavan, were with the people officially responsible for the final decision, but the repetitions of farce multiplied with regular recourse to stories about Afzal himself wanting to be martyred, wanting to die, wishing it was over. Another example in May 2010 reported by Anshuman Dutta quotes Afzal saying that his hanging would not cause communal problems. Curiously, we also have news that he is reading books by famed Indian Communist Party founder Manabendra Nath Roy: 'He is reading Politics, Power & Parties and New Humanism both by MN Roy' according to his lawyer, N. D. Pancholi (Dutta 2010). Described as a 'scapegoat and a boundary sacrifice', finally on February 9, 2013, Afzal Guru was hanged in secret in Delhi's Tihar Jail. Mathur summarises several sources: 'The President's denial of the mercy petition on February 3 was not made public and Guru's family was not informed in advance ... The body was buried in Tihar Jail and not released to the family ... The secrecy ensured that the courts could not be approached to delay the execution, thus denying Afzal the final judicial recourse' (2013: 442).

There are obvious ways in which legal and ethical standards are compromised when the justice process is played out through the televisual public sphere. Arundhati Roy and other prominent intellectuals speak out, television stations stage set-ups with opposing views and spokespersons of note. This is an celebrity pundit mohalla discussion with commentary by SMS and phone-in that has the quality of a lynch-mob. 'The Big Fight', hosted by Chandra, claims to 'pit those on opposite sides of an issue against each other' in a 'thorough 360 degree view of the key national or global issue at hand'. This rhetorical theatre can be disturbingly literal as performed in the case of Afzal where critical evaluation of the actions of the surveillance state was wholly blinded by commercial imperative showing little interest in questions of justice, fair review, legal consideration or due process. Certainly not an issue to be trivialized as sport since the case had to do with a man's life and a nation's attitude to the death penalty, the 'Big Fight' reduced significant concerns to a question of point scoring and viewer ratings, using a format that replicated reality TV, quiz competitions or a spelling bee.

Adding a tremor of controversy to the semblance of reasoned views sampled via SMS is a deeply problematic mode of 'news'. Perhaps with South Asia's venerable dramatic traditions in mind, Mehta noted the thousands of messages solicited by the stations had 'actively sought to construct a united nation' by way of this 'new and revolutionary theatre' (2008: 6–8). The 'Big Fight' host, Chandra, had been on NDTV since 1994 and significantly was its special correspondent covering the Siachen and Kargil wars and the conflict in Kashmir. He won the Indian Television Academy Award 2008 for 'Best Anchor for a Talk Show' – award shows themselves being part of the ideological manufacture of 'Experience. Truth First'. Of course SMS should be considered a part of participatory media which requires that we should also evaluate the framing of 'vigilante reporters' armed with mobile phone cameras contributing to what must now be called the world's largest 'tele-democracy' (Mehta 2008: 257). Television worldwide also provides, and may be examined in terms of, an emergent public interface of which SMS is only a part and to which it is now commonplace to add multiscreen, phone-in, and handy-cam video contributions (Zimmerman 2000: xxi). This is in fact an old model, largely pioneered by music television stations and the shopping channel, and only recently adapted to news, especially in India. The commercial and pop origins of this managed interactivity are significant but should not be overplayed. There has been considerable complaint in the past that television was a 'push' media. The 'pull' factors discussed here, however, are significantly constrained by form, so that it remains an open question as to whether these technologies imply a transformation of media space or otherwise. Surely we are not yet unable to judge if the popularity of the NDTV style of current affairs debate should be attributed to an 'argumentative tradition' or to versions of 'adda' as suggested by Mehta (2008: 245), or if, as seems more likely on the other hand, the incorporation of SMS and commercial consumer consolidation mixes with national security and anxiety management of the incorporated public to provide a mere semblance of debate in the 'Shining' India of twenty-four-hour news.

Mohammed Afzal was on death row 24/7 until his death and of course experienced the time as a kind of torture. He went so far as to request President Patil make her decision quickly. The trouble apparently was that there were fifty death penalty clemency applications in the queue, NDTV 24x7 reported:

> Parliament attack convict Afzal Guru is not the only man waiting for his death pardon to be reversed by the President. Sentenced to death in 2005, Afzal Guru may be the face of a raging debate on death penalty and clemency. But a Right to Information activist who petitioned the President's office

found that the number of pending mercy petitions of those who want their death sentence changed to life is as many as 50. (NDTV, 27 August2008)

In perverse mode I have imagined how television might otherwise handle the hanging of Afzal. I have suggested there be commissioned a satellite Hanging Channel slot that could aggregate scenes such as Saddam Hussain's hanging, and so also a sick opportunity exists with Afzal Guru. Could the station then go all out for a 'reality TV' scenario like the Afzal appeal, again with SMS voting to allow the people to decide? I suggest this of course with considerable bleak irony and reach for absurdist parody because of the slim prospects faced by anti-capital punishment campaigns that periodically arise since their media face does not chime with national and international requirements.

Instead NDTV go on to host a new edition of the *Ramayana* serial directed by Ramanand Sagar's son Anand (2008, dir. Sagar), and the successful show 'Airtel Scholar Hunt: Destination UK' – a mobile phone company sponsored reality TV vehicle to bring a media and cultural studies scholarship student to Cardiff and management students to Warwick and so on. This programme is a great publicity coup for UK regional colleges, in which the cultural construction of fantasy India, a UK vice-chancellor's dream of subcontinental expansion of the teaching factory and a tamed public sphere without a hint of critique proceeds apace – it was once thought the university was a place 'where there romped a rampant intelligence that was clever enough to know something better than just cramming' (Sloterdijk [1983] 1987: 157), now it's sold like soap in TV, not even as smart as a quiz show like 'Crorepati'. It has not gone unnoticed that television has been particularly bland in its programming in the wake of the invasions of Afghanistan and Iraq and the subsequent chaos theory policy of destabilization pursued by the Western powers. Journalists seem to be subject to the same eradication programmes as other privatized sectors. For example, Daya Thussu quips that 'even serious news networks, such as NDTV 24x7, have increased their quota of talk and chat shows' (2007: 104). There was of course significant 'serious' media coverage of the hanging of Saddam Hussein, as well as considerable mention of the fiascos of Guantanamo and Abu Ghraib (and Sangatte, Harmondsworth, Woomera, special rendition, wikileaks etc.) but predominantly television tends more and more to avoid even the unregulated 'live' talk-show news format. Accordingly, it is not accidental that we see a saturation of domestic programming with game shows, cooking, reality TV, police dramas and parodies of the format of the court highlighting questions of judgement and voting. This is what Avital Ronell diagnoses as a 'repetition compulsion' that is an 'incessant petition to the law' which is in turn 'frustrated by the endless postponement of justice' (2010: 52).

Terror as a cultural system

The direction of travel for this chapter must of course be about how this played out globally over and over again, for example in relation to the Mumbai attacks of 2008. Another NDTV 'Big Fight' debate on the terror attacks at the Taj Palace Hotel and Victoria station lines up a number of prominent pundits in similarly tactless, though perhaps more atmospheric, surroundings. Available online, the pundits – including Najma Heptullah, Imtiaz Ahmad, Aamir Raza Husain and Waheeda Rehman – sit in the open-air garden outside an impressively lit Indo-Gothic building, possibly the hotel forecourt. There is a 'studio' audience in attendance, though they are not inside the studio, and the compere chairs a passionate, wide-ranging debate that only sometimes steers beyond – though importantly it does go beyond – the protocols of expectation: speakers question the requirement for all Muslims to show remorse that the attackers were Muslims; the requirement for Muslims in India to show they distance themselves from Pakistan; routine denunciations of the State of Pakistan; praise for the Indian police and anti-terror forces; concerns about lapses in security (solution: better funding of security forces and more training); calls, from the compere for the guests to think of 'ways we can channel our anger' and be 'united as a nation'; and so on. Watching NDTV on another occasion offers further opportunity to see the nation affirmed and confirmed through the response to terror – this time viewers are able to watch 'Walk the Talk' with J. K. Dutt, Director General (DG) of Security (now retired), speaking of Operation Black Tornado, the response by the security forces to the attacks in Mumbai in November 2008 (NDTV, 4 April 2009). Once again the SMS facility, the backdrop, the polite reporter allowing the DG to 'finally' speak out, always in a tone that affirms the 'job well done' congratulatory and civil society affirming success of it all.

Complicity in 'the legitimization of violence around us' (Bharucha 1998: 115) is achieved by way of television screens. The audience that watches, by watching, convenes the community of television within which these complicities are played out, and indeed enacts the violence depicted in such stark colours. It is clear that the varieties of 'terrorist' now 'known' so well are in fact shaped and constituted alongside the equally fictive moderate citizen or model television audience that viewers are presumed to really be. In the movies the terrorist of course has bombs strapped under her shalwar kameez or rides in wearing a black hat and laughs a wicked 'Gabbar Singh laugh'. The audience, both nationalist and economically aspirational-ascendant, is conjured into existence by way of a commitment and relation to the terrorist-as-other out of proportion to the extent of actual terrorism, thus tempting fate and manufacturing expectations. Framed above by the logo of NDTV and captioned below by a rolling ticker giving headlines and stock prices – though too fast to give any meaningful correlation between shares and events – the low resolution CCTV footage of the attack on parliament in the 2001 raid is contained in the same frame as the honoured guests on 'The Big Fight'. Equivalences are not intended, but inevitably made – viewers become inured by way of format. Indeed, viewers are encouraged to be vigilant and provide commentary, perhaps even on occasion be the eyes and ears of NDTV, recording mobile phone video of events and providing it to air – the development of the citizen journalist as 'vigilante reporter' is now anticipated as with fanfare (Mehta 2008: 257). Phone-in and twitter commentary runs like the stock prices too as viewers provide a new layer with the station logo still another 'level' back. Isn't it strange this television news developed its distinctive screen architecture at the same time film worked so hard to clear the screen, to give us the unmediated fiction of the widescreen letterbox format, with at most only the broadcast logo feint stamp in the top corner – so neat and subtle compared to the clutter of the real. If cinema retains pretensions to a seemingly effortless realistic presentation in contrast to the news, or to MTV, or even a cooking show, then making so much effort to conceal the marks of its staging of the live 'eyewitness' news is all the more deceitful. Such divergences are of course co-constituted, and the one is no less trustworthy than the other, despite appearances. Fiction is real reality is not, 'liveness' is manufactured (see Roy 2014).[2]

Terror events will catch us all with live movie format reports by way of networked personal media produced by and available to viewers who could just as easily be caught up in events as be watching at home. In this way modernity and postmodernity are both manifest in a low-level everyday fear or anxiety about security and prosperity. This security and this prosperity both rely upon the smooth or full space of electronics – and thus convergence entails the simultaneous promotion of robust surveillance and a widespread plastic consumer sector. The work of promoting this doubled platform combines design, framing, training, organization, intellectual labour and celebrity punditry, infrastructure and planning, coordination, and luck – none of which appears as a seamless whole, but which nonetheless gets results.

Terror is presented as effecting everyone and yet it comes from outside – it is both familiar and alien. It is to be discussed, analysed and detailed. There is a concerted effort to combat and contain it – inspectors of police are interviewed, experts arrayed and displayed, Pundits confer with their close-up cameras. The correspondence of despair and celebration is written in the meta text of NDTV. The double façade of presentation on screen – the double framing of each item, not only the content of what is said – is the preserve of media and especially news when it stages traumatic events as shared, and reassures itself that everything will be okay, that the nation is defended. Terror strikes, police cordons go up, bombs fall, politicians debate. Stiegler tells us that the media 'co-produce' what happens ([1996] 2009: 115–116). Inside this theatre there is no place for recognition that this framing is constitutive of terror; that the police, the promoters, the formatting specialists, the political grandstanding, the policy platforms, the talk back style, all this legislates terror and bombing. The decoration of the screen with shocking, gruesome horror – news flash, breaking news, scoop – manages this uncertainty with the live ticker, updated scripts and item 'idents' that reassure continuity, even while leaving ambiguous gaps in the record. This is a globally adopted, locally focused anxiety trading on domestic concerns in a pattern that navigates a geopolitical hierarchy. In this way everywhere our co-production as viewers is involved, we contribute attention by looking and perhaps more problematically, we concede a kind of inattention, flitting channel to channel, from debate to debate, internalizing the parameters of the 'Big Fight' as if the format were our own, as if this were the nation, or the planet, as we would have it, as it would be, never otherwise, just so. It is the obligation of critics to open up these problems, not to let the frame close them down.

NDTV is television in the service of selling mobile phones and demonstrating their functions to the enormous consumer classes – the Airtel and SMS links. That this is then grafted onto the current incarnation of the 'nation' or national-modern as subject only updates Nehru with Noida. The *nation* building project becomes the *national* business model with aspirations in all markets. It is not merely a national question, but url, a time slot and a global segment, Global South Asia. The overseas settlements and global diasporas are accessed now as NDTV 24x7 becomes available in the United States and Europe via satellite, online and from 2010 in Android and IOS app. Again the format is twenty-four-hour news, with an added strand of reporting from home to those NRIs abroad or who have business interests in the subcontinent – and the occasional media-interested cultural studies scholar. The format of the 'Big Fight' debate remains popular internationally also, perhaps because, like sport, the action is always at the spot scheduled and covered by the cameras placed on location in advance.

There are protests of course, duly reported. Dissident voices are part of the entertainment of 'The Big Fight'. There are exposures of corruption that lead to resignations – every week a new scandal – or apologies. Government leaders may be voted out of office every four or five years – only to be replaced by another horror show compere. There are theorists of change, and even sometimes the advocates of revolution may be invited on stage to be interviewed – for example, self-described 'last Maoist in France', philosopher

Alain Badiou, as well as the then Nepalese Maoist Prime Minister Comrade Prachanda have appeared on the BBC (for Badiou, see the 'HardTalk' interview broadcast on 24 March 2009) and Prachanda was seen on NDTV reports where he was said to 'clearly mean business' on a visit to recruit Indian investment (broadcast 18 September 2008). As ever, the format of the report and the time slot – in Prachanda's case a breakfast news item of forty-five seconds – determines the extent of the discussion. It is a matter of 'First Punch, Second Punch' and then there is a restoration and return to the normative format.

Fascist TV?

Where have we seen this before? This horrible combination of police violence, constant surveillance and bureaucratic proceduralism – sensation and formality, the script of all news programmes – reminiscent of nothing if not a latter day Gestapo operation. Bharucha cautions that 'the charge of fascism ... can be a violence in its own right, and therefore the word should be used sparingly and consciously. While acknowledging the burden of the terrifying legacy, one should not censor it automatically from contemporary usage' (1998: 116). In this context, in his book on social activism in India, *In the Name of the Secular*, in a particular nuanced passage in the essay 'On the Border of Fascism: The Manufacture of Consent in *Roja*', Bharucha cites Chomsky and writes that:

> nationalism is mediated and disguised through layers of cultural expression, which have been consolidated through a 'manufacture of consent' engineered by the local agencies of the State in the market and the media. (1998: 115)

If we must be careful not to make the charge that there are fascists in the sense that there is a brown(or saffron)-shirted phalanx marching towards a pogrom, we can certainly speak of fascist structure to a system that has rewired social life in the manner of the work camp and the concentration camp and how – this is the most grotesque element – we have become more and more acquiescent towards the impossible outrages that are telecast before our eyes. We go on working and concentrating while persecution is made routine, in our name, in the name of the audience, the public, security or peace. Brother of the accused Geelani writes that Kashmiri Muslims are often portrayed in the media as terrorists. 'Films like *Roja, Mission Kashmir* [(2000, dir. Chopra)], *Maa Tujh[h]e Salaam* [(2002, dir. Verma)], *The Hero* [*: Love Story of a Spy* (2003, dir. Sharma)] and even TV serials have systematically constructed this image'. He reports that in a 2005 serial on ZEE TV called *Time Bomb 9/11* (2005, dir. Mehta) bin Laden himself surfaces in Kashmir (Geelani 2006: 26). The all too common police procedures of torture, interrogation and detention described by Geelani are harrowing at the same time as they are just what we have come to expect from the demonic register of Global South Asia. Extra-juridical killings by police of Kashmiris in 'encounters' (Geelani 2006: 94) are not dissimilar to those made famous in an earlier era when it was Naxals who would meet such fate at the hands of the state, duly reported as another triumph for order. Such horrors – and the bombings, detentions, imperial wars, fratricidal aggressions – do not disrupt the rampant pursuit of wealth and the subservience of political figures to real power, as executive committee of the bourgeois class they are for nothing but the facilitation of wealth. Even Communist Parties in Bengal encouraged big capital, and the slaughter in Nandigram leading to the election of Magmata Banerjea was the consequence. The 24x7 talk show is the bureaucratic form of the parliamentary fiasco that provides the unedifying spectacle of a bland and phantasmatic version of politics alongside entertainment – as containment of debate. A 'Big Fight'.

But too easily the talk show abdicates the responsibility of the critic to tread carefully, thoughtfully, yet forthrightly into the political scenarios that critical thinking must address. Bharucha points out the dangers of the 'seemingly reasonable and self-righteous' stance of the commentator who end ups contributing to 'thought control' and the manufacture of consent by playing within the 'rules of the game' (1998: 133). Polite discussion and conversation can be applauded and declared necessary and I do not always want to disagree, but too much well tempered conversation could also leave everything intact. In such circumstances we remain unable to address necessary redistributions – of power, of economics, of desires – we remain uncomprehending of what would be adequate to help win through to a radically different world, and in the end we serve up only the oh so satisfying prospect of our being knowingly in the right, while all around innocents are hanged. The really existing Right as such is in ascendancy – as in the racist parties elected to government, such as the BJP in India, and the rise of the British Nationalist Party and the English Defence League in the United Kingdom, and the ultra-Right in Europe, Tea Party and Trump in North America. Bharucha in an expansive but judicious tone says: 'Obviously, there are different levels of expertise in reinforcing the premises of the State, but they meet through a common ground of complicities that are manufactured not by force, but through the most open and, at times, inane of exchanges' (1998: 133).

The inanity Bharucha has in mind here is that of the 'magazine culture' which propagates vacillation as a norm. This has been often mentioned, for example by Thussu in his study of satellite television where television news seemed 'to take on the worst aspects of the tabloid newspapers' (2007: 5) and became 'a powerful discourse of diversion ... taking attention away from, and displacing from the airwaves, such grim realities [as] neo-liberal imperialism ... tyranny of technology ... freemarket capitalism and ... consumerism' (2007: 9). In my first year of university, in a journalism class I ultimately failed – taking anthropology as a catch up – I was taught that the formula of good writing was to argue both sides without bias so that a reader with a reading level of fourteen years could comprehend the debate. Even this could be a high standard for some parts of the media today. Bharucha demands a writing that is not subsumed by the 'trivializers of free speech in the mass media' and thinks that something more can be done with other forums, including 'songs, poems, pamphlets, documentaries' [and better films than *Roja*] (1998: 134). These might provide a more meaningful and detailed picture upon which something 'beyond crude associations with terrorism' would be demanded and acted upon by 'all citizen groups and public forums in India [and elsewhere] concerned with democracy'. In this comment, Bharucha is talking particularly of Kashmir, but with wider relevance his assessment that it 'is shocking to realize not only how little we know, but how we *accept* this fact' (1998: 134) might be considered equally important in many other theatres. We know we are ignorant of the way the war on terror has transformed our lives, but with our heads down, we studiously ignore it.

Is it that the images and the effort have become incomprehensible, or that the atrocities have been forcibly banalized? The endless wash of images no longer shock, the everydayness of camera-phone footage, the seamless 'news' without commentary (but plenty of diagrams), in the press or TV. In Kureishi's novel *Something to Tell You,* the main character (and psychoanalyst-murderer) Jamal has a friend called Henry who wants to go to Kings Cross to lay flowers after the July 7 2005 London bombings. He says: 'How can I stop thinking about the horror of those bomb-blasted trains, the ruined bodies, the cries and moans and screams, which segue, in *my* head at least, into the diabolical killings of civilians in Baghdad – severed heads, blood underfoot, children eviscerated, limbs blown into treas. Could only Goya grasp it? Why are we making this happen?' (Kureishi 2008: 314). That he can ask the question – an intellectual playwright – is indicative of its own malaise. The conversation does not broach an alternative even when critical.

Scripted discussions

On NDTV, nothing unusual can happen. The debate is already scripted. The separation between extreme entertainment and considered argument has been fudged by lazy and cynical media operatives and the national agenda that is, however, not an agenda worked out with a five-minute delay by the prime minister, but a national project, of 'Unite the Nation', that deploys anxiety and hatred – of Afzal, of calls to 'hang him' – and links up with a global media thriving on the 'same' anxieties, the same 'Unity'. All the better then that lucrative commercial subscription rates are achieved through sensation-attention, and the more controversial the debate, the greater attention from a wide and diverse audience and the greater containment (this is not to see this audience as conflicted and confused, but the format possibly encouraging traffic in, not critique of, the format). Here, some say attention is the premium; I would add that there is also a production of an attentive inattention. Something like this is suggested by Beller where he argues for the 'productive value of human attention' (2006: 28) and says that the labour theory of value must 'account for the systematic alienation of the labour of looking' (2006: 23). He suggests:

> equally significant [is that] in viewing the image, we simultaneously and micrologically modify ourselves in relation to the image as we 'consume' it – a misnomer if ever there was one, since images equally, or almost entirely, consume us ... this production of both value and self (as worker, as consumer, as fecund perceiver) through looking ... [means] visual culture must be set in relation to the development and intensification of commodity fetishism. (Beller 2006: 24)

Beller's work accesses another model that can supplement media theory for a theory of the media. The media work offered by Marxism is of course vast, and a survey of its parameters is the other dynamic of this book insofar as it seeks to learn from Global South Asian media studies, such as those by Madhava Prasad et al. Relevant to this commentary, there are some staple perspectives offered by Marxist film studies redirected to television as I have hinted in cursory form above (see Wayne 2003). More explicitly, the task set out is to take the appearance of news and examine what kinds of labour go into its production. There are new elements, and old. I think it is the case that a series of sensational 'breaking news' terror events have transformed the appearance of news, and yet often nothing much happens on screen – often the appearance of news is still distanced, with nothing to 'eyewitness' or 'experience'. Considering the few occasions where mobile phone uploads of CCTV footage are offered, usually the 'same' images over and over on very high rotation, the 'live' aspect of the news story consists of a presenter standing before the police lines, or the cordon tape, reporting to camera. The camera will very often then zoom-in over the presenter's shoulder into a cleared cordon space while we are told what we are seeing – a distant building with smoke, a ruined bus, the smoking towers. A city where nothing happens, live.

Of course uploads must be uploaded, and framed. They must be introduced; they are captioned. Some presenter – formerly a journalist, now a desk bound reader of the tele-prompt – is required to decipher, and speak over, the images on the loop or the live scene shots of the requisite police stand-off, ongoing investigation or security barrier. Such imageries are of course 'news', but someone is editing them, framing them, adding a station identifier and an item logo is superimposed, and elsewhere the ticker strap info must be typed in, the stock prices checked, the wiring to the stock exchange maintained. Cameras must be set up, purchased, built, tapes stored, catalogued, reviewed. And satellite up-links are not spontaneous, as there are shifts of workers – it is 24/7 recall – producing the news that the audience attention then consumes – even where the audience is solicited to participate and gives their attention for minimal subscription charge, this labour is not offered free and is certainly not the supersession of paid skilled work of many kinds. It is true that increasingly the formatting, idents, studio props and so on are always prepared in advance, as are the trucks, catering, tailoring (for the presenters' suits) and the research that identifies which pundits might be called upon from the little black book of punditry, but even all these events are produced. Nothing is happening on screen, the camera stands still at the side of the police chief managing the barricade, images of the burning hotel, the damaged bus, the shooters, the towers, all these are what Stiegler calls a 'tertiary retention' ([1996] 2009) but this does not mean the economy of contribution has changed the ideological field.

Attention to the 'attention mode of production' would not displace or replace older prevailing productive regimes or critiques (of manufacturing, ideology, nation, service sector or digital) but offers a frame to think the real subsumption of more and more parts of life to commodity logic. All the time we are tuning in we are further attuned for training for a constant contribution to consumption and production – and even as we participate in complicit unacknowledgement in yet another round of surplus extraction and valorization, the attention we reflect back upon television only confirms this exemplary form. TV is mundane reproduction and emblematic of our circumstances, even as the debates are staged.

It is still the case that in the mix of multiple satellites and constant 'debate', the evidence before our eyes – 'Experience. Truth First' – means all the work that goes into representation of these tragedies can be understood as necessarily contained by a modernity that presents itself, for a certain constituency of television viewers in India, South Asia and internationally, as the work of 'the nation'. What it also, more worryingly, means is that in screening and containing anxiety in these formats, the possibility of a Global South Asia different to that scripted in the 'national' imaginary is left off screen. Most relevant here are Spivak's commentaries in *Other Asias*, and especially her consideration of which parts of Asia register, and the chapter 'How to Be a Continentalist', where she argues – in telegraphed form: 'There is no original unity to the name "Asia". When we claim the name today we are divisive. To repair this, Social Sciences and Humanities must come together. The production of knowledge must be supplemented by the training of the imagination' (2008: 209). So too for other alternative worlds, other possible lives. To combat [and repair] this, a concerted effort to tamper with the framing of terror might do three things:

1. develop an attention to Global South Asia that can rethink television in the context of financialization, commercialization and vernacular globalisms (Mukhopadyay 2012), such that NDTV's 'The Big Fight' and the like will be recognized as a locally produced framing of the same, an appearance of television doing ideological work at home and abroad, for home and abroad;
2. recognize the residues of nationalist and national construction project television, and cinema, in the context of geopolitical reorientation as well as a neoliberal vernacular that trades on a globe-facing specificity, where local incidents articulate with international themes, shaped by commercialization, financialization and neoliberal political alignments and;
3. develop popular access and studious comportment towards both the news channel and the film archive of examples that shape the globe-facing home-audience as well as the contingent incident-related global scrutiny that comes from outside. Do this in a way that foregrounds all the varieties of labour that goes into framing news as entertainment and as ideology, which redirects this labour and media towards critique and develops an open, interpretive, conviviality of media reception in social and political life.

If I were a little more confident of grand projects, I would suggest it is worth attempting to develop these three points as a new interpretation of Global South Asia that could comprehend the media without media theory, would critique of fascism without fascists, can combat terrors without terrorizing, and as a way of learning to watch our screens without getting square eyes or drawing strict and straight borders around cultural forms.

Subsumption and sublation of critique

Is there something larger to be learnt from the critique of news television as ideological framing, as sensational but faked 'debate', as a sop to entertainment and commerce, which also cows viewers into a 'nationalist' security in anxiety? The speculative context for media politics that broaches political work alongside transforming media studies adopts Madhava Prasad's theoretical deployment of subsumption along with a critique of regionalism as foreground. This already exists as a massive commentary on Global South Asian media, but to scale-up from Afzal Guru through The Hanging Channel from discussions of the 'political implications' of popular cinema (Vasudevan 2000: 2) to a political diagnostic for the Global South may be recklessly ambitious. It is not simply a matter of adding geopolitics to the heightened concepts of representation, community, identity and sexuality. The baggage in the terminology is heavy (Vasudevan 2000: 8) but it will now be obvious, I hope, from the literature peppered throughout this book, that the overlaps of politics and screen make it no longer difficult to distinguish where desire for a truly relevant media studies should mark and cross the boundaries. Anticipating yet another sort of critique of the 'who are you to say?' variety, is it still worth the risk of temptation to suggest that Global South Asian media studies itself be thought of as a struggle for justice? Well-informed writers generating relevant and argued concepts and detailed research and commentary on matters that mean a great deal should surely be heard, and the new Global South Asian media studies overflows its demarcations in ways I think promise much. Not only the old film festival prominence to 'world cinema' or the celebration of auteurs like Ray or Sen, but tampering with *Kali-Yuga* to suggest organizing a disciplinary formation that develops from street corner *adda* to total institution, and even to total insurrection. To then introduce the critique of state violence in a geopolitical setting of the world to rights is already be exoticist overreach, and all the more necessary thereby. It will be countermanded below, but if the alternative news forums of *adda* in which I first heard intensive *filmi* discussion in Kolkata was any guide to how film studies could be practiced as political critique, then this really appeals as the metaphor to be expanded to manage the overwhelming abundance of discussion and fight that Global South Asia generates. Sure, this is no longer a single-issue justice campaign with special pleading but an all-comer invitation to aesthetic appreciation in the commercial hub, now sponsored and the entry fee paid to the greater panchayat council. Replacing public desire with gross domestic production and international revenues, military machines and mass mobilizations has been a too easy containment.

Global South Asian media may be 'at once located in the nation[s], but also out of the nation in its provenance, orientation and outreach' (Kaur and Sinha 2005: 16). To take this seriously means the politics of 'our' desires, and in Nandy's terminology it also means asking 'whose desires? Hence the haptic, the ideological, the -scapes and the -izations, as well as the provinces and diasporas, the in-nation, the outer-nation and the imperso-nation (Chakravorty 1993) all must be discussed somewhere and must mean something. The discursive world that is Global South Asia is connected, through all the opinions cited here, to a sometimes exhausting and always tendentially intensifying politics of interpretation. It may be too much to expect any immediate implementation of the effort required to learn new modes of putting knowledges together critically and imaginatively and institutional support for any such attempt would need to acknowledge high stakes and long indefinite durations to grasp the epidemiologies of research. But these are epic stakes. This is why it is noteworthy that Spivak was apparently working for a time on the text of the *Mahabharata* – let us hope she will take it up again, and perhaps share views on elder brother Karna and the repeat visits of television and film to the mythological. Though Karna is not exactly subaltern, his position on the side of the Kauravas is at least interesting and the archival exclusion is operative, gridded over by a counter-female patriarchy and, as national and global reworkings of the narratives insert stories into developmental teleology, neo-liberal hype as well. No surprise that in order to shift the frame of the epic Spivak would take up the case of the tangential character. It is because of this careful, critical, but oblique style of reading that Spivak can smuggle an entry pass into the archival with the possibility of progressive intervention even if it requires more effort and competence than we usually can manage ('more' – means persistent, language learning, privilege-unlearning, patient, painstaking scholarship). This too would require more work on television than 'activists' could afford, though since no media theory is enough for a theory of the media, it is her work on terror, suicide bombings and planetary justice that is crucial.

Thus on the telematic, from Spivak we might determine that Global South Asian media would be something like knowledge, reason, responsibility, and so the interpretative effort must be to conjure with and be interrupted by a persistent non-fascist discipline that would exercise self-critique to rearrange ordained and pre-coded assumptions. To watch and learn from Global South Asian screenings at the centre, not just to fill up on knowledge but to further transnational literacy and an ethics that does not succumb to hierarchies and rankings of 'others', 'over there' and different. On terror: the ethical interrupts the epistemological. There is a point at which the construction of the other as object of knowledge must be challenged: 'the ethical interrupts [law, reason] imperfectly, to listen to the other as if it were a self' (Spivak 2004: 83). The task suggested here that seems most difficult to get our heads around is to accept complicity in a way that makes possible an identification, 'alive to visible injustice' (Spivak 2004: 89) as well as 'not to endorse suicide bombing but to be on the way to its end' (Spivak 2004: 93). Is there a message we can hear without an automatic move towards punishment or acquittal? SMS texts are not audience participation and an NDTV SMS poll is nothing like democracy. Here the ethical and archival task of knowledge is to learn to learn what is in the mind, and what is the desire (or motivation?) of the media just as much as of the terrorist bomber. Perhaps this is a way to combat the fascism of manufactured 'Terror'.

If the motivations are many, the ethical is a problem. Consider that someone in the newsroom is paid to put the terror images together, and someone else profits from their labour as they do it; consider, a vast apparatus of production orchestrating news as infotainment and archiving the nation and the global in this way and not that. The terror event lights up a shocking and systematic public awareness at the same time as it activates circuits of production prepared in advance to contain it. Consider that there is no terror without the social and media relations – class, work, ideas – which make it possible. Consider that these are interpretations, and that interpretations are the stuff of a struggle over meaning. This is the point of the obligation the well-intentioned critic has to raise questions, to challenge perspectives and framings, to explore alternative possibilities and to insist upon, and to provide, with an eye to education for emancipation, a critical debate that moves minds rather than affirms stability. Consider the frame must be shifted.

In this context, consider how new media is said to have finally come to South Asia and that sometimes it still seems possible for commentators to act as if no one has really noticed its impact. Of course this is not to say there are too few champions of the view that new media has 'arrived' with an explosion in the subcontinent – that is now standard, often reiterated. Instead, it might be possible to reverse engineer the technology and make the obvious argument that there has always been a media sphere in India, that it has always been a contest, that there are conservative elements which often prevail, and that these can and are always being challenged, and they change. The suggestion that cross-platform televisual media, satellite with talkback and audience participation via phone, SMS or street interview, has always been a subcontinental phenomenon is one I would only contingently claim, as I have done at the start of this chapter with reference to *Kali-yuga*. The status of this perception of television news as being twenty-hour horror show is just that – a contingent interpretation. The terrible thing is that an analysis attending to the mechanics of presentation on screen – the format, the peripheral text, the framing – may miss the very content that framing contains. This is the catch, the terror is already there in the fascism without fascists who have already framed the frame. Does the reiteration of the NDTV 'Big Fight' slogan 'How can we Unite the Nation?' not already affirm this? Even when – as in 'The Big Fight' debate over the Mumbai attacks – there was a forceful critical Muslim position complaining that every time such an incident occurs Indian Muslims would be expected to publicly distance themselves from terror, from Pakistan and from violence; even when critiques of the security state are aired; even when the constraints of globalization and geopolitical regional strategy are questioned. Again, all this affirms the notion of a nation and a public – the civil order of viewer-consumers, each contributing to this market, either nodding their heads in agreement or shouting at the screen.

Is 'The Big Fight' all there is? The revolution does not happen precisely because it *is* televised. I do not think the positive idea that there is an 'argumentative tradition' or some other exceptionalism (Mehta 2008) can offer a reinvention of the form. Rather instead it seems to reinforce the same in the new. With that said, we do have to welcome further research on the various imbrications and innovations that bring *Kali-yuga* to the screen, as well as those forms offering *adda*, or *cybermohalla*, or Media *Nagar*, even *Doordarshan* again, or which posit the information age as 'Sarai' – a term duly explained on their website front page as a forum for discussion of the future, which is good news for a new media research group that locates itself physically at the Centre for Study of Developing Societies in Delhi (in passing I notice there is something slightly, and usefully, heterodox in this name 'Sarai' – CSDS is not exactly a street people's scene, nor is it a tavern, as might be suggested by the word). What SARAI stands for however in the context of local and global media is more important – a hitherto somewhat neglected area of academic and creative interest, deeply marked by a version of a technological cringe. The idea that new media is somehow new to India is also marked by a realization that the old politics will of course be played out also in the new news formats. This has not been missed by those that work with care and imagination in this field. Or at least, it should not be simply set aside. In any case, to offer the mischief of electing the dual co-author-producers – continuity editor and scriptwriter – of the extended family drama of the Pandava Five, Sage Vyasa and Elephant-head, broken-tusk, copyist Ganesh, as the patron deities of the media age, is probably a little far-fetched and of the order of 'social science fiction' (Visvanathan and Sethi 1989: 54). Alongside any rehash of the epic archetypes, I think perhaps there are other possibilities; think again of Karna, the disenfranchised sixth Pandava brother, son of Kunthi – this sixth brother might also prove to be significant, as Spivak suggests. I remember there were rumours, were there not, that six attackers stormed the Parliament on 13

December? Mohammed Afzal was not that brother, on balance – it is never balanced; he was innocent, but now his televisual murder can only show us how the media makes its case.[3]

Who is Karna today?

The predictable equation for the end of this chapter would be to claim Afzal for the critical tradition, but he is dead and did not want to be conjured as a martyr. Yet at what point does the screening of his life provide life lessons? It is not a matter of alienated receptors governed by remote control, where you cannot change the channel because the channel has changed you. The slumdog million strong audience responds to the same formula with a flicker of recognition that tuning in to a frequency and time slot is not the bland stupidity of television but a deceptive transparency awaiting instructions and destructions. New popular critiques morph from terror into anger and there are many who latch onto contemporary provocative offerings served up through the image machinery that cannot sleep. Although the challenge of producing cinematic material contrasted to and as critique of real news on delay is part of the dilemma of trying to be serious, there are significant investments in an edgy counter-narrative that plugs into and the psychic disturbances offered up everyday as real. As it becomes clearer that a kind of orientalist two-step is involved when terror and exotica dually totalize South Asians, both in South Asia and beyond, the grid of reified and abstract concept-identifications is challenged by new material. Often, but not in every case, the complicities are debilitating for those subject to them, and anyone who adopts any part of these frames runs a material high risk. Adopting degrees of unexamined culturalism is endemic where capital is neo-imperial in scale but a local goonda in person, and racism takes the form of white supremacist social aspiration. The challenge of a dexterous intervention that works inside exoticism and terror, that makes films with guns – and a girl, Godard – is not obviously outside of the context of screening terror for terror's sake. If perhaps unwelcome, to the extent that I can understand it, working at complicity is a perpetual and necessary labour especially as Global South Asia now exports both the 'commodified and globalized ... "feel good" version' of South Asian cultures (Rajadhyaksha 2008: 37) and Taliban, ISIS and CIA-funded head-chopper gangs serve as shock feed 'news' for the terrorist side.

It may have taken quite some time for the Left to realize that news reporting followed a formula of broadcast that seems indistinguishable from fiction. Today however this awareness has been hammered home by many films – for example, see Shah Rukh Khan in *Phir Bhi Dil Hai Hindustani* (2000, dir.

Mizra) – and this thereby means ideological manipulation is readily available to all political parties, commercial films and the fascist Right. The dissemination of ideologically managed truth extends internationally through care packages, hit films and family connections that solicit return remittances sent from abroad. What chance then of tuning into this in a critical and progressive way that at least tries to disseminate the groundwork preparing cultural uplift as a contextual support – habitual critique, ruthless, of everything, plus care and inclusion, and the refusal of complicities by making our exchanges dysfunctional for capital. Perhaps. But even to sell the connectivities we tell stories on screen to mass audiences in the expectation that in different ways audiences will get something, more or less intended according to circumstances, from their active participation as audiences. Despite the barrage of terror, this is of course shaped by the technological, paraphernalia, atmospheric and haptic surroundings or contexts of the film mis-en-scene – back to the connectivities again, as if in a spiral or circuit.

On the other hand, what I call Global South Asian film and television studies and its critique entails an engagement with diverse products and challenges in so far as they are media subject to questions from an also diverse but at least alternative critique of the dominant. The Global South, as good, bad or indifferent category to one or the other dimension of the exotica-terror spectrum, means a space where a wide set of texts are shared, and released, by long critical reflection on the problem of what is variously (mis)named as Bollywood over against Hollywood, or the 'intimate enemy' over against 'the West', or against some other 'hybridity' of here and there, alongside which a struggle to not adopt the exotic compromise of being hybrid or being either Western or non-Western releases deeply engaging work. A provocative cinematic example that stitches film to the diasporic musics I had been reading my way into for thirty years would be the Bengali film *Gandu* (2010, dir. Mukherjee). The film follows a moody but charismatic Bengali teen 'asshole' ('*Gandu*', roughly translated) who creates a lyrical world of rap in Kolkata while living off his mother's sex work – a mild form of compensation dating with the very 1980s looking Dasbabu. Mother colludes in Gandu's pick-pocketing of her lover, though her fragile psychological state seems to be dangerously passed to her son, who angsts about his thefts while happily eating the meals she provides. Gandu's bicycle rickshaw friend, a video arcade and an occasional heroin smoke are his only distractions from a fantastically imagined world of musical success and pornography. Drug dream sequences, a datura trip in hallucinatory black and white and an erotic feline bedroom romp with the director's reputed girlfriend, in colour, allows him at least to star in his own film. Reconciled with his mother – a cash payment will do it – Gandu decides to make a demo to send to Asian Dub Foundation (ADF), who, as luck would have it, are appearing in Kolkata and will need a support act. The film ends on a high. Dedicated to sex and drugs, director Mukherjee went full exotic but ironic in response to an interview question raising concerns about the 'explicit' scenes. Linking the film's message to Shiva, he said: 'we have every bit of this in our bones and blood. We have just forgotten it in our moralized years of oppression and repression. Look at the story of the Shiva Ling, and you realize what the power of that image can do' (in Kamath 2010). Whether ADF had further involvement is unclear. There is no cameo, unlike, for example, the appearance of Beckham at the end of Chadha's soccer film. The colour insert and the knowingly edgy credit intertitles and text on screen do show a distorted homage-like residue of the styles of Mrinal Sen and film school renditions of French new wave, Trinh T. Minh-ha and Dogme. But it is possible to still push forward these challenges to conventions and defend against the other side of horror where paid civil servants torture teens for the nation. Even if only beginning to read a way into an alternative tradition, and I am a beginner in this sense, it is possible to see that the conventional two-tone renderings miss a subtle nuance that is there if one cares to look. I feel the same way about Marxism, should anyone like to note.

5

Mela

What is it to settle down in front of the screen and think such a simple yet now universal experience might still have anything to teach? Without even specifying yet the 'where' of the here, or the 'us' of the us, first of all let us agree that the world needs to be more open to the pleasures of interpretation now, and we – who 'we'? – all of us – who 'us'? – need to learn from experience elsewhere. This chapter examines recurrent film motifs across a number of films, mostly called *Mela*. It also offers some observations on melas, actual and allegorical, as represented in the films but often seeming to exceed their containment in context so as to say more about the conviviality of life, where this is at issue; where life is at a juncture in need of resolution within the cycle of becoming. The chapter begins in the United Kingdom with an example from the already discussed work of Gurinder Chadha, and an early film from her that I want to identify as particularly marked by a Global South Asian aesthetic, if not also its politics. The rest of the chapter is more focused upon *Mela* films themselves, and the allegorical insofar as this has a well-known and well-worked theoretical treatment in the debate between Frederic Jameson and Aijaz Ahmad, which I review with the help again of Gayatri Chakravorty Spivak and others writing on Global South Asian film and television.

The dialectic of terrors and festivals

Often, perhaps too often, a film festival is also a festival of violence – but the conviviality of the festival may also be an antidote. Film has long experience dealing with the celebration of violence, and a double vision here offers a first moment of learning. Violence and rebellion in a history written 'in letters of blood and fire' (Marx [1867] 1967: 502). In the subcontinent, this is history itself: colonial violence and resistance, leading to independence; partition violence as a needless tragic consequence and – another whole book here – the posturings of nationalism that impact brutally on lives bifurcated by policy; independence was then grasped enthusiastically but in due course leading to elite betrayal, neocolonial reassertion, complicity, complacency, renewed aggression, internalized, externalized, patronizing aid, development hypocrisy, geopolitical machinations, and proxy wars – the violence takes many forms, but more often than not is continually *projected* from the West *upon* and *against* Global South Asia. It is also on screen. Violence is news, revolt is cinematic, and the theorists writing about film and television in this book address such concerns because there is violence on their screens, and mechanisms of denial are more or less inoperative.

The story is also one of resistance through projection – the necessary containment and occlusion of alternatives, and a long struggle; annals, blood, fire – inversely documented in the ways the Global South as revolutionary anti-colonial movement is both screened and not. The interpreting reader should not fall for a sensationalist focus, as if all that is newsworthy is scandal. Of course cultural festivals have their non-violent sides, but scratch the surface enough and the hierarchical jealousies of any community emerge in anxious concert. It is a good thing that theorists of Global South Asian film and television studies also write about much that is not sensationalized – so it is not too hard to find studies of everything from the 'curry mile' in Manchester (Dudrah 2012: ch. 5) to the haptic around cinema halls, assemblages, bodies and affect (Rai 2009: ch. 1). While not 'enough' studies are given airtime – what would be enough? – there is also a need for critical evaluation and forums for discussion as a vast archive on the regional variations in diaspora, settlement and movement around Global South Asia is slowly put together. Guyana's fourth and fifth generation 'Indian' population watching old and new Bollywood film as a mode of access to a culture no longer directly 'refreshed' by new arrivals is reported by Narain (2008: 165); there are studies of economic 'pirate technoscapes' in Angoori Bagh by Delhi's Red Fort, with its piled-full stores of 'TV, CD, VCD, and DVD players, audio goods, and surgical components' in Sundaram (2009: 103, reporting work by Rakesh Kumar Singh). Many other studies have been mentioned already, from Nigeria, Australia, Fiji, Senegal. Yet even in these assemblages, deliciously full of melodramatic detail, violence and hierarchy do not always frame the story, at least not in every case, and other events, styles, changes and continuities, even consequences, demand a response.

Exotica too manifests as the well-disguised partner of the violent 'trope', in another media phantasmagoric. Just as any reporting of police violence and corruption across Global South Asia has an invariably dubious provenance, the exotic romance of patronizing racism in revolutionary tourism or even explicit anti-racism and multicultural celebration, of activism, diversity, piracy or conviviality in the capital city, can hide racist attacks in the suburbs, regional street violence, rural desolation and terror from the sky by drone or by F15, F22 or B52. Sometimes this is made to seem so very far away from the studio news and the audience 'at home'. Sometimes it is fuel for moral panic attacks disguised as calls to both keep calm and to carry on. This exoticism is routine and it is (not) reported everyday, and exposing it is not all that media-friendly a project and is not readily welcomed because it targets a subtle violence that is too often excused and given an alibi. The aggressive repertoires are coded and worth extra attention precisely when not reported, even as reports of violence proper are highlighted in the exceptional 'few rotten apples' argument, dubiously deployed. This is how the everyday outrage of violent romanticism becomes commonplace and needs to be made more than merely material for Booker Prize winning novels like *The God of Small Things* (Roy 1997), which is nuanced and effective, but a drawing room discussion that circulates in rarefied air, with no popular film version while Roy refuses to sell the rights, on admirable principle, and yet. The work of Mahasweta Devi, made globally popular by Spivak, offers another version of the already noted example where the term 'encounter' in reporting is registered as a euphemism for police execution. Films about the affective consequences of the Naxalite persecution are devoured in the festivals when they do appear – *Mother of 1084/Hazaar Chaurasi Ki Maa* (1999, dir. Nihalani) was lauded, then forgotten – even as it was widely recognized, and denounced, that any 'miscreant' could be murdered, labelled and tagged by the police, and were too often found to have been 'countered' and in subsequent investigations found to have already been handcuffed when killed. Mrinal Sen's *Calcutta 71* is also one of these known but not so often screened stories. In this case, a youth is chased and brought down in the street, killed in the prime of life, in the centre of the city. Sen was restating and emphasizing the grotesque regularity of this as a politics of fear, and was aware that media exposure of extra-juridical killing did not necessarily undo the real or the ideological threat. What was a national controversy in the 1960s and 1970s soon escalated to global proportions and to be 'countered' now also refers to those subjected to counter-terrorism measures, drone strikes and extra-judicial assassinations, but even this awaits better film treatment.

The Global South Asia register of war as terror is also the threat quotient that allocates South Asia as a place where violence and terrorism incubates with worldwide implications. Here, the Taliban prevention of schooling for women and harbouring of international fugitives – who are later found quietly watching videos in Pakistani safe-house compounds adjacent to the national secret service (see Hersch 2015) – is uplinked to a global register which implies the intervention of bombing for democracy everywhere. As if they cannot govern themselves, there is a return of imperialist ways to pacify and re-educate, supplying weapons to allies, and bombing yet again when the allies turn out to be less than reliable puppets. This chaotic destabilization becomes the preferred option for mismanagement from afar, with the function of media imagery doubled as a threat to stay in line at home – for settled migrant diaspora and less recent migrant alike. Witness the piling up of images of the dead in the Muslim lands in the unsafe 'foreign' theatre, or occasionally at 'home', with 'sexed up' dossier justifications for revenge. The 'spin' innovations of the UK Labour Right Blair government were also taken up by Bush, Obama, Cameron, May and Trump in turn. 'Fake news' one day; policy photo opportunity and indiscriminate bombing from the public relations playbook the next. The doctored dossier on weapons of mass destruction on the one hand and celebrations of cultural diversity on the other are manipulated as tools of statecraft. The Global South Asian alternative would be to oppose the ideological investments of public televisual displays with stories of affirmative conviviality and legitimate calls to take seriously the humanity of those you otherwise bomb. A film like *Bhaji on the Beach* (see Desai 2004, Sharma 2006) of course cannot be expected to balance the scale of the massive escalation of violence in the Global South Asian theatre, but its appearance in 1993 was already something of a call to arms even when couched in the guise of a melodramatic road movie and festival day out, a family comedy-drama with tug on the heart strings appeal.

There are a number of films that counter violence with affection; an intimate and domestic alternative to policy and war. This is not just a subcontinental thing, but it was evident in the early partition films, it is there in the resolution of those films where warring brothers in the end reconcile, and it is the undercurrent of every scene of melodramatic action that has a heroine capable of dancing on broken glass to save her beloved from death. The oscillation at the scene of violence is pronounced, and wherever the global war on terror is 'news', cinematic, and screened, humanity's collective (in)ability to cope with its depiction entails an outpouring of emotion and a charge that expresses frustration when the need to actively intervene is compromised, disregarded, disabled and somehow not taken seriously despite the evidence before our eyes. Do we admit we live in a world that self-represents as contradictory and chaotic, with pervasive modes and varieties of death smuggled into our souls? Or are these love stories in a war zone a way of coping with this glaring contradiction? Comedy-drama. Humanitarian interventions of another order.

Bhaji on the Beach

I am writing this text on Global South Asia from afar, but thinking of England as a remote corner…

Haven Sachdeva Mann refers to the 'spectacular popular cultural as well as economic "arrival" of post-globalisation India in London … a veritable explosion of Bollywood culture in Britain' (2014: 487, see also Rajadhyaksha 2008: 18). The rest of Mann's list of indicators includes,

> 'the British Film Institute's … 300-film strong film festival entitled "ImagineAsia" … Lloyd Webber and A.R. Rahman's musical "Bombay Dreams" … Amitabh Bachchan's and … Aishwarya Rai's wax figures at Madame Tussaud … Channel 4 Television's "Bollywood Women" season [and] "Bollywood Celebs." … the release of 74 Bollywood films in UK in 2005', the OED listing Bollywood as an entry (online edition) and Om Puri being awarded an OBE, Bollywood fusion dance, the 2010 London Indian Film Festival and a "Bollywood dance spectacular" [in Trafalgar Square as] … part of the run-up to the huge London Mela (fair) in August. (Mann 2014: 487)

Writing about films in a comparative here and there perspective, filtered through more or less contrived sets of lens, and feeling in need of contact and content, it made sense to look again at *Bhaji on the Beach* because it was the high point of an emergent on-screen British South Asian sensibility. This was at a time when anti-racism and anti-imperialism were prominent, if difficult, concerns for the Left (see Sharma, Hutnyk and Sharma 1996) and I turn back to the film both because of its importance and, somewhat gauche, because a dimly recalled festival sequence at the eponymous beach offers the chance to mention the director's inclusion of a significant 'vomit cut', expressive of an attitude a long way from the complicities of her later *Bride and Prejudice* or *Viceroy's House*. I have learnt much from the already mentioned diasporic approaches championed by Kaur and Kalra (1996), Sharma (2006), Narain (2008), Rai (2009), Dudrah (2012) and others and following them I will take up diaspora, though in a more conversational style perhaps, having watched the films so that you will too. I recognize that the classic films have accrued massive critical literatures already. I do not propose to pursue a survey, but without ignoring them I think there are aspects in this film that can be brought out to set up the argument that follows. One in particular that serves as a vehicle for this chapter.

Chadha's breakthrough film was *Bhaji on the Beach,* released in 1993 as her second and to that date most successful, and arguably still her best, film. In

Bhaji a group of women of various ages take an outing to Blackpool pleasure beach. Starting as a road movie set to a bhangra version of Cliff Richard's 1963 hit 'Summer Holiday', the film plays on the premise of South Asian women doing something archetypically lower middle- or working-class British, and doing so with a view to yet again another angle on the bonds of community. This time they do this against the backdrop, ever more significant, of Blackpool's somewhat faded seaside pleasures. The nuanced film presents a coming of age moment for the community, both within the film for the community centre group of women, and for South Asian audiences at last able to see themselves in cinema halls in a commercially successful crossover film which was almost universally applauded. *Of course* South Asian women can go to Blackpool as normal Britons, *of course* there are family and relationship dramas amidst the picnic and seaside romance, and *of course* it is the curiosity-but-normal factor upon which the comedy in the film relies to achieve its idiosyncratic but familiar appeal. All well and good, but it is striking to notice how first travel from their Birmingham home (Desai 2004: 135) and then the pleasures of the fairground rides at Blackpool serves to loosen social constraints and occasion a release of dramatic tension for the characters developed in the film. This is the genius of the film and the work it does to unpack social concerns and unfold dilemmas in a one hour forty minute package.

After the women first dip their toes in the water at the shore, the initial amusements we see are a mechanical camel race concession with arcade attendants dressed in exoticist sheikh-style headdresses, significantly not kaffiyeh style, more Lawrence of Arabia than authentic Middle Eastern. Desai explains that 'many of the local "sights" have an orientalist theme because the seaside resorts functioned to consolidate British identities for the white working class through tourism based on experiencing the exotic' (2004: 152). This makes sense of the conflation of saris with sand, bhajis on the beach, chips with masala spice and other seeming incongruities, all of which are made to seem not so exotic after all. Immediately after the camel race, the next scene has the camera enact a kind of vertical realization as it rises up on a Ferris wheel overlooking the water. The camera rides up and then in reverse shot we see the wheel take up the entire screen, towering over the viewer briefly showing the full cycle at just the moment when the women are beginning to enjoy themselves among the festive streetscape of Blackpool. In their openness to the out of the ordinary 'amusements', they are on the path towards resolution of some of the social dramas of their lives. The wheel was sponsored at the time by Burtons' Wagon Wheels, and it is fitting that this commercial confection appears symbolic of the circuit of change that would absorb 'new' migrant arrivals into cultural forms within the informal British order, though the teenager Ladhu, played by Nisha Nayar, does not quite comply. As if illustrating Desai's point that 'motion sickness' is a 'site of inquiry for understanding gendered agency within postcolonial agency', Ladhu and her sister Madhu, Renu Kochar, seek out two local boys and ride with them on the wheel, where Ladhu suddenly gets sick and spews. Chadha's achievement here is perhaps one of the most viscerally brilliant camera cuts in Global South Asian cinema as Ladhu vomits directly into the lens and the next scene is the older white gent taking Auntie Asha to an old school English music hall event. Statement.

The culture clash built into the film's title is endearingly tongue in cheek, but the script has serious and significant anti-racist and domestic political agendas. The film was made long before the war on terror; yet the mode of anti-racist pro-immigration intervention in the cultural sphere that *Bhaji* represents is not unaware of the kinds of conflict that would escalate after 2001. The everyday racism of early 1990s Britain was no picnic and *Bhaji* was a welcome contribution even as comedy-drama. It deserved praise for presenting a feminist and multicultural viewpoint, but was also not without critics. In *Multicultural Encounters*, Sharma notes Chadha's propensity for 'using "English" (working class) humour' (2006: 150–151) and in *Bollywood Travels*, Dudrah refers to the opening sequence as setting up the kind of film we expect to see: 'a grocery store, which is next to a closed shop front whose security shutters are daubed with a racist Nazi swastika. This in turn is revealed as standing next to a white male who is seen graffiti-ing another closed shop front with more racist slogans of the Far Right over layers of posters and fliers professing a multicultural Britain…' (2012: 68). Against this opening, the film works because it relentlessly strives towards resolution of its internal, melodramatic, issues and achieves in the end what can only be described as an age appropriate outcome in the affirmation of community in the conviviality of shared experience and bonding.

More politically aware expressions of conviviality exist – for example, in older works of scholarship that offer a language of potential hospitality evident in abundance, even in adversity, an irrepressible humanity. Under the theme of mela as a condensed alternative to dominant representations, we can open up such possibilities. There are multiple examples of the festive expressed in *Bhaji* as one pole of a critical directive that learns something from celebration and adversity held together, celebration of shared adversity perhaps called double consciousness with good reason. In *The Karma of Brown Folk* (2000), Prashad offers a tribute to the work of W. E. B. Du Bois and clearly a great critical literature resides among the references and inspirations, flowing from Du Bois, and through Paul Gilroy and Fred Moten et al., this sensibility can be shared, identified and distributed against the odds. If the work of such academics, an effort against the dominant compromise (Du Bois [1935] 1992,

Gilroy 1993, Moten 2003), can still inspire and reference what is going on at Blackpool, then also here, with community, there might be reason to revisit a history of the festive as counter-violence in the cinema. In even the most abject national contexts and difficult external conditions, there exists the possibility of dealing together with the conditions that oppress. The certitude that imagines community or diaspora as always in the making, as constructed, contested, invented, occluded and reified, is one which would surely contest myopic vision, tone deafness and inhumanity with an operating care. The consequence of going to the seaside in Blackpool, or to the mela despite the injunctions of parents and the dangers of unregulated festivity and commerce, has a spin-off potential and is a signifier of humanity that can neither be ignored nor contained.

Ferris wheels

A feature of the films discussed in this chapter is the presence of the most popular of pleasure park joy rides. Everyone remembers the Ferris wheel as fun, especially as I suspect that revisions of the experience have changed interpretations so much over time that it is difficult to remember the wheel as anything other than a good ride. Visitors to London since the millennium have hugely enjoyed the big wheel of the London Eye, despite British Airways sponsorship and a not exactly inexpensive ticket price. The attraction stands out from afar. Only 'the great wheel at the Empire of India Exhibition, Earl's Court' in 1895 (*Times*, 21 July 1895) rivalled the first large Ferris wheel, made for the World's Columbian Exposition in Chicago just two years before. A competitive sport, replications of big wheels worldwide, including plans for wheels in Kolkata, Mumbai and Bengaluru, have been floated with enthusiasm. As an unanticipated popular architectural structure, competitive urban posturing manifests in curious ways. Here it comes as bread and circuses, festivals and giving the public what the press says it wants.

What if it were plausible to propose an inversion of the usual perspective experiment and play out a scenario where an analyst would take the main tropes of Global South Asian film studies, and indeed its wider context in Marxist, diasporic, post-colonial and subaltern theorizing in general, and look as if anew at the cultural function of mela on screen? The inclusion of what will come to be known in multiple versions as the mela motif, arguably and controversially – the vomit cut as quintessentially British – can be seen as national allegory and this deserves extended treatment in this chapter. It is at least necessary to question if national rivalry was at all intended by the producers of wheels or melas for reception by commentators and viewers.

What perhaps is less readily accepted is that all cultural production can be seen as allegorical and within this the nation will try to capture the exuberant space and affect of mela for affirmative ends. *Sholay* however is always more than a national film and how it has travelled beyond expected audiences and genre designation – it is after all a 'Western' – should not be a surprise. It should also not seem strange to readers of Benjamin, Kracauer or Adorno to find the ideological is not contained in the national, but to read further into the circuit of mela in a way that can be derived from Global South Asian film study topics in ways that might make it possible push further than the Frankfurt School could in terms of culture industry and its meanings in an international frame.

The *Mela* films

The unavoidable key references forming a Global South Asian film and television studies remain, see for example Madhava Prasad (1998), Rajadhyaksha (2009), Rajagopal (2001) and Niranjana (2006). Among the subsequent academic commentators that need to be added are the authors of a range of studies released by their work – a voluble reading list I have tried to include, but by no means have I tagged them all. The sheer exuberance of the screen apparatus imposes itself all the more when the plethora of magazines, newspaper *filmi* sections, star appearances, radio shows, talk back and social media are taken into account. Further, a few minutes listening to talk back radio will show the experts to be relatively ill-informed compared with film fans. Alongside watching the necessary films, reading the available 'Bollyliterature' is a considerable commitment, and a secret pleasure (*pace* Nandy 1998), even if that carries with it ideological dynamics that also need to be sorted.

That said, I have searched far and not found much in the way of significant commentary on the *Mela* films, at least with regard to any comparative study of multiple versions of the film *Mela*. And yet like other big-ticket titles, *Mela* comes in multiple versions. To date there are three in Hindi: *Mela* of 1948 (dir. Sunny), *Mela* of 1971 (dir. Mehra) and *Mela* of 2000 (dir. Darshan); there is a remake in Telugu from 1956 (dir. Raghavaiah) renamed *Chiranjeevulu* but which sticks close to the 'original', then there are two somewhat divergent versions in Panjabi, the first called *Bhariya Mela* in 1966 (dir. Irani), and the second *Mela* from 1986 (dir. Askari), there is one called *Mela* in Bengali in 2010 (dir. Mondal) and one in Malayalam in 1980 (*Mela,* dir. George). There are also many instances of melas in other films and of course a large number of documentaries that I will only mention in passing. The point is that despite a significant repetition complex, *Mela* is not a film title around which any critical literature is organized, unlike say *Roja* in the *Economic and Political Weekly,* the South Indian socials (Madhava Prasad 2014a), any particular auteur, or the Bachchan genre films, though the much-storied *Sholay* has its mela sequence. A not quite comprehensive search found only two instances where scholars mentioned *Mela*: Rosemary Marangoly George (discussed below) and Istiaq Ahmed in the introduction to Gera Roy's edited collection *The Magic of Bollywood: At Home and Abroad* (Ahmed in Gera Roy 2012: xiv). If only for this reason I will risk a discussion of *Mela* but it cannot be neutral towards film scholarship. My readings in this are influenced by the extension of film studies in South Asia 'beyond' Bollywood to regions and diasporas, and to objects and contexts that are more culture industry or political movement focused.

There are different contexts for the same patterns in the films I will discuss. In these films we can quickly find narrative material that indicates fairly obvious allegory-making. The allegorical supports various projects: national reconciliation after partition in *Mela* #1948; agricultural campaigns and resolution of resistance under Nehru and in the early Indira Gandhi years in *Mela* #1971 and then organized 'terror' gangs with politicians in their pockets, versus worldly batting-above-average muscular prowess providing economic success in the *Mela* #2000 version. After introducing the films in this way, it becomes possible to consider the development of the politics of fear as a rhetorical ideological framework for nation and national imaginary in different modes, though each with psychological characteristics that reach intimately into identitarian desire, bodily and haptic affect, and restitution of family and national bonds through the elimination of either personal regret, resolution of internal injustice, and/or unity against 'external' threats. At least, as far as these films might show.

There is a diversity of style within the collection: the three in Hindi all called *Mela* are the same but different: two are 'remakes', but they have varied success, different stars and different contexts. All three are melodramas, but *pace* Madhava Prasad (1998) how would you write your way into thinking about films that are 'the same' across three very different time zones? They are not the same of course. There are also remakes in Telugu #1956, and films of the same name in Punjabi #1966, #1986 and Bengal #2010 but the storyline is significantly changed. The differences are subtle or not so subtle in each; there are differences in the set pieces as well as in the recurrent images and contexts in which they were made that can perhaps tell us what changes across time. Yet, how to present an analysis of this? Perfunctorily, first of all there should be a quick synopsis of the films, noting also their date of production and perhaps some salient points of context. That context could of course expand exponentially, but not yet. Next should come some identification and detailing of key tropes in the film, for example the opening sequence of a fairground Ferris wheel (*bada chakka* in Hindi), the scene-setting song and singer, then the key romantic story, the challenge to the hero, the main character roles, opposing figures through plot development and on to some hints – spoiler alert, the rhetoric of terror – at the resolution. Without ever risking the suggestion that the plots can be anticipated as always 'the same' – they most definitely are not – audiences do have expectations, and have learnt and even become habituated to certain narrative moves. Explicating these, and any disjunctive related notes, would then be the basis for expansive exegesis that made more of the context, showing a development across decades, broad brush and close argumentation both to make an overall case about the national or regional working through of issues such as power, violence, class or caste, development, commercialization, aspiration and perhaps even geopolitical position. If all goes well, then marketing the films also gives rise to comments on markets in general, and here there is cause to risk some implications for film theory as a diminutive coda, and the credits roll out some citations and influences upon this book. Might that be a convincing way to go? Let's see.

The relation of *Mela* to the three-worlds theory debates or about globalization, media-scapes, or even Bollywoodization may seem forced; I concede the conceit that sees *Mela* as a convenient vehicle for wider exchanges. Yet, as with Madhava Prasad's 'speculative proposition' about discussing *Roja* as a way to trace 'the work of the "political unconscious" ' (2000: 165), it would only require slight indulgence to allow that the variants of the film *Mela*, in the editions I focus upon here, can be interpreted to confirm my diagnosis. If it were not clear that real subsumption is replacing formal subsumption in the family drama of *Mela* #1948, the repetitions between versions confirm it, for example when Mohan is waylaid and cannot marry his childhood sweetheart, and she must choose to join the family of orphaned Indian children as newly consecrated, yet calculatedly ascribed, mother protector. In the Telugu version, this plot is repeated with only a slight variation where the lead character suffers not jail-time but a temporary blindness, although still following the same responsible path and tragic resolution. Rajadhyaksha might further diagnose this in line with several films of the early post-independence period that offered a bleak prognosis. Mela interrupted: not mentioning the films but one of the stars of *Mela* #1948, Rajadhyaksha makes a significant claim. In the earliest films of both Raj Kapoor and Dilip Kumar, 'happiness is not possible in the space of the new nation: in their early films you have to leave by either going away to another country or, as what happened in Shahid you can only find happiness in the afterlife' (2013). Here, the films work with an idea of the national, which asserts, through both autobiographical individual and filmic testimony, that independence was not an easy transition. It may be that the allegorical is undecidable in the end, even when it is clearly possible, plausible and legitimate, the broken relationships, the broken dolls, the couple as smaller manifestations of the many, of the structural and of the geopolitical, we can see that Pakistan and India cannot get along. The couple can be together only in some other space, after passing through the unbearable trauma of the actual and complicated real, through separation, yet these best people in the village can only realize their error and commit to an otherworldly (re) union.

In *Mela* #1971, at the outset, tradition is frozen and must be reaffirmed by stressing the difference between the traditional and the modern while protecting the village family romance – Kanhaiya comes to farm and restore the broken village with agricultural science learnt in university, yet he does so by way of marriage to a favourite village daughter and thereby reconciles with his wayward, dacoit brother and placates caste prejudices.

Although it would 'be a mistake to see these films as simply reflecting the changes that are underway, of being superstructural representatives of what is happening in reality', the 'ideological resolution' of real subsumption in *Mela* #2000 does seem to confirm that the tradition-modernity difference has been displaced. The village and family romance is not rescued by any 'efficient army which captures the terrorist' (Madhava Prasad 2000: 165), but by the substitute brother and his pirate trader business partner, whose postmodern pastiche of theatre, music industry aspiration, Rambo posturing and wisecracking humour – plus a bumbling comic cop 'Pakoda Singh', played by Johnny Lever – show that commercial opportunism can still appropriate a place within village India and win the day.

Mrinal Sen and Satyajit Ray

Everyday expectations of scholarship also should be tampered with. So, begin again, with another film.

Mrinal Sen got his start in the Aurora Cinema Company (as mentioned in Chapter 3) but left there to make feature films and in 1960 *Baishey Shravana* appeared. This film is a profound commentary on poverty in Bengal around the time of the 1942 famine resulting from British wartime grain manipulations. A key sequence in the film is a five-minute section that drives the plot in a way that becomes familiar. This sequence seems to repeat and condense a motif that appears in many of the mela films, both the one in 1948 and those made after 1960, including some of classic standing. No doubt comparisons of *Baishey Shravana* with *Pather Panchali* are plausible, but the capacity of Sen to go further into the condition of the oppressed and to go with less sentimentality, is impressive. The film is already a critique of Ray, but the part identified with *Mela* offers the pattern of public and private tragedy, and the brutal reality of the wheel of life that in some fundamental way repeats what fast becomes the *Mela* formulaic – a dramatic sequence in which the festival is interrupted by a howling gale, and violent nature causes the death of a mother. It is worth being specific: thirty-six minutes into Sen's film, building monsoon storm clouds and a Ferris wheel (*nagardola* in Bangla) express a growing anxiety. The storm destroys the fairground, people run helter skelter and in this instance, the protagonists, Priyanath and his wife Malati, make it home, but a fallen mango tree spells disaster. A festival of fun becomes chaos, destruction and a family is torn apart.

On the wonderful resource that is Indiancine.ma, the Jadavpur University Media Lab have annotated many of the films of the Bengali new cinema. For Sen's *Baishey Shravana* they offer interesting observations such as that about the common childhood experience of being caught, or almost caught, stealing mangoes. In Sen's film as well as Ray's *Pather Panchali*, this endearing moment, with accusations and excuses, is played out. The Media Lab annotators also describe the mela sequence:

> A fair [is] organised during 'gajan', a Hindu festival starting at the last week of Choitro continuing till the end of the Bengali year, associated with such deities as Shiva and local deities like Dharmathakur. A festival marking the marriage of the gods, it is an important event in the rural calendar with the fairs as an important commercial event of the year, drawing visitors and devotees from far and wide. A mix of ritual practices and revelry, it marks the end of the year with the 'Charak' puja done on the last day. Scenes of revelry, throngs of people, merchants and shops, are intercut with shots of Priyanath and Malati enjoying themselves immensely in the fair. Malati drifts away in the crowd of people and gets separated from Priyanath who frantically begins to search for her. Rapid shots of the two searching for each other, accompanied by the cacophony of the soundtrack, heightens the tense nature of the scene. Adding to the tense, manic energy of the scene, clouds are ... have gathered and a storm lashes onto the fair. (Maharghya 2015).

The separated pair soon reunite, and with a sense of relief at a close call, the pair return home. Yet:

> Rather ominously, the walk through the woods is constantly interrupted by a series of things on their path. The dark, oppressive mise-en-scene, along with the howls in the background heighten the sense of foreboding. The discovery of the tragedy is not immediate; he [Priyanath] first sees the mango tree behind his mother's hut missing and from then on it gradually

> builds up to a crescendo to the discovery that the tree has crashed through the roof into the hut, killing her. It only serves to heighten the gruesome and devastating nature of the tragedy. The long shot at the end of the sequence is dominated by the shot of the mango tree through the roof; it harks back to the last scene with the mother where she had changed her mind about re-thatching the roof. That there has been a definitive shift in the tone of the narrative is immediately apparent. (Maharghya 2015).

The storm interrupting a mela and causing death of the mother, or in other versions waylaying the hero, could be read without too much of a stretch as an allegory with clear reference to the impact of the British bringing their war to Calcutta. It could be interpreted as a displaced critique of British colonialism as such, or the advent of capitalist relations and mores. The idyll of a pre-conquest marketplace of South Asian generosity and openness – a mix of entertainments, pleasures and convivial trade – is swept away and scattered by the violent tempest of fate's arrival, causing traumatic loss that will be mourned for some time before events assimilate even these tragedies into the cycle of birth and rebirth invoked again in the Ferris wheel.

Sen's five-minute sequence in 1960 is telegraphed as if in a code. As we will see, it invokes the essence that drives the plot of *Mela* #1948 and it anticipates the powerful opening years later of both *Mela* #1971 and *Mela* #2000. The Ferris wheel features each time, it too is potent as allegorical image for the karmic ethic of temporal return that some will say governs Hindi cinema. Gera Roy (2015) points out that this is not the only factor, and other philosophical and religious elements demand account, but the repetition is insistent, and how it is read matters too. In Bengali cinema the formulaic is repeated later also in Aparna Sen's film *The Japanese Wife* (2010). Indeed, the film features a mela with a very small Ferris wheel appropriate to the restrained romantic, even syrupy, story.[1] The storm that comes only much later nevertheless portends disaster, although the exotic trimmings, the wrapping papers for the gifts from Japan and the beautiful and colourful kite sequence, all charm in ways that do not at all prepare us for the unbearably sad ending. Nevertheless, as well as drawing Japan into the orbit of Bengal in a delightful way, that should also be examined as allegorical meditation on alliances invoked but unconsummated in a bifurcated nationalist 'Asia', the film is a tribute to the motif.

Baishey Shravana compares favourably with *Pather Panchali*, perhaps not in terms of cinematography or the poetry of some images – Ray's water, his insects, his rain and the train – although many of Sen's scenes match for poignancy – Sen's clouds, Sen's faces – and exceed Ray's masterpiece as a social commentary, as a political version of a well-known story of poverty and famine. The parameters of family and community in conflict and despair are all there, but Sen's resolution is more potent because it is not merely sentimental. In addition, if it were plausible to compare Apu's life course as tracked by Ray with the composite figure of the angry youth that is shown in Sen's later Calcutta trilogy, it seems the explicit political content to do with revolutionary politics, in the later films the Naxalite uprising and its consequences, provides a more urgent context. Working through those consequences was Sen's contribution not only to film, but to sociology and an urban political ethic, even as the texture of the films are as cinematic and auteur-masterly as any of the careful esotericisms of Ray's rural idyll. The difference is worth noting, not only as an antecedent of a contest between these directors, but because a shift in approach to these years, shown in a comparison of the two films, is from an idealized India with romantic tragic resignation, to an anguished but real-world ethic interrupted by the storm of famine. Both are ostensibly responses to famine of 1942 but their universalizable appeal can extend to other and similar trauma, and for this reason it may be plausible to see this as an allegory of the market before and after colonization; mela as an open market and a festive space that, with the arrival of the colonial powers and their forts, became a closed and protected market, a series of walled compound as built by the Portuguese, Dutch, French, British and Danish.[2]

A mela for the memsahib

In Bollywood as a rule, the British colonial record is, to put it mildly, of 'a type'. And probably deserved. Not half an hour into the film *Mangal Pandey* (2005, dir. Mehta) the recently introduced characters all attend a colourful mela, with Ferris wheels, food stalls, acrobatic kids, a painted elephant, barber, bangle sellers, snake charmers, promenading guests and musicians pounding the ubiquitous dhol as if all for the entertainment of the very English visitor Emily. This sequence sets out the familiar tropes as if citing other *Mela* films in homage, the same scenes in the same order, but moving through a discursive parable about the East India Company excusing slavery and interrupted this time not by a storm but by money and the buying and selling of female slaves. Ostensibly a celebration of resistance against the British, *Mangal Pandey* can best be interpreted as a series of clichéd set pieces, for example the classic white man saving a brown woman from brown men, though with the assistance of one brown man, Pandey, as Tonto to Gordon's repressed Lone Ranger figure as the one honourable white man. Of course Gordon takes the sati as his lover, but is unable to rise to Pandey's defense even though he knows he should. It is not impossible to think the film's writing team had access to the reading list of certain post-colonial teachers. The plot surely here is the colonial era working as allegory for the present, not in any simple way that Jameson would call national or homology, rather a circuit (1986: 73), nevertheless, national chauvinist on both sides. The Indian state foundation myth is given a heroic back-story, bolstered in real life by exhibits such as those at the museum at the Red Fort. The British are portrayed judiciously, with some mad-in-the-noon-day-sun puffed up popinjay generals, but Gordon learns to be honourable through his association with Pandey, no longer merely conflicted and paralysed by a system that does not reward true valour. Happy ever after.

This colonial fantasy can be kept in mind when thinking of mela as allegory, as a festival in the sense of a bread-and-circuses event that, subtly or not, provides ideological cover for the development of market and state control. Control may be too strong a word, but I am taken by Madhava Prasad's picking up on an observation from de Pangerville that 'melodrama, as a theatrical tradition, was defended as a means of popular education, in which "people were not shown the world as it is, but how it should be"' (1998: 70n). Madhava Prasad's own take is that melodrama 'aspires to the transcendental, ceaselessly sublimating the realities of existence into mythical moral categories' (1998: 71). Here we can then see how 'foregrounding the political' (1998: 20) in a 'representative aesthetic form of a democratic society' (1998: 56) can permit films that are not explicitly about politics to be understood if melodrama is taken as a 'symptom of the ideological resolution of conflicts within the social formation' (Madhava Prasad 1998: 23). At the most general level, mela as a site of exchange should be a bazaar and a meeting place, a cornucopia of variations upon pleasure, desire, commodities, consumption and connections. There are food stalls and trinkets, rides and speakers, show tents, traders, gambling, pickpockets and illicit labour of many kinds. Mela as metaphor for hustle and bustle is not accidental.

Perhaps it is the most obvious thing to say about how the mela is framed in this sequence that the motif presents itself as an allegory of conviviality disrupted. Whether national, colonial or post-colonial, the invariable repetition is understandable both as a representation of lost idyll and as a plot device reliant upon the crisis of adolescence or naivety that will be overcome via adversity, the liminal movement of maturity. Depending on the subsequent picturization, any resolution is either despairing resignation or nostalgic. Neither option is fully redeeming of an eschatological hope where wish fulfilment has stalled, is postponed, or must be traded for a lesser realist resolution on the road that unfolds forever further. Despite their setting, in mela, the films discussed under this motif cannot show the particulars of market exchange nor do much political work explicitly – although there is a reproductive health booth in the background of the second *Mela* #1971 and a government minister is, almost incidentally, assassinated in the third *Mela* #2000. The films do not celebrate the market as market so much as threaten it, or update it with development of a small trader ideology. Of course in other film genres the shop or the circus could be tracked, but what confirms this significance is that even in the paradigmatic bromance of *Sholay* there are several shots of, and from, Ferris wheels at the mela, but little time is given to any commercial aspect. In what looks like a screenwriting staple, in *Sholay* a colourful celebration of a Holi festival is loudly and violently curtailed by an attack from Gabbar Singh and his bandits. A firestorm leaves the mela rides burnt and the town in fear – *Sholay* still translates as embers or cinders in Hindi – the pattern is affirmed again.

Given the terror angles, it is plausible that we call these melas 'festivals of fear' because the politics of fear is marketed as if at a stall. Each film starts with a song at a fair, and at the fair with a Ferris wheel as a feature, and also balloon sellers, dancing, and the male-female dance negotiates the wiles of seduction and power, so things begin as in many similar films – each aspect discernible at the level of motif. But there are different contexts for this same pattern. What can be singled out is that each film opens with a fairground song sequence: in *Mela* #1948 we are first introduced to a singer – the music is by Naushad, the song is sung by Mohamed Rafi (see below) – and a world weary or aged character, Mohan, wandering through the mela past the balloon sellers, the Ferris wheel, the merry-go-round and the stalls. This is a retrospective moment however, before flashing back in time to a framing shot of the market as the village community, and the fateful childhood meeting of the characters who will motivate the dynamic relationships of the plot. In the two later Hindi versions of the film, there is a return to the scene of the mela in order to move the plot towards its denouement. In *Mela* #1971 the song – music by R. D. Burman, sung again by Mohamed Rafi but with Lata Mangeshkar – establishes the close relationship of the male and female leads. Without any flashback needed, here it is through the dance that they move from being practical strangers, having met just once before, to, by the end of the song, being able to contemplate marriage, as of course the audience fully expects. Quite differently, then, the song in *Mela* #2000 – music by Surinder Sodhi, opening song sung by Roop Kumar Rathod, Sonu Nigam, Shankar Mahadevan, Alka Yagnik and Jaspinder Narula – has a deeply nationalist introduction, but then the danced narration of the marriage arrangement, enacting Roopa's importance to and immanent departure from the village, is one that brings order to the chaos of the marketplace, only for this to be disrupted by an attack by dacoits, who have their own more syncopated musical theme – and markedly less colourful clothing.

I will go further into a description of each of the films in a way that tries not to give up too much in terms of spoilers, nor impose anything but the most obvious, and even intended, interpretations of the meaning of motifs. Yet the arrival of the dacoits to the drum pattern refrain of the opening song sequence in *Mela* #2000 does indicate a trajectory that is important for both the ideological work of each film, and how this changes according to 'externalities'. Another echo with *Sholay* is the fact that the dacoit leader's name is Gujjar Singh, channelling Gabbar, and the film starts with a tribute to every film that ever had a police or army hero figure return to the village of their birth – no surprise this happens in each version of *Mela* – but in the 2000 version the dacoits-miscreants have taken on the universal look of the pagri-wearing 'terrorist'. It is unfortunate that the actors, led by the totally unsympathetic Gujjar, have trouble trying not to march in step to the hulking beats, and they do not match *Sholay*'s bandits for grit. Unlike the bad guys in the previous *Mela* films, the contemporary terrorist has no chance of redemption, and is neither a lovable rogue nor a lost brother separated in a storm.

Mela #1948

The film begins with the release from prison of Mohan, portrayed by the legendary Dilip Kumar, and we see him wandering through the mela detachedly observing the joyful celebrations of the people. A few congress-suited figures lead the crowd in dance as it arrives in the background at the fair. Mohan looks at the singer and at the worker turning the (wooden style) Ferris wheel through his own awesome strength. He soon has walked to the edge of the village and contemplates the spot where, as we will find out in the flashback, he passed blissful days of youth in the company of his beloved, played of course by Nargis. The story begins again in the past with the children arriving at school, the scoundrel who will cause Mohan's tragedy is caught smoking by the teacher, covering the teacher with itching powder, and picking a fight with Mohan. Later he becomes the somewhat slapstick army returned, bad English-Hobson-Jobson style troublemaker, and contrives, after Mohan is waylaid by a storm, to have Mohan's bride-to-be married off to an old rich widower. The two who were destined to be together cannot meet, and even when they discover a chance to come together again, they refuse to meet because of propriety and reputation. When it finally becomes possible to be reunited, there is disaster. The meeting is impossible, against nature, in this lifetime at least. Perhaps in another.

The opening feature tune sung by Mohammed Rafi in *Mela* #1948 is *Ye Zindagi ke Mele*. George sees that the framing song urges 'acceptance of life's ups and downs and the inevitability of death, and can easily be glossed as referring to the losses induced by Partition' (2013: 196). Although some viewers insist they did not watch it that way (personal observations of Fiza Vasudeva's grandparents, with thanks), certainly the timing would suggest no reasons to withhold such an interpretation and as already noted by Rajadhyaksha this would confirm taking the song at an even greater metaphysical register. The availability of multiple interpretations is obvious, and each not without interest. This was noted in a contemporaneous *Film India* review where the film was denounced for 'emotional masochism' and the 'illegal' portrayal of suicide (Indian Penal Code 309) with calls for censorship according to the then production code which specified that 'no crime shall be presented in a way which will create sympathy for it or inspire its imitation. Sympathy of the public shall never be thrown on the side of crime, wrong-doing or evil' (Anon 1948).

Other *Melas*

The Telugu version of *Mela*, renamed *Chiranjeevulu*, appeared in 1956 and it reworks the story by changing the affliction of the Mohan role – played by N. T. Ramarao – so that he must overcome blindness rather than a jail term. Some other changes include a younger widower, a more dramatic denouement, and notably at the start an extended song sequence by the co-stars as childhood best friends together, just as in 1948. Unfortunately this aspect is not repeated in later versions, thus abandoning the scene-stealing skills of the child actors in this case, Master Babji and Baby Sasikala (as the younger Mohan and Sarida). Nevertheless, the convolutions of this plot add to the suicide theme, death by anguish, and the final stormy sequence, with the younger widower elevated in the plot as a complicit agent/saviour of Mohan. Far from South India, this time in the Punjab, there are two films worthy of attention: *Bhariya Mela*, the 1966 Pakistani reworking with Naghma, Akmal and Munawar Zarif, does include the usual components of the sequence – the fair with Ferris wheels and balloon hawkers, a storm that disrupts the festivities, and violent consequences – the rural story has close affinities with the Hindi *Mela* #1971. What it adds however is yet more melodramatic tension, which by the time we get to its reappearance in an even later Punjabi version, *Mela* #1986, we see that the theme of blindness features again. This itself can be interpreted as a question of interpretation, with echoes of the blind Imam S'aab Chacha in *Sholay*, or later again the Om Puri figure in *Viceroy's House*. In the Punjabi version of this story, this time an action drama directed by Hassan Askari and featuring Sultan Rahi, Anjuman and Mustafa Qureshi in leading roles, the action begins with the now expected sequence of a mela interrupted, a stand-off and fight results in tragedy – eyes taken out with two spears – which in this example emphasizes the accumulated themes of gangsters raiding the festivities, killing, brothers separated, revenge declarations and a heroine fighting for justice resolved in another bloodthirsty dénouement.

Mela #1971

The first Hindi remake of *Mela* #1948 came some twenty-three years after partition and no longer had this backdrop so clearly as context. In *Mela* #1971 two brothers bunk off school to visit the nearby festival, are separated in the storm and as they are returning late, their mother looking for them in the forest is killed by a falling tree. The boys are orphaned but still separated, with the younger one of them suffering amnesia. He runs from the hospital and is hit by an automobile. The car's Muslim owner cares for and eventually adopts him. On account of him having a Hindu pendant, she brings him up loyal to his birth faith. The older brother is meanwhile brought up in his home village by an abusive and drunkenly violent uncle. Eventually this brother becomes a bandit, Shakti Singh, played by Feroz Khan, because his sweetheart was raped and killed by a landlord, and for this reason swears an oath to never allow anyone to plough the family field. The grown-up younger brother named Kanhaiya, after Krishna, played by Sanjay Khan, after passing first at college, comes to the village and unknowingly buys the family field from uncle, planning to farm it with modern methods – and a tractor. A romantic song sung by the village girl Lajjoo, played by Mumtaz, seems almost as much in devotion to the tractor as to Kanhaiya. Permission to marry the beautiful Lajjoo is refused to Kanhaiya by the village panchayat council as his caste is unknown, and it is inevitable that if he plans to plough the field he is likely to be shot dead by Shakti Singh. However, after sneaking in disguise into the mela so as to donate gold bars to the goddess at the rural temple, Shakti Singh's escape from the police is aided by Kanhaiya, albeit under coercion. The police trap was ineffectual and somewhat slapstick, but shots are fired and the bandit later sneaks into Kanhaiya's camp looking for bandages. As an upstanding and humane citizen, Kanhaiya dresses Shakti's wounds and they form a bond, with Shakti noting he owes Kanhaiya a debt. Because of this debt, still not knowing they are really brothers who had again met as foretold by goddess Kali, Shakti hesitates when Kanhaiya begins to plough the field. The scenario almost inevitably leads to the brothers fighting a to-the-death battle, and only towards the end, having wounded each other and ripped their shirts does Shakti see that Kanhaiya has the tattoo – of the sun god – which he and his young brother had both had done at the mela twenty years before. Mortally wounded, Shakti has at least been reunited and redeemed with his lost sibling.

The bandit here is someone we can understand and have sympathy with, despite his murderous ways, and his opposition to ploughing the field. He cannot however survive because the agricultural sufficiency of the nation is more important than the specific – read regional – grudges and complaints that stem from past injustice. What should be recalled as context here is how Indira Gandhi led a government as prime minister which still followed, in some sense, the Nehruvian path, but with the introduction of green revolution technology and anti-poverty drives, self-sufficiency and rule of law... despite hidden corruption, vote-rigging and favouritism that was to be exposed in the coming years, leading to the 'Emergency' suspension of democracy for two years from 1975.

Mela #2000

In the third Hindi edition of *Mela* #2000, it is surely worth noting the deaths at the beginning. Ram, played by Ayub Khan, is crucial only to the plot. The movie opens with his return to the village to arrange the marriage of his sister Roopa, Twinkle Khanna, to a border force army comrade. This plan, and the mela to celebrate the nuptials, is interrupted, as noted above, by the murderous intervention of Gujjar Singh. Ram, a terrific shot, is nevertheless overwhelmed by the band of 'terrorists', who had also killed the parliamentary dignitary and all his bodyguards. Also killed is the small boy Gopal who had been prominent in the opening dance sequence, with Ram and the boy both taking the lead for large sections of the first two songs. No other male sings apart from the eunuch, Ghungroo. These key figures, Ram and Gopal, are killed less than fifteen minutes into the film, so as to set up the rest, in which eventually Roopa teams up with itinerant lorry drivers Kishan and Shankar, played by the 'real-life' brothers Faisal and Aamir Khan (of *Mangal Pandey* fame).

The story of *Mela* #2000 is of the precarious working-class fighting against corruption and terrors that destroy forever the village idyll. That such a narrative should not inspire immediate mass audience support perhaps has to do with the opportunist pay-off of neo-liberalism in the rhetoric of 'shining India'. The film flopped at cinemas. Nevertheless, in terms of the production it works as a fulfilment of the pattern identified. The transformation of the market in the first decades of the century this film inaugurates offers a clarifying context. Moving towards an online and cashless economy – consider Modi's one fell swoop erasure of large denomination bills in December 2016 as a forced roll out of card machine tech – erases mela in the old frame. Already *Mela* #2000 was marked by such tendential shifts, with post-MTV Bollywood fantasy sequence, a terror image evoking the sort of siege soon to afflict the parliament and Mumbai, and a road movie car chase sequence format that displaces the 'space' of the mela. In the previous versions, transport was by foot or bullock cart. Even as *Mela* #2000 begins within village space – the dance ground wholly within the village – this presentation is a frozen nostalgia, with nationalist character, soon destroyed by foreigner intervention. The music sequence confirms a heavy-handed modernization: the special effects contrast starkly with the rest of the film, even as it offers a tribute to slapstick fight sequences and other routines. The early but extravagant divergence into fantasy – Kishan's musical item dream has him achieve MTV level celebrity stardom – comes at a crucial moment in the plotting, its incoherence as a dream sequence unlike any other style of the film. In *Mela* #1948 the doll figures play out the symbolism of home and family. In *Mela* #1971 it is chalk drawings on the wall of the house, and a tattoo of the sun – an icon inscribes first the family connection then identity across difference. At this point *Mela* #2000 forgoes inscription in favour of a fantasy item number in which our protagonist imagines celebrity success in a way that makes sense only as the phantasmagoric aspiration of the precarious in post-idyll neo-liberal Asia. Aspiration shifts from family to village to globe.

This point had been made already in the 1990s by various authors, for example Nandy (1990) and Pinney (1995) who indicated a shift in Bollywood film address from the national uplift narrative of family and Mother India, to films directed at an audience figured as 'the urban single male migrant in search of sex, violence and the remembrance of his absent family' (Pinney 1995: 11). This indexing of the male migrant labourer marks a moment of nostalgia here as well, still perhaps before dislocation of Global South Asia from a geographical referent in the war on terror, although Nandy (1990) was already alert to this part played by terror long before, but what is conspicuous is the agency of this migrant labourer. In turn, the seeking subject of a commercial film that panders to lowest commonality will of course seem to favour sex, violence and amoral dislocation, but another possibility is affirmation of community, longed for reconnection, and marking time in a global struggle that would be the condition of Global South labour universally. This of course is not what *Mela* #2000 demonstrates, even as it can also be understood to conform to the argument made by Nandy and Pinney. In contrast to an affirmation of community, in *Mela* #2000 by the end the village has been irrevocably changed by the battle against terror, the protagonists no longer have a rural place, and must return to the road. The inconsequential consumer pleasure of Aishwarya Rai's cameo drop-in at the end is a last ditch effort of Capital to tempt the globalized working class with the luck of the lottery. Fighting the terror has not brought rewards except through the sweet luck of fate, and this is dangled seductively before the audience. Along with the 'Mera Bharat' sing-along at the start, this happy disposition at the end means it should be no surprise that the film is often screened on terrestrial channels for 26 January, Republic Day.

Yet, this recuperation of the wayward and precarious to the fictional-national and emblematic village gives us a reason to recognize *Mela* #2000 as unsuccessful because it does not offer a Global South Asian nor a specifically local reference. Nor does it do the work of redeeming convivial association, except perhaps as linked contingent individuals performing unfounded or ungrounded ambition. It presents no future for either the national or regional, and indeed it is wholly precarious in terms of theme content and plot. Episodic narrative dominates after the disruption of the village mela tradition, a roadside cafe, temple, picnic grounds, and celestial reward all appear along the road, the truck drivers keep driving on their never-ending quest for the main chance. Unlike the nationalist promise of an emergent economy, this precarious allegory cannot guarantee success – not that shining India can, but its entire content is that it makes the claim. Precarity cannot make an allegory cohere as it remains a string of episodes and the audience has lost the habit of collective interpretation with reference to a recognizable (re-cognizable) frame. Neither partition nor independence contain the aspirations of this unfolding and unpredictable path.

Why did *Mela* #2000 have to kill off Ram at the start of the film? There is no indication that Ayub Khan was too expensive to hire throughout – indeed, his ghost appears again briefly at the second mela toward the end. No indication is given in the movie gossip press that Khan's role had to be truncated, so far as I could see, the plot scenario that called for his demise is not a surgical repair. While a speculative explanation is proffered below, it is perhaps first worth looking elsewhere to realize that such plot devices are not unknown, and indeed fairly frequent, in cinema. As we saw in an earlier chapter, in Mrinal Sen's *Ek Din Achanak*, the professor walks out of the film early on, and never comes back. In using the same device in *Ek Din Pratadin,* Sen had refused to answer viewer requests to know where the daughter had been when she did not come home on time – although she at least did come home in that film. *Ek Din Achanak* returns to the 'same' device some ten years later, with the film's internal time frame longer, a year rather than a day, and the father has still not come home, and never will. The family falls apart in the aftermath, as we perhaps too willingly see. That Sen is showing the inner demons of the middle class to the middle class is all the more disturbing given this familiar framing. In *Mela* #2000 Ram's death after the first song, inaugurates a story about repairing the damaged family, afflicted by terror from outside.

There is perhaps an oblique commentary in another of Sen's works, where an early death, a mother hangs herself, sets up Sen's film *Mahaprithibi* (1991).[3]

The use of newsreel footage may invoke associations with another film where an early cinematic death features – a character who exits in the first reel was already on display in Orson Welles's *Citizen Kane* (1941) with opening scenes showing Kane's death followed by a newsreel summary of his life. Even if the rest of *Mahaprithibi* is not so much a sequence of flashbacks, the removal of a key character to drive the plot is an uncommon motif. Whether it works or not, the dilemma that drives the film becomes one of understanding why the mother has hanged herself after the return of an estranged son to the family hearth. She leaves a diary, and the 'repair' of the family occurs through another significant motif to do with setting pages alight. Shomu, the returning son, proposes to read the diary so as to discern his mother's state of mind and find clues to her suicide. It turns out that none of the grieving family can face the task, and only when the diary is burnt can Shomu be reconciled with his father and take his place with the rest of the grieving family. In an echo of recognition of more global significance, Mukhopadhyay notes:

> As the flames leap higher and higher, we remember the foreign network footage, incorporated earlier in the film, showing the burning of Marxist literature during the last days of the Soviet Union. It brings out the essence of change in the greater world in the context of a small family. (Mukhopadhyay 2009: 198)

Again we see burning books attend a history of violence; reified in mythical stories and in figures as diverse as Ram, the Soviet Union and topical newsreels of violent protest. It can be expected that each director and/or writer of the later *Mela* films had seen the previous *Mela*(s), and so some degree of historical inter-reference could be built into the subsequent versions. Also, everyone has seen *Sholay;* so it is not only coincidence that in *Mela* #2000 at one point Kishan is renamed Kanhaiya as the village prepares the mela as a trap for Gujjar. This name change is poignant as at the same time he is (too) slowly falling for Roopa, which means basically he is transitioning into a replacement for the murdered Ram. The new son of the village no longer redeems the broken sibling relationship to heal rifts and reclaim a lost brother from the strayed path of dacoitry, but instead enlists his reluctant brother in the work of out and out revenge.

In *Mela* #2000, Kishan is afflicted by a near inexplicable despondency, until one remembers that in *Mela* #1948 and *Mela* #1971 the promise of an idealized marriage was never questioned. The lead couple were always a couple, always committed to each other, even when forced to marry someone else – they never betrayed true loyalty. In *Mela* #2000, Roopa is loyal only to her brother, but Kishan does not know that. He has resisted the matrimonial path until now, but once he meets his match, he is fully committed – only to find it was a false move. Roopa of course is slowly realizing that she does love Kishan, and actually wants to marry, but only through the mediation of replacing her brother with Kishan's friend Shankar and in the collective, defeating Gujjar Singh. In this process, Kishan as Kanhaiya shifts from being the heroic but aloof and individualistic Rambo – his poses and dress evoke the Stallone icon – to reaffirming his commitment to fighting alongside Shankar and then as part of the collective. Ram died to be replaced in Roopa's hopes and desires, after a time, by Kishan. The potential military match was ditched, giving way to a convenient husband found on the road, reworking an exogamous alliance in precarious times. While the village structure must be defended, family structures have suffered a devastating blast and the couples, with Shankar delivered of his celebrity cameo love interest, drive off into the uncertain future. The village idyll has been redeemed symbolically but not practically, the heroes cannot settle, and so drive on and out of the film.

Parched

All of which raises the relevance of yet another film featuring a mela, Ferris wheels and more or less intended allegorical projection. In Leena Javed's *Parched* (2015) the breaking of patriarchal normative sexualities gives the film a joyous and successful escape from poverty and prejudice. Although despite uplift – that mocks the trinket-exotica NGO handicrafts project that brings satellite television to the village – the film also shows the practicalities and setbacks of informal sector survival. At the end of the film, Thelma, Louise and Lajjoo are still left with nowhere to go but out of the film theatre, and in this it also echoes the non-resolution of *Mela* #2000. Of course films often may set their finalés in fairs, and fairs will almost always have Ferris wheels. In *Parched* the various interrelated strands of the plot converge in the spectacle of the Dusehera festival, itself represented by the construction of the effigy of Ravana and the giant wheel. The spectacular denouement resolves the plot in terms that promote the triumph of love and sisterhood over traditional sexism. Tannishta Chatterjee, Radhika Apte, Surveen Charla and Lehrer Khan are actors able to ensure that *Parched* does justice to the significance and sweep of the story. It was made with high production values and a dramatic, sometimes profound and other times funny, plot that seductively modulates affective associations. There are similar camera angles on and from the Ferris wheel featured in *Parched* as there are in each of the other mela films discussed. This accesses a by now established repertoire, even as the film also sometimes has the look of a Rajasthan Tourism Board promotional feature and surprisingly does not end with the dulcet cadence of the Discover India in-flight arrival video or the mobile phone ring-tone that so much product placement seemed to anticipate.

The motifs of mela in heavy rotation

Consciously planned or not, discussion of *Mela* as a film staple allows historical commentary and reflection on how approaches to allegorical 'topicality' might change over time. The films do not shy away from that allegorical charge, Ahmad and Jameson notwithstanding (see below), some films do explicitly embrace the role of translating national concerns into the register of the family drama – trading rhetorical formula for allegorical purchase and doing duty for chauvinisms or their debunking, according, in turn, to interpretation. The degree that audiences, and critics, buy the story is not necessarily dependent on the degree to which the film evokes or occludes its pertinent renderings. Sometimes a dacoit is not the Maoist insurgency writ large, sometimes the drunken uncle is not the wasted potential of a narrow-minded peasantry that doggedly refuse to adopt green revolution technology, genetically modified seeds or development loans. The taxi driver in *Sammy and Rosie Get Laid* might just be a haunting image rather than the representative of all those subject to the state violence documented in those blood-and-fire-fuelled annals.

Mela #2000 was not a box office hit: perhaps because its narrative failed to sufficiently invoke points of topical connection in changed circumstances, perhaps because the heavy-handed recycling of motifs was too subtle – the registration of the getaway truck was Hum 420 invoking the spirit of Raj Kapoor's Japanese shoes. I am inclined to favour an interpretation that suggests that a too ready acceptance of a central government line on terrorism made the film unsuccessful because this line was either not criticized or was not anywhere near allegorical enough. While elements of *Mela* #1971 are blatantly pro-Nehruvian in theme, and hardly subtle in negotiating Hindu-Muslim relations or the caste hierarchy, by way of a resolution it turns out that caste prejudices soften over time and 'different' couples can marry after all, especially if it turns out the boy from a Muslim family was really Hindu and of the same village from the start. In a hardly subtle way, there is at least recognition here through an explicit reality-fiction compact with the audience. More curious is that the separated brothers acting in the film are 'real' brothers in real life – Sanjay and Feroz Khan – and as their names suggest, Muslims playing Hindus, with one of them brought up in a Muslim household holding on to his Krishna devotional identification.[4] Distance perhaps makes it more difficult to judge the topicality of *Mela* #1948 where the contrived or forced separation of the two who were from the start meant to be together may or may not provide grounds for an instructional reading of how they let pride prevent any reconciliation until it was too late, but I do not know how to, or even if we should, decide. What is available is the possibility of reading the film in this way, and mapping that onto the subsequent versions and the different instructional topicalities provided there. By the time we get to *Mela* #2000 however, the fissures of caste and hierarchy are occluded in the all-singing, all-dancing opening scenarization songs, with the variety of regional identities rendered as if they were only styles of dress amidst a multicultural ensemble of village unity, threatened only by the stereotypically dark material outfit of the terrorists from abroad.

In *Mela* #1948, Mohan could be considered an example of what Sumit Chakravarty calls 'imperso-nation' (1993: 4) where the self-questioning of nationhood is offered as exemplar. Such self-questioning can include Rushdie's Farishta in *The Satanic Verses*, or better, Saleem Sinai in *Midnight's Children* asking himself just what the point of 'all this writing-shitting' might be, as Padma the dung lotus demands he spend more time with her (Rushdie 1981: 20). Mohan's point of view, wandering through the mela years after events that will be told in long flashback, could be the apotheosis of the tragic hero who dies with redemption and knowledge in a world that no longer has a place for any regret for what is lost. This is utterly useless for the protagonist, since he falls off the cliff and out of the movie, but as an instructive parable for the audience, is possibly also useless because it is patronizing in its allegorical bludgeoning.

In each of the versions discussed here the village can be understood as a more or less unblemished fortress of identity, with, in the remakes, the mela as its performative laboratory through which process and change in the eternal and cyclical path of life occurs – explicitly associated with the Ferris wheel in the first song of *Mela* #2000. Kaur's study (2003) of the Ganapati festivals of Maharashtra illustrates well how the political space of a festival can be used to work through political meanings, incorporating many contemporary issues and imagery alongside the icons of tradition and faith. In *Mela* #1971 the film does need to work through old prejudices about caste and community by getting the village panchayat to permit love match marriages and a marriage between Lajjoo and Kanhaiya despite no one then knowing Kanhaiya's caste and having to get past the revelation that his adopted mother is Muslim. And then also to accept the marriage of Billoo and lower caste Bansilal, achieved through the wiles, and finances, of the prospective wife, but perhaps accepted because both characters are somewhat comic, and the father-in-law is a sweet softie who only pretends to be a strict stickler for tradition. The panchayat itself performs a similar role to the mela grounds in that it provides a protective moral space around the village. In the *Mela* #2000 iteration the mela itself is physically surrounded by the village. In the earlier versions, first it was the village surrounded by a wall, and the open mela, through which Mohan wanders, is far from home, reached by bullock cart. In the #1971 iteration, it is the mela that is surrounded by a wall, perhaps an allegory of private property, and thus the space of the market festival changes over time and in each film it may be showing the encroachment of privatization, against which, even when as in *Mela* #2000 the wall is a line of people that an outside threat must first break through. At the end of the song in *Mela #*2000 the way the terrorists walk up in time to the dhol drum rhythm of their signature tune helps mark them as outsiders as much as their much plainer, less colourful, clothes.

A catalogue of blood shots might be another way to get into the melodrama of it all. In the second of the films here, Shakti Singh is shot twice, and in each instance his brother's hands are covered in his blood. Both times he holds his hands up to look at this, the first time of course not knowing it is sibling blood – they were separated in youth. The viscosity of the scene, and the era of splatter effects, may seem dated now, but the charge and the meaning of negotiating blood lines is vibrant. I thought of collecting similar scenes, but then realized this is not a catalogue volume. The trinketization of motifs is evident in the repetitions we will discuss here. The Ferris wheel and merry-go-round motifs are seen in each 'remake' – and of course also found in *Sholay, Mangal Pandey, Parched, Bhaji on the Beach* and as we will see in *Pinjar*.

The convivial idyll of the village mela interrupted by the storm of colonial arrival, partition, loss, Naxals or terrorists is the rite of passage hook for the films. A cinematic working out of trauma through back-projected nostalgia and the wheel evokes the cycle of life, its profound meaningless, ongoing-ness resolved – as also with collecting, often noted – through the circular play that moves those currently incarnate as life forms inexorably along a cycle. If you could hold up the hands of the collectors of trinkets, you can see a political and family affinity in repetition. The point is that with mela the turning achieves resolution through revolution, and the set fails or succeeds according to how the participants perform.

The contradictions that come with globalization also seem right up front in *Mela* #2000 and not so confused after all if thought of as a mediation of fear and nostalgia. Although not a box office success, the film plays regularly on national television on 26 January. Does the overdetermination in the repeat of motifs mean these usual winning formulae were inserted into the wrong plot? Did the judgement of the director – and the problems in initial casting – misfire, or was there a lack of connection with the unfolding development of the proliferating media assemblage (Rai 2009: 115, 176)? The repetition of aesthetic elements, such as the crane-shot of the mela with a carriage of the Ferris wheel in the left of the frame, gives only a formal continuity. However, plot and characterization, as well as moral or ethical instructional intent, provide a greater sense of continuity across the films. Between these two poles, the recurrent song emblem is not the 'same' in terms of instruction, but does replicate the structural pattern.

Another continuity across the films is memory and loss, with Mohan in a coma and then years of prison in *Mela* #1948, Kanhaiya injured and suffering memory loss that only the tattoo reveal at the end can resolve in *Mela* #1971, and Ram killed but his memory and role as village protector replaced by Shankar – and a miraculous reward in Aishwarya Rai's miraculous appearance. The differences between the films however also indicate some level of overdetermination. *Sholay* in 1975 had copied, and perhaps perfected, the *Mela* #1971 song sequence with Ferris wheels and merry-go-rounds, but by *Mela* #2000, the masala formula that worked in the 1970s had become mere genre confusion by the end of the century – which may explain the difficult and breathless failed resolution for the village. With set pieces that are in turn romantic, devotional, ensemble and nationalist, followed by a terror-action sequence, fantasy futuristic modern dance, then road movie, bar brawl, cabaret variety, slapstick toilet humour, love story, wet-sari waterfall item number and a marriage celebration giving over to Rambo-esque village unifying Magnificent Seven Samurai reconciliation, revenge and development narrative… there may just have been too much going on. The film incorporates the repertoire of previous films to excess, readily identifiable with industrial level production values of the Bollywood system, but offering nothing new or stand out.

Interpretation and stormy relations

If the interpretation of multiple versions of 'the same' film is to be taken seriously, the argument might hinge on an evaluation of the allegorical in narrative. The prospects for this are challenged from the start however, as Rai writes:

> Modes of production analyses such as that by Madhava Prasad have the overall effect of presenting a cinema of static reproduction: reproduction of ideologies, narratives, social structures, identities and even prefabricated heterogeneity. (2009: 57)

The static interpretation would be challenged by a conception of allegory that shifts according to interpretive frame. Consider how *Sholay* has meant different things to different audiences over forty years. In a somewhat exoticist comment for the BBC, Dudrah calls it 'the ultimate masala film ... Because it has all the spices – drama, melodrama, romance, action, family – and they're blended perfectly' (Durdrah in Verma 2015). Dudrah redeems this excessive appreciation with critical work later on *Sholay*'s queer readings, at a seminar in Manchester in 2017, but even earlier in a popular forum he makes the allegorical point: 'it is not just thrilling entertainment. The nation is writ large in themes of law and order, justice and revenge – they reflect anxiety around India's Emergency from 1975 to 1977' (Dudrah in Verma 2015). What the variety of appeal offered by *Sholay* also achieves is attraction for different generations from different perspectives. This does not mean suspending older interpretations of *Sholay*, as Curry Western and so on, but that other not necessarily commensurate interpretations accumulate in a critical community of self-recognition that works at the dialectical end of perspective. The 'buddy' relationships in *Mela* #2000 could also be read in these terms with added, but secondary attention paid to Roopa and Bulbul as 'structurally' paired women given a large role in the mela dance sequence, though fading thereafter. *Parched* also explicitly focuses upon fluid sexual and erotic pairings, to the delight of some activists and the scepticism of others who saw it as pandering to cheap thrill marketing (class discussion, Jadavpur 2016). These dynamics of interchangeable relationship and identity calculus make interpretation a variable of scope and orientation in which the politics of the 'same' film may significantly change with the times – as I argue, does *Mela* – and yet still reference, for example, anxieties about particular events, as well as present-day ones. It also means the mode of production analysis can reappear as surprisingly resilient.

In perhaps too simplistic terms, would it be plausible to say that the different versions of *Mela* provide differing moments in a dynamic of the public's relation to social politics? To interpret *Mela* #1948 and *Chiranjeevulu* as only searching for ways to move past the trauma of a broken relationship and serious childhood attachments would bring out only one aspect of the films: the impossibility of the relationship between the two protagonists interrupted by real-world concerns, storms, prison, honour, so that there is no place in the film for the couple – in this imaginary, the unity of Global South Asia – and only being thrown outside of the film into the next life can bring the desired connection. So also in *Mela* #1986 and *Parched*. In *Mela* #1971, we again have the storm of separation, but a reconciliation of communal and family partition is seen in the suture of the brother's two divergent paths, one legal, and one illegal. This resolution follows the village farm development model, the heroic Nehruvian path, a misguided but understandable individual distortion into rebellion is forgiven, and – in the lesson of the film – can be reconciled by coming back into the nation from insurgency, albeit in death. Think here of how the Comintern required the national Communist Parties to intervene and suspend sub-national uprisings like Telangana in the interests of the emergent nation state. A less socialist narrative in *Mela* #2000 has commodification and terror join hands to disrupt the ideal of the village, yet in the journey towards modernity new alliances can be found to satisfy the lost ideal – of Ram. This ideal can be offered even to those who are not of the village if they can prove themselves in aspiration and effort to be worthy of the rewards of belonging. Yet the effort of fighting to defeat Gujjar has Kishen and Shankar perform a mode of slapstick rather than full-blown heroic action, also in an embarrassingly jingoistic way. The scenario is unsatisfactory because it offers no content or commitments that can become attachments beyond the pursuit of individual gain – there is no ideal attachment beyond that which was already in the village at the start, nothing has really moved forward, the Ferris wheel has only turned, no one even got sick. Nothing is made of the turning of male desire towards heteronormative romantic convention (think also of *Sholay*), but this cannot find a place within the old structure, and the future has no content but hope. Is it not in a similar way, the bifurcation within the notion of the Global South that separates socialist historical origins from its current rhetorical deployment as economic advantage? We see no substantial attachments and nothing to secure the habit of earlier motivations born of anti-colonial struggle against imperial violence because success today is couched primarily and merely in terms of economic and financial survival, therefore affectively empty and individualist, even neo-liberal, gain – however lovable the two itinerant heroes are, they will never match Jaidev and Veeru for 'buddy' altruistic commitment.

Framing frames

Perhaps the thing to do is to suggest each of the *Mela* films can be placed in an interpretive frame – a Ferris wheel carriage – to do duty as examples of the unfolding of Global South Asia over time. Rai gives grounds for doing something like this when recognizing 'specific topological changes in [Global South Asia's] media assemblage' (2009: 176). Conveniently, the *Mela* films might be pre-selected illustrations for this point, but then, the imposition of general stages on the coordinates of cinema studies could be welcomed by some, even if speculative.

An initial frame suggests itself at the level of the nation. Even as I am aware Jameson also prefaced his remarks about national allegory as 'speculative' (1986: 72) nevertheless it is impossible not to notice how a certain rendering of national level violence and personal experience of suffering is shown in *Mela* #1948. The lovers are separated by a horrible storm even as the prize – marriage, jewels – was close; then, however painful, they maintain the terms of their enforced separation – partition – and only in the next life can unity prevail. Message: this life and its pain are illusory, and to see so, and stick to duty and your own, can redeem hurts in the long run – while others build the nation. *Mela* #1971 comes as a heavy-handed agricultural allegory, also explicit – the wayward brother is a worthy fellow maltreated, not nurtured, in the past, his younger brother, not knowing of their bond, nevertheless shows care, and has a tractor to grow the nation. Through the younger brothers' selflessness, the wayward brother is released from his pain – the psychological dynamic and the secret desires both coincide with the national agricultural development, but the 'problem' the plot works through is the psychology of nurture and care – important for plants, relationships, and politics. *Mela #*2000 shifts the context in which the village sits to the outer-national where the threat is from abroad, and cannot be reconciled without going through the traumatic conflict. The terrorists are vaguely Muslim, coded visually at least as from Pakistan, or as the Taliban. They arrive and destroy the village, kill Ram and capture Roopa. A worse storm could not be imagined. But despite the odds, what must be done in response is done through a scrupulous resolution of cultural traits, prowess and skills found in unlooked for specificities of the home-grown make-do. Roopa escapes and teams up with two brothers whom she sees as no-hopers heading at least in the right direction. The resourcefulness of a fortuitous preparation however means that whatever is needed is already at hand – as if the gods provide the needful by arranging for whoever and whatever is required to have always-already been available. The brothers turn out to be allies, even they did not know they were waiting as if for the right moment for their true vocation to appear from behind its slapstick disguise. This latter formula is clinched over and over as the brothers move closer and closer to a confrontation with Gujjar. Their fighting skills and teamwork in the cafe brawl sequence and again in the abundance of desired items found in their truck – beer bottles for bribes and relief, a star for the show, apples that are grenades, grenades that are apples, and (huge spoiler alert) best of all for the Shankar, Aishwarya Rai, who drops from the roof to fall instantly for him at the end. The truck is almost the paradigm of international just-in-time production and deregulated commodity market filling the new shopping malls with an abundance of things, and fulfilment of dreams. In turn the political ideological, the psychological-ideological and the globalization-ethnographic commodity-local can be mapped almost too neatly onto each film.

Only the most inflexible concept of interpretation would insist that the films here are always national allegory, or, conversely to categorically deny that they never are. In the court of arbitration, who will decide if I contend that *Mela*, in each of its versions, is not *just* national allegory? At the same time, to think that a determination for or against national allegory amounts to analysis is to make a joke of the need to understand even national allegory as the allegory of former elites renegotiating their position in the shifting economic class hierarchies of independence, neo-liberalism and digitalization. Much more is at stake when, over generations and in different ways, former elites renegotiate their status. Against those left to lead precarious lives, the elite manoeuvre within a hierarchical polity, their aspirational self-reconstruction must be considered in its continuity with the fortunes of the early collaborating classes under formal subsumption.

It may be plausible to rethink these films in broad terms related to social class in the colonial frame. Since the very onset of colonial occupation, the local elites had seen opportunities to renegotiate their prominent positions through alliance with global capital and geopolitical intrigue. At any point in the story it is possible to identify links between those who saw advantage in collaboration and the upward mobility of aspiration. Over time however, the coordinates of this aspiration change and a trajectory can be plotted from the early comprador advantage of the emergent merchant class and its facilitation of extraction, through the canny reinvestment of anti-colonial independence movement credentials – Congress cap, fidelity to Jinnah, reinvented Sinhala Buddhism – which proffered positions in parliament and advantageous opportunities. Then, in the early years of independence, the old institutional formations where military training, uniforms and traditions have some ongoing gravitas. These symbolic and actually powerful roles could be targeted for families wanting to get ahead – the army career and its status is still potently operative in the cantonments and in the context of governance, though increasingly this newly reconstituted old order is undermined by media reports and public awareness of corruption, baksheesh, encounters and complicity with terrorist intrigues.

Perhaps another run through the film plots will allow us to better read this trajectory in the three Hindi versions of *Mela*. The Congress figures enter the mela field at the beginning of *Mela* #1948 and after the idyllic village scenario goes wrong, an older businessman assigns stewardship of the young to the heroine. Our hero Mohan, waylaid by events, can only be an observer of a difficult compromise, resolved ultimately only in a death that recognizes that life must go round. The message, if any, is of accepting assigned verities, while not permitting opportunist manipulation of the new structures. It is the too-easily manipulated panchayat and the conniving figure of the returned soldier, who must be rejected so as to avoid tragedy. In *Mela* #1971, the separated brothers of the sun god, their allegiance tattooed on their arms, are ultimately redeemed and affirm the village in a makeover via agricultural science and development – even the panchayat sees the advantage that permits a small trader to marry up the caste hierarchy, having convinced the father with the cunning that belongs to business acumen. Kanhaiya gives us tractors, sophistication and medical aid to win over the village suspicious of his origins, while filial piety in the end shows the wayward brother to be true. In more complicated times, but still to confirm the trajectory, we can read significance into the early disappearance of the soldier brother from *Mela* #2000 – the death of Ram in the first reel. The inexorable decay of standards is evident when his army friend, to whom he has arranged his sister Roopa's marriage, turns out to be a boorish fool. The old promises, as is often narrated in literature, fall down – the heroine is left forlorn and desperate. Guarantees of the emergent developing non-aligned nation and its society of patronage and place have been eroded in the face of terror and complacency. What Bulbul endorses in her song in praise of village tradition is threatened by an uncertain modernity in which international terror, corrupt commercial networks, and the flat competitive realities of having to make your own fortune have become the norm. That our heroine can then step up to the challenge with the help of two otherwise unremarkable but honest lads is a story of hope and restitution. In effect Roopa replaces, even remakes, her dead brother Ram by means of an opportunistic deception that luckily can access emotional and affective investments in love and family-affirming 'marriage' to Kishan, the resolution of the entire romantic Hindu pantheon coded here in the pay-off their individualist aspirational outlook needs. Those who live by their wits and sale of labour power in the new modernity are structurally superior in new times to Ram and his military friend, prospective in-law. The film displaces one pair – with their outmoded institutionalized soldier roles – in favour of the less structured, neo-liberalism-compliant truck driver friends. The message again is that the village must move beyond reliance on the old institutions so that the restoration of old values in new times can work through symbolic negotiations: such as that a commoner truck driver can meet and woo Aishwarya as a reward for being loyal to the abstract ideal of family and village. Again, the soldiering class cannot be redeemed but the middle level trader class can step up to develop those values that make the nation proud.

Narrative allergies

The diagnosis of 'a' film as reflection upon socio-political abstraction assumes much that is tenuous if consideration is not given to multiple audiences, competitive and indeterminate 'readings', unspecifiable 'authorial' intent or just plain variance of possibilities for meaning making. Images and sound arrive as assembled, jumbled, ordered disorder and are reordered and reassembled by interpretation all along the way. Responses and readerships are organized by training, context, planning, accident, time, frame, distance and so on. Some of these vectors can be iterated, and belong perhaps in the credits. Interpretation is necessarily or inevitably supplemental, though always anticipated, and more or less visible in the film apparatus, and considered in preparation by writer, director, producer, star, crew, editors, sound, publicist, critics, audience and the like – well, we can probably omit the Google-eyed film scholar from this account so as to protect them from the ignominy of being appended to such lists.

The gap between film studies and those who are complicit in a rigid, self-regarding, ontological and aesthetic contemplation and those seeking openly for a politically viable film activism is huge, and determinates hires in industry, press and academia far too much. Film schools can be demarcated into the categories, and a good indicator is the staffing, level of discussion, frequency of publication and production, or reproduction, of critique. Here there can be impressive formations, such as the one I am tracking as a critique of Global South Asia, and there can be false trails with both tendencies, I think, expressed in the impasse between Frederic Jameson and Aijaz Ahmad.

It seemed a whole generation was made uncomfortable writing about literature and film as national allegory as I have done above. Suspicious of any allegorical designation, it does nevertheless seem possible to discern a development in the national-political use of class and fear, demonstrated here in different ideological stances portrayed in the three Hindi films, and different because dated from 1948, 1971 and 2000. The films have the same name, giving some justification for shared analysis, and each follows a variant of the same story and scenography, yet each portrays a different politics of fear as a national allegory. This suggests a revision of some aspects of Ahmad's famous polemic against Jameson, not so much to defend Jameson's position, but to recognize that perhaps sometimes films *are* national allegory, or explicitly try to be, and some of Jameson's distinctions were 'speculative' and perhaps wrong. The Hindi versions of *Mela* certainly look like they are intended as national allegory at first viewing, even if perhaps they more and more exceed their intentional brief.

Ahmad's point was that Jameson had conflated a variety of literature together when saying 'all third world literature was necessarily ... national allegory' (1986: 68). The critique most powerfully centred on the presumed unity of the 'Third world' (Ahmad 1987). Before Ahmad's rejoinder, Jameson had himself acknowledged that his use of 'third world' could be criticized for 'obliterating profound differences' among countries. He meant the term as a reference to 'countries which have suffered the experience of colonialism and imperialism' (Jameson 1986: 67). When dealing with texts from such countries that specifically emerge in the representational form of the novel, Jameson states thus:

> Third-world texts, even those which are seemingly private and invested with a properly libidinal dynamic necessarily project a political dimension in the form of national allegory: the story of the private individual destiny is always an allegory of the embattled situation of the public third-world culture and society. (1986: 69)

To defend this statement by saying transposition to film texts is unwarranted is ... unwarranted, but we will get to that later. First it is worth noting that Ahmad has a case, and it relies not so much on the issue of allegory as on the distinction Jameson makes about such texts and those of 'the West'. Jameson explicitly distinguishes those texts where 'the relationship between the libidinal and the political components of individual and social experience is radically different *from what obtains in the west*' (1986: 71, my italics). I find this just as strange and as problematic as Ahmad does, but then I had already read Ahmad... and indeed Jameson, as well as Spivak who will come to this party as well soon. But why is it so strange, and yet so strangely familiar?

The familiarity has to do with a personal connection, sharing language and references and an intellectual and political commitment. So when Jameson says third world texts 'come before us ... as though already read', I thought hang on, that sounds familiar but not quite right. First thinking it was a misquote, it is worth expanding the quotation for context, and to see who's been eating my porridge, sitting in my chair, and sleeping in my bed – allegory of the bear – if the text is already read when I get it. Who is this other reader? Jameson writes:

> A popular or socially realistic third-world novel tends to come before us, not immediately, but as though already-read. We sense, between ourselves and this alien text, the presence of another reader, of the Other reader, for whom a narrative, which strikes us as conventional or naive, has a freshness of information and a social interest that we cannot share. (1986: 66)

Jameson is saying these texts come to us already mediated. The word excised in the version of this sentence used by Ahmad is 'immediately'. This carries a greater weight than usual and like Ahmad perhaps, having read Jameson a lot, I anticipated at least some of his moves[5] and was deeply surprised by others. In particular, that Jameson only seems to identify a narrower location for the other reader in his 'Third World' text even if what we have to remember is how he also sees this other reader in all texts – the always-already is generalized.

A solution to the paralysis that confronted readers of this debate is not then to steer away from terminological anxiety in discussion of the 'third world'. The dilemma Ahmad rightly identifies is not magically resolved by simply importing some other neologism – 'developing societies' is bad for dependent reasons; 'Global South' is better, but this has peculiarities to do with its geographically specificity and the bifurcation among elites and internal colonies; 'non-West' is perhaps the worst of the lot, being derivative, geographically non-specific, and of course unable to deal with Nandy's (1983) argument about the 'intimate enemy' and what happens to the Westernization of populations in the supposed non-West? Or periphery? Often underdeveloped – all hierarchical. Perhaps instead, the use of allegory can be redeemed, as applicable to all texts as mediation; if and where the interpretations are adroit enough we can see how they work and how they fall apart. We might recognize that motivations of an individual in any particular text can be understood as 'merely private' not just Western ones, but conversely, any merely private individual obsession can be read allegorically west or east, north or south, centre or periphery, local or global. What matters is the power of the interpretation. Later in the article Jameson does suggest that some 'Western' texts are also national allegory, and he quotes Deleuze and Guattari in a way that could argue the case: 'every delirium is first of all the investment of a field that is social, economic, political cultural, racial and racist, pedagogical, and religious' (Deleuze and Guattari [1972] 1983, cited in Jameson 1986: 79).

Nikos Papastergiadis approves Ahmad's criticisms of Jameson, but then also adds a critique of Ahmad's 'moralising over the difference of cultural difference' (1993: 88n), which is an elegant point that evokes the spiral to come perhaps. It is here that the point Spivak brings to the debate seems all the more important. She argues that class and nation are assumed references for both Ahmad and Jameson. Certainly if we tracked these concerns through the *Mela* films, we could see different ways such nuances become relevant. The national story is sutured together differently in 1948 than in 1971 or in 2000. Indeed, by *Mela* #2000 the village is a propaganda ideal much more than a really existing domesticated space. It is a psycho-social rite of passage that stipulates required behaviours. Where in *Mela* #1948 the necessity to sacrifice love in favour of the upkeep of orphaned children is strong, we see this give way in *Mela* #1971 to a development narrative where the tractor and farming are doggedly pursued so as to heal internal conflict and prejudices in an otherwise well-meaning village. In *Mela* #2000, the village is nominally fine, and while our heroes do not belong to the village, by defeating terrorist forces from abroad, they gain honorary villager status, though they neither farm nor bring up children. They join the village despite their clear itinerant, precarious worker and outsider positions, and their class and national ascription is not so foreign that they cannot aspire to belonging. Give or take some pop culture fantasies of stardom and the life of the road, their aspirations match any who are born of an emergent economically prosperous South Asia wanting to do well, make a 'good match', and without much hesitation, be ready to fight external terror threats to village harmony and order even if they do not live there.

To clinch the point, consider the shifting motivations of the dacoit figure in Shakti or Gujjar Singh. Whereas Shakti Singh in *Mela* #1971 is the wronged and misguided but ultimately reconciled dacoit-brother, the class ascription of Gujjar Singh as rendered in *Mela* #2000 is of an unsavoury and irredeemable terrorist sex-pest miscreant with foreign connections driven to crime through lust and greed. The context in which *Mela* #2000 depicts a 'terrorist' with rustic Islamist coding should not need to be stressed: attacks on Muslims in Gujarat, Mumbai and elsewhere across nation, region and globe, involving rape and torture, with popular prejudice repeated over and over. The didactic socialist realist message of communal reconciliation in *Mela* #1971 cannot survive into the time of *Viceroy's House*. In any case, reflecting and reversing the pogroms on screen does not totally replace the news. The codings are clear even where *Mela* need not reproduce newspaper headline type scandal. Not every commentator is fully ensconced and so somehow immune from another, rival, turn of perspective.

To identify a change of characterization as either allegorical or merely bad writing can nevertheless still signal important contextual aspects of the ideological framing of village and nation. Does it matter if the allegory is heavy-handed, unacceptably cartoonish in its stereotype, yet instructive – about precarity and aspiration – in its popular and unpopular choices? It is possible to note the relevance here of how several times Spivak has spoken about teaching literature where, with a good teacher, and with better students perhaps, there is a possibility of learning to read in a way that breaks with the certitude of unmediated authority. With Gujjar Singh so badly maligned in the later film, there might be a chance to see where to begin to unlearn the privileged arrogance of belonging to the culturally dominant, even perhaps learning how an opening to the difference that enters with a politics of interpretation which cannot be finally 'won' in certitude might be a good thing: might be 'salutary':

> When we seem to have won or lost in terms of certainties, we must, as literature teachers in the classroom, remember such warnings – let literature teach us that there are no certainties, that the process is open, and that it may be altogether salutary that it is so. (Spivak 2003: 26)

It is then also salutary, for me at least, that in not winning this debate, Jameson still can be read as providing hints about the need to 'rethink our conventional conception of the symbolic levels of a narrative (where sexuality and politics might be in homology to each other, for instance) as a set of loops or circuits which intersect and overdetermine each other' (1986: 73). Except that perhaps 'we' have moved on in regards to the 'our' here – who? – and the rethinking has been going on regardless of any imperative 'must'. Now, shift this homologous series of looping circuits – is this a disguise of the phraseology of dialectics? – to film 'texts' and the insecurity that stalled Global South Asian film criticism until Madhava Prasad's intervention, can perhaps be understood, and short-circuited. And, anyway, what if only some parts of the text – the film narrative, its image motifs, and its resolution for 'problems' – were allegorical? That *Mela* involves a number of different films cannot be unthought and removed from a history that is also not the only context in which the viewing might take heed – Ferris wheels, agricultural sub-plots, assassinations and army intrigues all give space to a range of trading stalls on a field of marketing, mixture and myth. The mela space where it comes together in multiplicity.

Crow film secrets

What if the argument about national allegory is only useful some of the time – about 10 per cent of the time, 20, 50? – and the argument about secret enjoyment is useful about 30 per cent of the time? We could split hairs or get a spreadsheet to decide. Twenty per cent to psychological drama; 17 per cent to aesthetics? Anthropologists put in bids for rite of passage and a liminal filmic plot structure. Mukhopadhyay makes a different case in consideration of Krishnakumal's travel narratives as allegories of national desire akin, but opposite, to Rousseau's *Emile* (2012: 77). Here we have the fruitful opening of another staged debate, so that solitude or solidarity becomes the frame – the contrast is Krishnakumal and Tagore – for debating the proto-national and *swadeshi* as working out of an oedipal conflict, where food, chillies, can also become a sexual taboo (Mukhopadhyay 2012: 96) – an echo of the aforementioned Adornoesque taunt that 'nothing should be moist: art becomes hygienic' (Adorno [1970] 1997: 116). If we must consider the allegorical as a generational conflict, I prefer to turn to a debate that took up a variant of the terminology used here, albeit in a fairly ferocious form. The question of allegorical purchase was to the fore in a controversial mid-1960s exchange of letters in *The Statesman*, with Satyajit Ray and Mrinal Sen trading insults over Sen's film *Akash Kusum* (1965), with additional contributions from Sen's co-writer Ashish Barman. Here 'topicality ... whatever its worth' can be social or intellectual, physical confrontation or value-judgement (Barman, 21 August 1965, reproduced in Mukhopadhyay 2009: 285). Chaplin is brought into the debate, by Sen, with the Hollywood tramp suggested as an illustration of topicality, given the poverty of the times in which the tramp emerged. Ray responds by calling *Akash Kusum* a 'crow's film', invoking the antique story of a crow who dressed up as a peacock. 'A crow's film is a crow's film is a crow's film' (Ray, 20 August 1965, reproduced in Mukhopadhyay 2009: 287). That such an image of dressing up can be dismissed by the master filmmaker and designer must surely leave no one in doubt as to why Ray and Sen thereafter rarely communicated with one another. The topicality of the film was found weak by one, defended by the other, but the debate itself still seems topical, or at least an allegory of our times and of the stakes involved in disciplinary debate.

That such debates are a struggle for prominence in a contested celebrity field should not obscure some wide political consequences. While Sen was popular for his 'internal' criticisms of the Marxist tradition, absorbed in a running debate with comrades almost as if all Bengalis had been issued manifestoes and primers on alienation or surplus value as part of their formation, the more globally famous and elite pedigree of Ray seemed to manifest in a penchant for making trouble in the 'industry'. *Pather Panchali* was described by Nargis herself as 'peddling poverty to the West' (see Gooptu 2010: 215). In mitigation, it must be recognized that the Bengali literature that Ray in part drew upon lent itself to such charges as a 'powerful storehouse of images and narratives of the rural life of Bengal' (Biswas 2006: 47). The cinematography does confirm a more mainstream affiliation, and Vasudevan points out that in *Pather Panchali,* Ray's children move 'almost mythically' through fields 'defined by textures of light' among vegetation and technology – the telegraph line, the train – that 'cannot admit of verbal communication'. Durga silences Apu, and gestures that he should listen, a 'billowing cloud of smoke emerges on the horizon' as the camera pans to catch Apu moving toward the train line (Vasudevan 2001: 57). Vasudevan points out a knowing self-irony later on in the distance shown by his characters who visit the rural from the city in *Aranyer Din Ratri* (Days and Nights in the Forest (1970, dir. Ray) – Ray himself had fled Calcutta during 'the Naxalite years' (Vasudevan 2001: 72).

Diasporic film

It is the versions of India abroad promoted in this abstracted Global South Asian media dispensation that might well deserve the kind of critique Mann seems to disavow when it is laid at the foot of diasporic film, which in her rendering has it that these productions evoke a 'a regressive Hindu nationalism-in-globalism' (2014: 494). Mann seems to prefer the trademark 'ambiguous' rendering of Nandy to the kind of critical interpretations offered by Kumar (2000, 2002), so my allegiances are split, but it is difficult to see how the crucial moment is anywhere but in that where a nostalgic exoticist version of India is defended by British force of arms. Hypocritical and inflammatory war on terror weaponry coincides with imperialist nostalgia for an all-singing, all-dancing uncomplicated exoticism we know we cannot have. If only a hybrid cinema did hold the 'potential for mediating the East-West divide both in the domain of the popular cultural and the socio-political' (Mann 2014: 495). This is where the 'vomit cut' in *Bhaji on the Beach* seems such a powerful but overlooked comment on the romance of well-meaning contact, alas a discussion lost in the subsequent rush to respectability. Worryingly, despite the glitter of *Bride* films, 'global chic' is indeed ambivalently 'godless', and not only through consumerism. Mann's discussion here though is of Indian films that locate London as a venue for celebration of the extended family underneath the cosmopolitanism of the urban middle class in India. It fits well as a foil to the domestic scenes in the versions of *Mela* considered here only if we periodize them, and so can see how the nostalgia shifts through variants of the national allegory, liminal growth, caste and class reconfiguration. Partition and longing for unity, Nehruvian agricultural and multi-community socialism, then family village Hindu nationalist ideal precariously meets external terrorist threat with politicians, families, comics and truck drivers all vying for position within the wider neo-liberal societal field. The place of the NRI film here as counterfoil seems to confirm the trajectory.

> [The] 'repackaged and retooled' 'imaginary village' (Nandy 11) is 'bound to fixed locations of home and heart' (Kumar 216), which neglect the religion-, caste-, class-, region-, and language-based schisms that have rent the Indian national fabric even (or especially) in the recent past. For the urban,

> globalized (upper) middle-class Indian viewers, there is the paradoxical portrayal of an urbanized, westernized India, that is, however, merely a veneer under which lies an imagined, deep religiosity and commitment to the Indian extended family. (Mann 2014: 495)

In *Pardes* (1997, dir. Ghai), Mann finds both an illustration of the allegorical register and all the intact arrangements for a story of family prestige as:

> an IndoAmerican businessman ... wants to arrange his son's marriage to a girl from India. But the girl, aptly and symbolically named Ganga – after the holy river Ganges and as a stand in for the nation-state, India – finds, on a visit to Los Angeles to her prospective in-laws' family, that her future husband, who has only contempt for India, wants to destroy her 'sanctity' – and that of India itself. (2014: 497).

The film includes a 'a paean once more to pre-modern, pastoral India' where the song repeats a refrain 'dusra Hindustan, dusra Hindustan'. This reiterates the phrase 'I love my India' in the next couplet and is not far away, though ever so slightly different from *Mela* #2000 where Alka Yagnik sings, while Ayub Khan lip-syncs, 'Bharat Bharat Bharat, Hamera Bharat, Tumera Bharat' at the festival for the arranged marriage of Roopa. This bucolically intimate village scene to be disrupted by attack by terrorists in a way that the stark issue of allegory need not even be mentioned. The twists and turns of the plot after the death of Ram in *Mela* #2000 deftly conjures with slapstick, deception, emotion and the desire for an outcome, so that the path of true ideology never runs smooth. The politician assassinated before Ram is effectively ignored in the film – a circumstance that in real life would be uncommon and it is the 'encounter' assassination of villagers which is usually not registered. If the explicitly political is ignored, then what can we learn from Mohan, Kanhaiya and Kishan? It is not lost on us surely that Mohan serves time unjustly imposed as his world is rendered by village backwardness; Kanhaiya fights against communalism and greed while redeeming his brother's love; Kishan and his best friend Shankar fight dacoit terrorism using only their wits and low-level commodity trade skills. Our attention is continually drawn to the ways the sons and daughters of the village morph in stages into secular nationalists, agricultural developmentalists, and finally the modern precariat, adventurer brothers who replace the upstanding soldier and are granted rewards – Shankar finds love – due to those who stay true. The ethical within the community survives even rootless mobility in the post-liberalization economy – and transportation vehicles replace the tractor that replaced farming in an economistic reading.

Markets and history

As the venue for markets and commodity exchange, mela's long history deserves separate treatment. Fairs, bazaars,[6] religious gatherings and Grand Durbars – when the Europeans came the containment of the market in the grounds of the fort or compound was a way to manage tax where previously Moghul rule had required tribute. There was always a hinterland of trade to mela, and it is not without significance that the market is the forbidden abode of romance at which the lovers escape the surveillance of parents and village. These too are the squares of public gatherings, the social movement of political communication and mobilization. While the conventions of anthropology look different from the market, no one instance of the market need be a model for the others, no revolution must follow the template of the previous, just as no one film, or three, or eight... but there is a market for Global South Asian film and television, and the commentary on all that is part of the marketing of the Global South as well.

Spirited work such as that of Neepa Majumdar (2007) that would 'complicate rather than fortify the notion of Indian film' (Desai and Dudrah 2008: 4) is once again on point here. Fortification as an enclosure of the marketplace exchange is the move of paranoid property-oriented security discourse and should be unlocked so that the cinema, and commentaries on culture more widely, can escape from state constraints and controls, from national allegorizing and chauvinistic merchandising, from regulation, however haphazard (Mazzeralla 2013) and from other containments. There are many celebrated examples – both Mani Ratnam's *Bombay* (1995) and Deepa Mehta's *Fire* (1996) could be candidates for discussion, especially where they can be contextualized alongside the creeping fascism emergent in insurgency of the type seen in the mosque destruction in Ayodhya in India, around Sinhala militancy and anti-Tamil actions in Sri Lanka, the Taliban in Afghanistan or the patricide/regicide within the ruling Shah dynasty of Nepal in 2001. While *adda* or mela might be uneasy exoticisms to smuggle as 'frames' into theoretical and political discussions of such gravity, the potential to make docile bodies 'uncomfortable' (Rajadhyaksha 2012c: 48) must be welcomed even when there is a 'transference' which reconfirms the 'abstracted spectator-position [and] reproduces the properties of the apparatus' (Rajadhyaksha 2012c: 49). The controversy over the sexual politics of *Fire* came at the beginning of a period of censorship, or Censor Board, involvement directly focused upon identitarian and communal sensibilities. Shabana Azmi's role had particular significance (Mazzarella 2013: 126). Similarly, the Censor Board examination of Mahesh Bhatt's *Zakhm* (1998) and Anand Patwardhan's *War and Peace* (2002) meant subjecting films to close scrutiny based upon communal sensibilities (see Kaur 2013 and Vasudevan 2011: 12) in ways that meant other films, say on cricket, would benefit.

Return to Rosie

Are such trade scenarios made more complicated when the context is the global parameters of diasporic film, when the representation of South Asia in Global South Asia is also an allegory of globalization, and it manifests in, at least, the two modes discussed in this book under the shorthand of terror and exotica?

> Diasporic viewers of Bollywood films are estimated at between 15 and 20 million. With some of the highest per capita incomes in their countries of residence, they contribute up to 40% of the total, current revenue of the Bombay film industry. The latter phenomenon can further be explained by the relatively low ticket prices in India as compared to the US and UK. (Mann 2014: 503)

Rajadhyaksha is somewhat nonplussed at this kind of 'hype' but finds the 'ancillary industries' that run alongside global Bollywood interesting (2008: 18). Bollywood is not co-terminus with the Indian film industry alone but rather a 'diffuse cultural conglomeration involving a range of distribution and consumption activities from websites to music cassettes, from cable to radio' as a small part of a wider phenomenon that no one has control of, can measure and really 'nobody quite knows the overall picture' (Rajadhyaksha 2008: 20). Mann herself seems more uncertainly certain, and goes on to argue that, unlike the earlier merely exotic use of London in foreign location filming, 'now NRI films reflect the *confusion* of a society in transition' (2014: 498, my italics). Mann formulates a new model to comprehend the Bollywood diaspora film's implied audience as being those that aspire to a wealthy middle-class lifestyle, who access the trappings of a Westernized life, but with values derived from a version of South Asian 'culture' (Mann 2014: 498). The Global South Asia named here would include homelands, travelling, diasporic and settler filmmakers of all stripes.

Global South Asian film and television studies here then operate with a range of perspectives and themes that could, for the purposes of experiment, be placed within the allegorical orbit of multiplicity and at least mark out a relation to a slightly more complicated tracking of historical developments. Without getting into the rights and wrongs of this move, reassessment of themes allows a summary. This would necessarily include the allegorical, as discussed, but perhaps just as powerful is the shift from 'high nationalism' to decolonizing psychological with studies like those of Nandy (1998: 18). In the return and realization, if not culmination, of ideology critique enabled by work of Madhava Prasad and those he released, or unleashed, openings like the *Journal of the Moving Image* at Jadavpur and the consolidation of cultural studies at Bangalore show what has begun. Work in the United Kingdom on diasporic film (see Kaur and Sinha 2005, bibliography in Dudrah 2012) also includes new ethnographic studies on venues, distribution, the extension of culture through family, financially driven migration and multiplying technological formats, but thus far this work still awaits mainstream influence with the disciplines or on production. By its nature, marginal cultural production does not command mainstream resources or airtime, despite heightened scope for innovation beyond the constraints of otherwise ordered frames. The time for change may be nigh however, as cross-border financing demands cross-border concepts (Caton 1999). Rajadhyaksha notes the efforts to get NRI investor support for Bollywood films as having a context where, 'at the back of it all there was the more complex political issue ... of the Indian state itself negotiating a transition from an earlier era of decolonization and "high nationalism" to the newer times of globalization and finance capital' (2008: 29).[7] He argues that if we saw 'the cinema as the suturing agency par excellence' of all 'displacement and mediation' (Rajadhyaksha 2008: 33) of national or geopolitical direction-setting, then alignments of film and television with the interests of corporate endeavour comes into focus. Which is not to say that all plotting is in the grip of state policy and national allegory, since the assumption of control of all aspects of a narrative in the interests of policy can never match up with the convolutions of family drama – melodrama must have its way – even as it makes little difference when chaos too is a policy experiment, as it is with the facilitation of terror and fear.

We can see some of the politics of this played out when Rafi from *Sammy and Rosie* escapes Pakistan with his loot – 'my life is in danger there'; he arrives with his corrupt fortune and commandeered assets ready to transfer to Sammy and Rosie if they will give him a grandchild. He is not the feted but ineffectual politico assassinated in the opening scene of *Mela* #2000, but he might have been the sort of figure that would send and underling in his place. Corrupt and calculating, Rafi can be seen as an update on the controlling, but misguided panchayat leader of the earlier *Mela* #1971, but more significant for any character substitution game between films like this would be to speculate on the appearance of Rosie as similarly placed as the sister of Ram – Roopa must step up and fight. Rosie never needed an AK 47 to fight, but her world had not been threatened and undermined in quite the same way as had that of Roopa in *Mela* #2000.This would be to expect too much of Rosie and her strengths lie elsewhere as she is on the spot to comfort and care for Sammy in her own loving way. To posit a difference between Rosie/diasporic film and Roopa or Kishan's Westernized aspiration may be too easy. The argument is not clinched merely by citing Moore-Gilbert's book on Kureishi to repeat the point about links between the actors in Kureishi's stories and Raj revival cinema, for example, Saied Jaffrey, Roshan Seth (2001: 73) and take Kureishi's word for it that his was not the sort of 'lavish' film set in an 'exotic' location that the revival films were. These films may well share more than the same target audience. Roshan Seth also appears in the Arundhati Roy-written film *In Which Annie Gives It Those Ones* (1989, dir. Krishen) as well as *Indian Summers* and in the Kureishi-written *The Buddha of Suburbia* (book 1990, film 1993). Nisha Naya, of the vomit cut scene in *Bhaji* was also in *Buddha of Suburbia*; Naveen Andrews in *Bhuddha, Wild West* and several significant period features; and the star of *Lagaan*, Aamir Khan also features in *Mangal Pandey* and is Kishan in *Mela* #2000. Om Puri was in almost everything before his much lamented passing in 2017. A register of the narrowcasting of actor types across genres is not just coincidence.

It is possible to comprehend melodrama as the narrativization of coincidence and mastery of chance (Rai 2009: 180). In between anxiety of the future and inevitability of tragedy in each edition of *Mela*, might we identify the emergent varieties of hope and hype that may be embodied in screen bodies as they obey national, communal and neo-liberal projections? This should not suggest a 'linear-causal relation to consciousness and identity' in the representational frame of cinematic narrative (Rai 2009: 3) but must recognize the 'patterning' of pleasures that cinema and television in their different ways circulate and reinterpret, especially in remakes and re-imaginings of previously popular motifs. Rai's ethnography provides thick material for thinking through this patterning especially where he understands Global South Asian cultural production as a place of unanticipated futures, where – in a usefully awkward phrasing – 'futurity combines, unmediated, with pastness, where outsides are infolded and sadness is happy (happy because the press to action and expression is life)' (Rai 2009: 137). Unpacking the terms leaves the emotional charge of *Mela* #1948 as so much more affective than the autonomist future of *Mela* #2000. It is the suicide tragedy of Nargis and Dilip Kumar united forever that stains the screen.

Border references

It is tempting to complain that this abundance of material, in colour, illuminates our now somehow less luminous lives of black and white. I don't mean just this however, even if the slow work of textual scholarship seems to occupy a tonal register several shades below the technicolour charm of the screen. The varieties of *Mela* were tracked because they offered a possible alternative path to cosmopolitan conviviality. This made it plausible to follow guidance from scholars of Global South Asian film such as Dissanayake, who in three steps could be read as directing attention first to 'cinema's overt participation' in politics (2003: 216). Then a 'second area of investigation ... is the interplay between globalism and localism' (Dissanayake 2003: 216). And then the suggestion that 'a useful way of coming to grips with the local global dialectic is through an examination of the production of newer localities ... to focus on the production of the local and its ever changing contours in response to the demands of the global. [Though] the local is hardly static' (Dissanayake 2003: 217).

These three steps could help unpack another mela scene in a film already mentioned earlier (in Chapter 1). *Pinjar* (2003), about ninety minutes in, offers a mela sequence with Ferris wheels and the usual celebrations, but this time closely intercut with tense scenes of the kidnapped Hindu heroine Paru going through a miscarriage, surrounded by – caring – Muslim women and a midwife. This is an explicit allegorical intervention into politics which uses the Ramayana story of Sita and foregrounds locally specific but tragically generalizable aspects of partition as a miscarriage of justice. The storm here is not nature, but the brutality of attacks of Muslims on Hindus and Hindus on Muslims. More than the rite of passage that the mela interrupted usually can be, here the film addresses issues of violence and its consequences for women, men, families and communities, including affective states of fear, as well as recognition, reconciliation, revenge and restitution. As such it has local and global relevance and does this in a way that shifts from previous partition films – and is different from *Viceroy's House especially* – by locating the necessary scene of reconciliation at the border. The film makes a great effort to avoid blaming one side more than the other, overcooking attributions of blame or overcompensating to show kidnappers as saints or demons. Although the Hindu kidnappers in the specific story committed their crime two generations past, they are of a type with some rather brutal contemporary Hindus who remain in the Pakistani village, where Paru is kept at first against her will by the Shah family.

Sometimes a deep appreciation of a single scene can tell more. Degrees of subjectivity no doubt apply, but demarcation variables are so many – class, caste, region, age, gender, faith, time – that no one should pretend authority. As Banaji poses the problem: 'who can say exactly what meanings' films have? (2006: 13). Mela is a festive event that can be derailed by storms or allegorical malevolent forces, depending on interpretation. In most instances, the traumatic event inaugurated by the mela crisis is a necessary call, demanding a response that would otherwise not have come. Resignation, repetition and resilience of a cyclical formation are symbolized by the Ferris wheel and merry-go-round, with metaphysical considerations that do not need to be spelled out. The mela acknowledges the multiplicity of life as interpreted by each of us for good or bad. A plurality of interpretations make up the whole, kept in mind as an ethical call to empathy with others.

Global South Asia is neither hybrid nor authentic or inauthentic; it does not contrast diasporic films with national allegory nor world cinema with selective interpretive chance even if the destabilization of certitude in interpretation at least means it might be possible to move via diaspora and vernacular globalisms towards an internationalist cultural studies. This would include theory-production within Asia not as afterthought or corrective but as starting point for global debates alongside the parochial US and UK academies and their recent pasts. Spending time explaining that something other than national allegory is going on in films too often becomes a necessary prelude. Of course a woman, a village, a vehicle, a fairground ride or a boat is not the nation, or not always.

At the border, questions of national allegory seem less compelling, regardless of whether Jameson's case is convincing in part or in whole, when viewed from a perspective that disavows or otherwise exceeds the national or the protocols of reference to a national research programme are undone. If the requirement to report back to the authorities is unmoored from the national, what then for evocations in literary or filmic texts where the coordinates of possible resistance and militant action for revolutionary change can be tracked in a new dispensation? Even tracking the image and plotting of street protests must look different if the map offers other scales of interpretation and other staging posts, new points of reference and desire for aesthetic experimentation, open access distribution of knowledge and a wild promiscuity of interpretation.

Global South

This is why the scholarship emergent from Global South Asian film and television studies is the kind of festival I want to join because it begins to articulate something that can shift, through critique, the dominant representations. This shift is not just away from Hollywood as the reference for film, or New York, Washington, London, Paris, Berlin as the centre for news, but also an escape from polite activism talk of ontology and effete disciplinary posturing, none of which can contend with how Global South

Asia can be read against the dominant at all. Through this book the dominant normalized interpretive grain was under reconstruction, or transformation at least of its terms. If the melas multiply in this chapter, concede at least that the interpretive scheme of burning books and brides gave up a register where some melas were more progressive than others. Global South Asia can be progressive or deceptive, and in practices of interpretation as regionalism with global aspirations, meaning becomes a universal time slot and classifications are up for grabs. My view, inspired by the critical studies assembled which deal with Global South Asia, is that a break with the practices and stereotypes of the dominant is possible only if struggles for justice, reparations, anti-war mobilizations and progressive movements everywhere are sufficiently informed to begin with, attend to, and embrace what can be learnt from the Global South at its best. Another world is possible, informed by Global South Asia. This is where Prashad can come in again, speaking of Global South but not with a capital 'G':

> The 'global South' has come to refer to this concatenation of protests against the theft of the commons, against the theft of human dignity and rights, against the undermining of democratic institutions and the promises of modernity. The global South is this: a world of protest, a whirlwind of creative activity. These protests have produced an opening that has no easily definable political direction. Some of them turn backwards, taking refuge in imagined unities of the past or in the divine realm. Others are merely defensive, seeking to survive in the present. And yet others find the present intolerable, and nudge us into the future. (Prashad 2012: 9)

I want to endorse this sentiment with more than a nudge for the future. It is important to put the battle for commons up front, and this must come before too-easily manipulated dignity and rights talk and support of 'democratic institutions', which are to be critically distinguished from lobbyist-saturated elections and vote block purchasing. Instead, a dialectical approach. Too often Global South has slipped from the grasp of a progressive tradition that can claim both heritage and resilience to instead refer uncritically to any destabilization of Western hegemony, even if it is rampantly capitalist, right wing, death squad jihadist or Hindutva chauvinism. There are also soft power versions of the same, and it is possible to almost, but not quite, endorse the triumphalist tone of those who greet China's economic rise as banner headline news.

For example, focused intently upon China, in *Adam Smith in Beijing*, Giovanni Arrighi writes primarily of the economic rise of the Global South even when acknowledging, via Samir Amin, a political movement as the foundation for secure economic advance – where the 'revolutionary tradition had endowed China's subaltern strata with a self-confidence and combativeness with few parallels elsewhere' (Arrighi 2007: 376, Amin 2005). He also writes favourably of the then Indian Prime Minister Manmohan Singh and the prospects for redeployment of surplus towards Southern emancipation – where 'stunning' conditions now exist that are 'more favourable than ever before for a new Bandung to bring into existence the commonwealth of civilizations that [Adam] Smith envisioned long ago' (Arrighi 2007: 384). Recall that Manmohan Singh had identified the Maoist threat as the subcontinent's biggest problem, perhaps overlooking Kashmir. But Arrighi travels to Beijing not with Mao, or on a delegation with Singh, but with Adam Smith as guide, and for sure it is the case that an economically robust Global South holds some promise and some funds, even as for Arrighi there are limits and no possibility for two large nations to live with the consumer lifestyle of the United States without choking themselves and everyone else: 'China's rapid economic growth has not yet opened up for itself and the world an ecologically sustainable developmental path' (Arrighi 2007: 389). That an update of Adam Smith offers no prospect of a Bandung-like alternative to Capitalist domination should be evident so long as the political mobilization of Global South Asia is captured in the pincers of corporate media and the terror war.

What remains to be seen however is whether a Global South as social and political movement capable of defeating the chaos policy of West's last hysterical gamble might lead to a different unity of the world movement. One that acknowledges the politics of representation that the Global South has as track record, since the marginalization of the Soviets, the Leninists, the Comintern, the Maoists and indeed Bandung, right up to the social movements discussed by Prashad, the social forums, alter-globalization, squares, Occupy movements and environmentalism – these might activate a genuine non-alignment with capital. But this is also something for deep discussion, and if the demonization of the Global South and Global South Asia under the sign of terror has shown anything, it is that the West is willing to use every dirty trick in the book of orientalism to secure its exclusive privileges. That such trick books are increasingly transparent now requires a still greater political organization, and a non-alignment of Global South Asian scholarship which can turn such kinderfables into the exposed bias of so much ancient history. Arrighi's somewhat breathless enthusiasm smacks of other recent bouts of creativity, whirlwinds of hope and faith in trade deals. As the date of Prashad's paean to the social movements perhaps also betrays,[8] the vicious rolling back of the so-called Arab Spring into 'Libyan winter' and worse, to adopt Prashad's term for what Chandan more aggressively and aptly calls the

'Arab sting' (Chandan 2015) leaves no reason to think there is an easy passage through the struggle against capitalism with tanks.

Even after fifteen years of terror war however, the Global South still comes with a leadership and organized social movements to articulate these sentiments, the ones also found in the representations of revolutionaries, militants, Maoists and those who battle oppression and exploitation wherever they see it. This means there can also be a cultural wing, supporting those resisting capitalist subsumption, multiplying those resistances, and seeking free expression, indeed freedom, while maintaining the happy disposition of celebratory communities of struggle and social conviviality as a component of reproducing revolution... well, that is a Global South Asian media studies I think we desperately need. Gandu can do the soundtrack. Crucial however is not to be taken in by the global in its propaganda mode of universalized and diasporized middle-class modernity and the signs of shiny development than manifest as chain stores, coffee house art gallery bookstores and mega-shopping malls. These of course exist, populated by multiple desi punters, latte drinking coconuts, radish, mango smoothies, health foods faddists, Bikram yogis, and all the vast variety of cosmopolitan conviviality we must nonetheless applaud as a first step of visibility, but where the uniform streamlining of monolithic globalization obscures the unequal economic and social foundations upon which the new genial urban, the post-Thatcherite updated neo-liberal urban, is built. Arrest under Prevent, Homeland or SUS is just around every street corner at constant CCTV command. Other globalizations do exist alongside plastic fascist modernity, but they contend with a well-entrenched and extensively exploited world of migrant forms of indenture, contract and remittance. The registers of different Global South Asias circulate differently, as sophisticated literary and art film forums, within film festivals embedded with in more public kinds of meetings, in melas and mobilizations, contested street level exoticisms, scamming through the trinket markets across the backpacker banana-pancake trail as tourisms become war-torn locations of desperation and flight needs must be towards economic restitution, so much owed over generations, owed what was stolen, plunder demands repayment, debt declared, battles shared, there is no one that doesn't really know its time to come to terms.

6

Conclusions and Further Viewing

This work explores variations of a hesitant conception of a Global South Asia. This means an interwoven – co-constituted, perhaps repetitive – analysis of the different yet simultaneous ways in which the phrase may have meaning:

- first, commercial culture industry, multiplex and satellite channel, time slot distribution and production for type, the largest film industry, saturation television, ubiquitous screens and thriving regionality;
- second, negative demonizing, hostile and racist stereotyping with extreme prejudice accelerated by the war on terror and the boom in arms trade;
- third, potential and transformative Asian turn, or return, for the former colonizing countries, driven by migration and settlement of diasporas;
- fourth, diverse vernacular globalizations, take up of Bollywood in all corners of the world, success of film export via festivals and video distributors;
- five, vernacular globalization as migrant class politics universalized from below and by necessity, bringing 'we are here because you were there' into practical co-constitutive multisite attention;
- six, mythic, religious, fantastical exoticist redeployment of a sea of stories archive in new formats.

So many avatars, yet for some time work on music and film has moved beyond boundaries and conceptions of discrete national, ethnic, stylistic or aesthetic communities and genres to consider transnational and global connectivities. This has meant renewed interest in the production and circulation of ideas and creative cultural expression, dating perhaps from Gilroy's influential book *The Black Atlantic: Modernity and Double Consciousness* (1993), but also reacting critically to the comforting cosmopolitanisms of elite privilege, putting a sharp political focus into play within the humanities, musicology, film studies, anthropology, human geography and cultural studies.

The director's cut – edited

To conclude this work, I have taken time to go over again some of the topics and films discussed in this book, suggesting other films and adding an evaluation and sometimes a new perspective on what has been achieved. The format here at first follows the chapters of the book, but the point is not simply to reproduce or repeat, rather to set out why these examples were important and what examining them now might mean for the notion of Global South Asia. It will then come as no surprise that considerable space is given to justifications of the approach and possible wider significances. A demonstration and speculative commentary on diverse possibilities serves in lieu of a conclusion to the conclusion. This becomes almost aphoristic on purpose since the ambition is really to suggest further reading and give enthusiastic recommendations for viewing. No assessment of the pleasures that such viewing entails is given here, but it should certainly be assumed as obvious, and I hope will lead to action that is not just sitting on the couch or in the dark, but that too.

Whatever the circumstances, I do think 'we' all could learn more through films. If there were ready access materials to screen for youth, and young at heart, or even those who like to watch, the inspiration could be contagious. This would mean making new films too – for example, there could be films about Global South Asian diaspora organizations that offer inspiration and tactical lessons – the Asian Youth Movements would make for great screenplays (see Ramamurthy 2013), or a biographical feature on the first Communist member of the British parliament, a Parsi in the 1930s called Saklatvala (Wadsworth 1998). The backroom story of the Communist Party of Great Britain and the career of its long-time leader Rajani Palme-Dutt would be the biopic we need – call it *CPGB Masala* – the factional fights would be high drama (Callaghan 1993). Instead of family romances about the Mountbattens, a global rerelease of the partition films of Ritwik Ghatak would be compulsory viewing – pristine prints please. Accompanying this, the Calcutta trilogy of Mrinal Sen would discuss, critically, the Naxalite and Maoist adventure in Bengal in the 1970s. Alongside many others, the films of Mokammel in Bangladesh must screen. In particular audiences can learn from the commentaries in cinema and documentary on the struggle for Bangladesh, for example from John Hood's *The Bleeding Lotus: Notions of Nation in Bangladeshi Cinema* (2015).

Necessary films from Bangladesh

It is worth seeking out the films. Hood's useful book tracks a bloody and violent history, from Zahir Raihan's *Stop Genocide* (1971), Tareque and Catherine Masud's *Ontorjatra* (2006) through to Nasiruddin Yousuff's *Guerrilla* (2011), all in the context of an extended commentary on Tanvir Mokammel's three-hour documentary *1971* (2011). An elegiac annotation of the horrors of partition, featuring a cast of grotesque characters, if they can be so described, including the rapist Pakistani military, the bloated bodies of murdered women, groups of dead children in a screen violence perhaps unprecedented, and in horrific witness: 'deeply moving, powerful visuals' (Hood 2015: 75).

The problem of circuits infects film distribution as it does publishing or politics, imposing a hierarchy of visibility and voices according to who shouts loudest with which speaker system. Distribution costs money or favours and without vast resources, sensation and political intrigue substitute for worth. Thus it can be that the most widely viewed documentary 'evidence' of the Pakistani army atrocities in the Bangladesh freedom struggle is a film that owed its international renown to a cross-border intrigue by someone previously not much into the business of facilitating film reviews. As Hood argues in discussion of Zahir Raihan's *Stop Genocide*:

> Released even before the war was over [this] was perhaps the earliest cinematic expression of a people's aspiration for freedom in the face of an occupation army's inhuman barbarity. Prime Minister Indira Gandhi bought the film rights and had it distributed around the world to project the excesses of the Pakistani military [and so] to justify the Indian intervention. (2015: 17)

Never before had a twenty-minute film found such unlikely international backing, as Indira also used the cover of the war intervention to quash urban Naxals at home. It is then not without irony that *Stop Genocide* begins with a quote from Lenin and a refrain from 'The Internationale', before shadows of palms and the sound of marching boots, barking dogs and gunfire. Lines of refugees – stop – close-ups of hungry faces and wide abject eyes – stop – the return of revolutionary anthem as a pleading dirge at the end smears misery across the screen, exceeded only with a reference to Auschwitz – stop, Stop, STOP Genocide across the final frames.

What further circulates, however, is the globally distributed image of Bangladesh as a space of trauma, supported in turn by the indubitably well-meaning and necessary 'Concert for Bangladesh', starring George Harrison and Ravi Shankar. The concert must be welcomed, but it is also true that abject nationhood sells. In the hands of philanthropic friends, the contrast could not be greater if the opening sequence of Morshedul Islam's *Khalaghar* (2006) were taken to illustrate the dual tendencies of more recent times:

> The setting is a lush and dense tract of riverbank. The camera focuses on a boat coming along the relatively narrow and secluded stretch of the river. Other than the boatman nothing comes into view; the only other sound than the splash of water by the moving punt is a gentle twittering of birds. It is a truly idyllic scene, which lasts for just about two minutes before the boatman draws to the bank under the cover of low over-hanging branches and in scary silence six young men emerge from the jungle behind the camera to meet the boat. Without a word the boatman proceeds to unload a cargo of arms, passing out guns to the men on the bank. Not a word is spoken. (Hood 2015: 122–123)

Reflections in the water play an important role in the sequence, ripples and shimmering in the image, the youth collecting the guns framed under the tree, before a bell rhythm introduces the opening credits. It is a full five and a half minutes before a word is spoken, when the teacher is informed of news about the fight for freedom. The idyll contrasts with an indication of the guerrilla war. Hood is right to double up on noting that words are unnecessary for the effect. Bangladesh, like Nepal, Sri Lanka and Afghanistan are rendered as paradise with violence; only sand, dust, mountains, or swollen rivers are interchangeable, and these stereotyped images, along with the all-singing, all-dancing Bollywood ready reckoner, circle the globe. Partition horrors, the emergency and the pogroms dull the tune. Of course other images and critiques of stereotypes are possible. A counter-narrative is found in Humayan Ahmed's *Shyambol Chhaya* (2004) where towards the end the Bengali freedom fighters approach a Pakistani army post disguised as musicians, who, when they get close enough, 'exchange their instruments for guns and grenades' (Hood 2015: 140).

Sammy and Rosie get laid again

The Pakistani military do not come out of this portrayal well, but that should only make us recall the taxi driver in *Sammy and Rosie Get Laid.* No doubt, those who do not know of it should educate ourselves as to the politics of Bangladesh's emergence and the role of torturers like Rafi Rahman. Rafi is accused of, and fleeing from, crimes he had been party to as a government minister in Pakistan. Is awareness of the torture and violence that appears in London in the form of the taxi driver the only responsibility viewers have to respond to the geopolitics of Global South Asia? The moves of documentary and feature film are of course different, and *Sammy and Rosie* is after all meant as entertainment, but pointing out violence does not necessarily repair the damage. In another context, but relevant here, Sanjay and Ash Sharma show that 'identifying white paranoia does not necessarily undo its agency or violence' (2003: 2). The reverse might not always be true. Rosie's guilt is not greater than Rafi's, though Rosie, despite always doing care work, is the representative in the new generation of white privilege and she gets off scot free, loving both Victoria and Sammy as she glides past any guilt of Empire in a multicultural embrace; meanwhile Rafi dies, the squatted camp is destroyed, but the terror and Rosie's credibility remains. The 'need for Europe to seriously consider the imperialist damage it inflicted around the globe' (Chen 2010: 266) cannot be addressed.

The point of discussing the contradictions of the position of Rosie in Kureishi's work is not to find despair in the predicament of the Left in the United Kingdom. It may seem so, with Thatcherism made out to be almost polite in retrospect after the war on terror, Blair, Cameron, May and the massive arms trade, chaos and return to even more vicious imperialism are on display today. The nostalgic view of Kureishi's work cannot be sustained, even as Desai appreciates it greatly:

> In *Sammy and Rosie Get Laid,* the city of London still remains that site of oppressions and possibilities. It is in the interstitial spaces of the city that Kureishi locates the successful and failed resistances to exploitation, racism, marginalization, and state violence (both of the postcolonial nation-state and the metropolitan nation-state). The film interweaves the lives of Sammy (a hedonistic Asian Brit whose father has returned to London from Pakistan) and Rosie (Sammy's wife and a liberal white social worker) into the network of lives in the communities around them. Its dystopic view of Thatcher's England is similar to that of *My Beautiful Laundrette* but is painted in darker hues. (2004: 57)

It is in reference to the earlier film that Andrew Hammond stresses the importance of the character of Papa, a kind of alter ego of Rafi, only pickled in vodka and self-exiled in his expatriate bed:

> *My Beautiful Laundrette* dramatises, through the character of Papa, the increasingly depleted status of the left during the struggles of the Thatcher era. Emerging from a 'rich and powerful' family this 'leftist communist Pakistani' ... had been a well-known journalist in Bombay, a popular cohort of politicians and a personal friend of Bhutto ... he believes [he] can challenge global capitalism, as well as by his advocacy of education as a tool for political transformation, emphasising the necessity of 'knowledge ... to see clearly what's being done and to whom in this country.' (2007: 235–236).

Sammy is somehow Papa's child too, a degraded version of Omar from *Laundrette*. In one scene Sammy is 'the perfect example of the excesses of capitalist consumption as he masturbates to porn while listening to music and consuming fast food burgers and cocaine' (Desai 2004: 58). Is Sammy hedonism, or a realistic deflated Omar? Without presuming any instruction or injunction, we might just watch the films, even if familiarity won't necessarily solve the world's economic race or political problems, any improving educational contemplative effort trumps the usual myopia. If we learn anything from the later fuck sandwich influenced by Bollywood it is that this influence matters as co-constitution of a significant trans-dimension. It does not make sense to consider diasporic film or existence in isolation from any of its influences in British, diasporic Asian, mainstream Hollywood or South Asian Bollywood, Third film, new directors or world cinema – whatever flawed concept that would be. In the same way someone might make a critique of world music. East and West are co-constituted in these figures as they embrace.

Thus, in the discussion of *The Satanic Verses* and his subsequent career, it is possible to recognize how Rushdie had held commonly considered progressive views up until the publication of that book – for example, his narrative on Nicaragua, his comments on colonialism, even if Nandy had said that the interesting thing about Rushdie was his unconscious, not his narrative prose (reported comment to Don Miller, personal communication). However, Rushdie certainly traded his progressive politics for celebrity marriage and turned to the warmongers' side in a series of ever-more shrill affirmations of military muscular secularism, while in contrast Kureishi tries to mediate between fundamentalism and the secular sentiment of a progressive intellectual Left. The problem with Kureishi, in turn, is that he can only do so as an individual because the Left collapsed under the weight of a sectarian factionalism that is the operational mode of most Trotskyite groups in the United Kingdom. This is where any collective campaign that emerged organically was, when it reached a certain level of media notice, then joined by opportunist Trotskyite cadre who worked to recruit the advanced activists and then closed down the specific campaign in favour of longer-term concentration on building their own factional brand. Of course this was short-sighted, and the decimation of content left only a cynical shell of fractional survivors, and a far larger rump of people who had left political groups or learnt through bitter experience the lesson of staying somewhat apart. The possibility of organizing within such a space was hampered also by unacknowledged privilege held in certain speaking places, and identitarian egotism. Local scale community work survived, but the bleak context meant those in the diaspora with a strong Left political formation were only able to operate without explicit acknowledgement of their effort, remaining, for various reasons, invisible to the host community among whom they settled. A difficult arrival in terms of labour relations, and migration itself often occasioned by political difficulties at home, meant that a level of political involvement within the first generations of migration was honed in the necessities of anti-racist struggles despite unwelcoming reception into the labour movement and/or the complexities of exile, economic and political. This was sustained in the face of white Left opportunism and subsequent drift, such that the later generations might not articulate this heritage in ways obvious to sociologists and ethnic studies scholars but it is not surprising that it can then be recognized, for example, in the figure of Kureishi's portrait of Papa in *My Beautiful Launderette* and his endearing care for Omar, despite Omar's ultimate degradation as a parliamentarian many years later.

Pages on partition

Perhaps each stage of this book is an example of the embattled political character of Global South Asia as it makes a major turn towards saturation media. This in turn invokes the possibility of turning that media back again to politics through recognizing that the Global South did not so much go away as get mediatized as a survival strategy – in piracy, in people's media – which must now be reincarnated. That it cannot yet be recognized as such has to do with individual agency as a dominant trope, as opposed to collective and organized solidarities nurtured by an active Left.

In the *Viceroy's House*, it might feel unseemly to insist upon more significant scholarship in partition – Butalia (2000) and Pandey (2002), again – but there is a responsibility to speak up for an elderly relative who just cannot hear what you are saying. The extent of Chadha's reading of partition literature is not clear, but that literature is so extensive that surely no one can read it all. Oral history, memory recovery, diplomacy, strategic intransigence, the interpretive divisions are as significant now as ever, the rifts harder to heal, the attempts to do so impressive. If a director chooses the dangerous path of personal or family heritage, as with all heritage projects there is a risk that any pristine originary moment is cleansed of lived experience and the fraying and messy fabric of contradictory textures disturbs and destroys any more nuanced possibility. Yet respect, as the commentary on Global South Asian film and television proliferates, it does become possible and perhaps necessary to speculate – wildly – about new theoretical frames. Political evaluations for an alternate global imaginary, a radical challenge to national and regional fidelity seek out a reconciliation between long lost brothers given over on the one side to the law, the other to dacoitry. Without reifying identity politics above class struggle, a challenge to the dominance of the Hindi language film channels is achieved through a reconfigured diaspora, as a time slot rather than dispersed space.

The Satanic Verses was burnt for the cameras in time for the evening news. Maybe this can be seen as a repeat screening of that night with the Nazis, if the uniforms were different, the event articulated as an emergent street politics that morphed within not so many years into terror-anxiety induced general fear. What it also was, before being distorted in the coded debates of freedom and fries, was an attempt to challenge the terms and terrain of a debate in which some protagonists had not had the chance of having their say being heard and considered. Debated even. It was something not too far from a sentiment along these lines that inspired Ambedkar to burn the Hindu book of laws of Manu, the *Manu Smruti* on 25 December 1927. Book-burning, burning down the television transmitter in the Himalayas, the staged protest of Bangladeshi booksellers against assassinations can be an intervention of knowledge. The Lama who instructs Bill Murray knows it, the Taliban know it, the CIA are fully aware of the power of burning books – squeamishness about such acts is only left for those not able to defend knowledge and books as a resource. Not as prizes or ornaments, though of course books also furnish a room and have an important and necessary display function to be indulged – but questions of participation and democratization in knowledge production require a political intervention. The transformatory event of reading for enlightenment even as staged awakening does not reside in the books or the films by themselves, but requires an agent, a reader of viewer, audiences themselves.

What perhaps the tourist and terrorist (Phipps 1999: 74) version of Global South Asia can never get – as Michael Palin flies in from on high – is that the burning of books or of studios is not only what it appears on the surface, a media stunt. Rather, it is dark and due recognition that convergence places the ideological firmly in the centre of a life mediated by technologies of the image. Palin is both the old master of this, and apparently the least aware of its pervasive power, possibly because his non-threatening avuncular production has meant a fairly free ride through television and cinema as convergence has moved from the days of Python through religious comedy to travel narratives. The book that is burnt in Bradford does not signal retrograde religious conservatism, though it surely was that in part, it also announces the fact that even the traditional is a saturated multi-platform mediatized reality. Any manifestation of God or Gods today comes via satellite and any profiled feature on Asia, Islam or Hinduism that is promotional as well as demonizing is digitally delivered.

Nostalgia or Mao

The presentation of South Asia to the world from on high in the mode of quirky nostalgia gives us a hill retreat Shimla versioning of the Raj, suffused with eccentricity marinated in Gin and Tonic or Tom Collins at the station club in *Indian Summers*. The distance to the rural terror of Maoists or timeless tribals, unwashed peasantry or other globally circulating clichés in the vaguest contours is part of the off-colour charm. In his documentary on the Himalayas, Palin is the lovely end of the British State, a friend of Gurkhas and Lamas – as is Joanna Lumley, still in 'posh Rosie' character – but Palin was unable to even find the Maoists, which is something any regular visitor to Nepal can do without much effort.

What is a comedian to do in this day and age when remaking travel narratives in a style that worked so well in Africa by train, or for Phileas Fogg, no longer deserves serious attention and recipe books sell better? Is even having the leisure to ask this question not exercising a popular aspirational colonial and bourgeois ambition that had been held in hock for his retirement years? The channelling of a celebrity format lacks no sincerity, national treasure after all, but did no one on the set bother to have a word with the Python as he seemingly without effort replicated the gauche arrogance of the colonial relation as if channelling the Empire at will? Palin might not be cut out to be the celebrity cine-star of a type that might seem reminiscent of the South Indian variety diagnosed by Madhava Prasad (2014a), but with more slapstick and ultimately of a kind with Mountbattenesque discombobulated apologies for a romantic Raj of kippers and Darjeeling tea. It is also relatively inexpensive televisual production, not quite reality TV or sport, but getting a camera in front of the 'action' in travel is logistically convenient and a well-worn format. The real problem is that it occupies prime-time space and resources that could surely be put to better use than defending complacent Raj-era tourism. Perhaps it is not the case that documentaries by Anand Patwardhan can be run back to back on mainstream television stations – but why not? – anecdotal evidence suggests at least with the availability of handy-cams and mobile phone video, the imperative of a proxy colonial tour in the hands of Palin is less pressing. The promised democratization of media presentation has not broken with the brand-name presenter game as yet, but there are those like Zimmerman who think 'transnationalization and alterations in national culture threaten independent documentary [as] new consumer technologies such as camcorders, digital imaging systems, and computers offer hope for democratization of access to production and for specification of cultural difference' (2000: xxi). It was not handy-cam that displaced critical documentary as much as exoticist mush masquerading as cultural insight. NDTV's 'Big Fight' is not any different (Mehta 2008: 8). While a few instances of award ceremony promotion of new talents alongside word of mouth viral success can be listed, it is more likely that similar to music industry digitization, the result of new technologies in film distribution will be that there will be space for only a few of the perennial big band names to tour and make money, the rest will struggle on in obscurity, with rather less chance of a breakthrough 'hit'. John Pilger is still around, though any comparison between him and an aging rock god is insulting to both. Zimmerman hopes for a proliferation of the ways people might 'reimagine and reclaim public space ... create alliances ... expose ... layers of contradictions ... [and] ... unsettle the gloom ... [with] ... a new dialectics' (2000: xxiii). Any alternative to Palin or Pilger would have to work against forces that seek to amputate and quarantine independent documentary in favour only of 'entertainment programmes produced by massive media transnational' (Zimmerman 2000: 4). Palin's affable man is the spokesperson for Fake News from Nepal in a handicrafted exoticist slapstick, a trinketizing souvenir cinema not far below the depths of dire alongside development videos or a city what's on airplane arrival feature.

The electronic palanquin over Everest

The emergence of Global South Asia then is not mapped by some comprehensive statistical accounting and comparison of films released globally or in global cinema chains – though laments at lack of recognition of the sheer volume of film releases can be found in many (most?) essays on Bollywood. Instead, the point perhaps is to track the influence of Global South Asia as a patchwork of cross-hatched reference in much else that is 'global': from the displaced 'Indians' that Columbus assumed were from

South Asia because they wore colourful cloth, to the very reasons why Palin would conceive of a colonial era touristic remake in the Himalayas. A huge array of research materials are then opened up, from Rajadhyaksha's much cited notice of the Selfridges refit, to the Karma Kabs taxi service plying the London streets in the early 2000s (see Graversen's documentary *Exotic India*, 2000) or in Melbourne the *Tramjatra* by Mick Douglas (2005).

Flying over Everest, Palin's electronic palanquin has become an isolated atomized microlite, detached from the remote control crusading Raj of drone strikes, which it nevertheless anticipates. Arriving just one step up from the situation room, the here and there forces itself back into focus as we remember the operators in tactical HQ Colorado or the Nevada training yard used by Seal Team 6. The distance is not so far since conflicts have become media events, in what Zimmerman tracks as a move from 'militarization to mediatization'. This new terrain is characterized as 'the transnational era of mobile capital, fluidity, global communication flows, digitality and diaspora' (Zimmerman 2000: 16[illegible]). Russian versions of the Great Game become media espionage, no longer just a battle for a sea port in the Indian Ocean, but also not the romantic boosterism of the new media professors who hope that digital media delivery brings with it some radical democratic impulse, rather than the more likely further consumerization of everything.

That said, not just consumerism. Every drone flight in Afghanistan is a snuff film watched from Nevada, and that is where the war crimes tribunals should convene. Who will sit on the tribunal to evaluate these moves if not every viewer in the promised democratic shake-up of judgement and aesthetics? We might take still more seriously the convergence of media and reality as it is already rendered for us in the fictive figure of the aspirational Global South Asian film reviewer. This imaginary figure conflates film fantasy and life – though of course audience members are usually and sufficiently cognizant of the gulf between life and the cinematic world, nevertheless the figure of the implied audience member who finds allegory for their own identity in cinema or television perhaps offers something worth retrieving from those who imagine they control the separation of ideology from consciousness.

So many news channels say the same thing over and over. So few news reporters with investigative skills are on the spot, and more is spent on logo screen furniture than on content. Digital citizen reporting has not yet developed an investigatory ethos, or rather, the conception of content providers on citizen content remains underdeveloped. Yet there are now such opportunities to inform, and be informed, updated and in awe, if not aware that it is not plausible to continue the same way. It is now possible, given a base-level economic access of internet and time (which is of course not nothing), to see so many of the films that were previously confined and corralled in elite festivals and one-off art house screens. The commentary on cinema and politics can be more available – though an impressive achievement of censorship, selective reviewing and product placement ensures that it is not.

Instead, the best critique allowed within the dominant is a contained critique. To return to *Taboo* (2017) the action drama seems to take over any naive expectation that docu-drama as tribunal might stick closely to the facts. Neither the writers Steven Knight and Edward Hardy, nor the directors, Kristoffer Nyholm and Anders Engström, thought of the series as anything less than an exotic gore fest. The heritage architecture and houses – and all the curio office trinkets – offer impressive detail that substitutes exoticist intricacy for fidelity and insight. The characters are framed in magic dream-warrior mysticism in just about as oriental-fantastical a way as you can get. Only the incest makes it seem racy. And while some violence is certainly appropriate to any tale about this most rapacious of corporations (see Robins 2012) the bias towards individual braggadocio, insanity and visceral affect is strong even where there is a satisfying resistance to the East India Company by the tattooed protagonist. However, the long list of crimes the real John Company did commit, such as facilitating the opium trade, exacerbating rural poverty and famine, and aggressively extracting revenue in India for centuries, are either assumed or written out of the entertaining-containing narrative; the narrative as entertainment makes the critique *only* entertaining.

The hook line of James Delaney – 'I have a use for you' – works in the series as ideological distraction. The addressee is the passive audience, who by the penultimate episode, if not earlier, must be rooting for revenge set up so clearly that only blood can satisfy the crazy desire and wishful thinking that 'our hero' can take them on. With its delectable writerly twists and betrayals at the end, however satisfying as drama, in effect the outcome is inconsequential and rather a smokescreen and alibi for rewriting a nation of rotting apples as just having a few bruised fruits. *Taboo* (2017, dir. Nyholm and Engström) for critics, despite its noir stylings, has a feel-good ending which is not unlike Edmund Burke's pursuit of Viceroy Hastings, a pointless court drama achieving little over ten years in the parliament, with no result, or perhaps it reruns the impeachment and suicide/murder of Clive, the East India Company's premier extortionist, conniver of the Bengal trade and opium profiteer, whose opiate death in retirement is still not a feature in any of the several Clive memorials. The effect of launching the fantasy of a self-made act of reparation against a particular representative of the East India Company is of course to deny the possibility of formal and legal action against the rest, or against the British State on that score, and it occludes the actual history of indigenous resistance to the Raj, as documented elsewhere: for example in Ranajit Guha's compulsory volume entitled *Elementary Aspects of Peasant Insurgency in Colonial India* (1968). The East India Company is bloodied in *Taboo*, but the target audience of today can too easily assume this comeuppance delivered to one set of corrupt officials is to be adopted and internalized more generally, in turn extending moral absolution to all the other crimes done in the name of British interests in general. Queen Victoria then steps in to shut the Company down, initiating a whole new official Empire of theft and accumulation, with attendant Raj apologism blockbuster movies.

The scenes outside the frame of our film and television screens begin to look like they were made for television, made to be screened. In the White House, Obama, Clinton and the others are pictured in a situation that has more to do with *the situation* in TV, as in situation-comedy, the snuff film photograph has little to do with any situation a president might really need to deal with. After all those years, bin Laden was killed for the media, for ratings in a long running TV war, staged for prime time, with so-called smart bombs that have cameras in their noses right next to the high ordinance explosives. Lynndie England at Abu Ghraib was not an aberration in the media, but of the media. We could say she had an eye for the media angle, performing for film. The book-burners of Bradford were just slightly ahead of the curve.

Mrinal Sen and Ritwik Ghatak

Mrinal Sen's films can offer a crash course in media manipulation; they might be described as city allegories, rather than national, though there is such a close connection there between city and film the space for allegory is thin. This applies whether it is the experimental format of *Bhuvan Shome* (1969, dir. Sen) or the Calcutta trilogy films that offer a commentary and critique of the street politics of Bengal in the early 1970s.

Sen's first film is 'lost' but his second film, *Neel Akasher Niche* (1959) tackles anti-Chinese prejudice head on. The stereotype of the Chinese as a hawker and supplier of opium are portrayed in two complex Chinese characters, Wang Lu and Maki. The hawker, of silk, invoking longer India-China ties across the silk routes, makes contact with and visits the swadeshi activist wife of an arrogant bhadrolok husband. There are beautiful interlude songs from fisher folk on the river, a closely shot sequence on new year celebrations in Chinatown and a dramatic story driven by exchanges of khadi and silk. The urban scenario of 1930s Calcutta is shown to good effect and the viewer's sympathy for the protagonist must also be afforded to his long suffering dedicated neighbour, the waitress/opium den/brothel worker Maki, who is dedicated but spurned by her beloved. The swadeshi activist housewife, Basonti, visits Wang's house in Chhatavala Lane in Chinatown against the wishes of her husband Rajat but also offending Maki. The sexual mores of an identitarian society are skewered; Basonti has to explain to Wang that Maki was perhaps forced into the opium trade because of difficult conditions in India, because of the need to help her family survive. The committed activist, eventually her freedom struggle activism means Basonti is caught and sent to Presidency Jail, while for Wang his home in China calls when Japan invades and he returns to take up the fight there. *Neel Akasher Niche* translates as Earth beneath the blue sky and makes much of Sen's almost trademark broody monsoon clouds, interiors and powerful still shots and newspaper inserts. The film can be read as a paean to unified China sent from Bengal, endorsed with the gift of familiar sister-brother solidarity in the Rakhi gift exchange.

Of course, as we already saw, the Great Game scenario is invoked in relation to *Viceroy's House*. The argument over Global South Asia is also one prefiguring the future superpower dramas of China versus India, the return to prominence of great civilizational powers. Was it this that Bill Murray was contemplating when his firewood ran out up the mountain? The clouds finally part for the view, and Nanking is in flames.

Ghatak's cross-border cinematic sensibility meanwhile can teach a sensible and sensuous, meaning-filled contact story across difference without prejudice, warning of the dangers of giving over to nationalist powers and turning upon each other at the behest of abstractions. If we also cannot see the Global South, or the idea of South Asia, for all the hype of national order, the work to imagine greater alliances must be enacted with care and compassion that films such as *Meghe Dhaka Tara* (1960, dir. Ghatak), *Komal Gandhar* (1961, dir. Ghatak) and *Subarnarekha* (1962, dir. Ghatak) display to acclaim. Ghatak's films appeal because they are 'the most prolific examples of the angst of a society that had experienced a weakening of community life and intense ethical crisis in the wake of political turmoil' (Gooptu 2010: 163). This might lead to an interpretation which judges that partition films that are not about independence have greater significance through marking a wider globally relevant humanity. The link with politics and the screen is not always activated in the national broadcaster and the film festival competitions, but the possibilities for other alliances are still active in the screening and potential retrieval of sentiment from sentimentality.[1] Ghatak's films evoke personifications, sometimes distressed, but always optimistically striving towards human co-feeling. In migration, across partitions within lives, the mass movement of the future appears to have found its best advocate, alert amidst the thrashing about for meaning, able to show a calm centre in personal connection and co-presence. Ghatak's pan-human alliances are fit to screen.

Can the Bengali intellectual, revolutionary and romantic figure still be seen in the older Ghatak when he is playing himself? Perhaps he is more like the grown up figure of the angry young revolutionary in the Sen trilogy than a later incarnation of Soumitra Chatterjee's Apu. Might it be said this is typecasting of the irascible maverick as revolutionary youth become louche intellectual, acting out the theatrics of Badal Sircar (Katyal 2015) but recast for new times beyond the war on terror? This retrospective Ghatak would seem needed now more than ever to intervene in the routine story that has Afghanistan and Pakistan in reconstruction mode under military rule firing rockets rather than building houses. With the rest of the region reported as a series of skirmishes, life cheap across the hills of Kashmir, Nepal, Chhattisgarh, Andhra, the North Eastern States and Sri Lanka, all ready to operate a police and army cleansing programme, where is the critic that can capture attention in the same way? The Global South is in need of leadership and coordination in ways currently lacking both politically and in terms of cultural expression, at least insofar as someone who has the force of personality to break out into public domains. Instead the opportunist parties are only opportuning, and the critic-pundits in International Centre are not even internationalizing, blocked at each turn by distribution control. Despite all that could be gleaned from the opened digital screen, perhaps the politicization of Global South Asian media studies must be rebuilt from scratch like the famous jalopy from *Ajantrik* (1958, dir. Ghatak).

Screens ablaze

There are many other significant book-burnings, not always of the same order of concern. The 1981 burning of the Jaffna library in the Sri Lankan civil war was of course disastrous, but of a different order was the burning of books by Bangladeshi publishers in protest against the killing of secularist publishers such as Faisal Arefin Dipan, who had published a book by Avajit Roy, himself hacked to death in 2015. Yes, the Taliban burnt the Pol-i-Khonri public library in 1998, but this event in Afghanistan is not singular. Indira Gandhi had burnt the Sikh library in Amritsar in 1984, and this sort of outrage of course had its antecedents in colonial times when the British burnt the Royal Library of the kings of Burma at the end of the Third Anglo-Burmese War in1885–1887. The list can be extended but book-burning cannot save the group from the environmental apocalypse – in the film *The Day After Tomorrow* (2004, dir. Emmerich) all the books in the New York Public Library are barely sufficient to keep out the cold.

In Sri Lanka, the killing fields of the Tamil North were only occasionally newsworthy. Historical atrocities, satis, the burning ghats of Varanasi, or films named *Fire*, even the mythic consideration of Agni ritual systems by anthropologists were more likely to attract the attention of the BBC. Yet television reports of the burning of the *Qur'an* in America foreshadow a vicious return to an unacceptable Inquisition-era arson. Kenneth Burke documents thousands of copies of the *Qur'an* burnt in Spain in the early 1500s (2016: 84). Sri Lanka appears in screen memory as a site of armed struggle, with fanatic suicide bombers and 'Tigers' armed with cyanide pills in a desperation of a particular ethnic type, the AK-47 and the sarong, sandy beaches and grainy footage of war crime atrocities. Perhaps an older generation remembers Buddhism and beach huts.

Archives and renewal

In archival work that inspired new waves of interpretive recovery, Tejaswini Niranjana tracks feminist film studies in India from the film reviews published in *Manushi* (1999: 93). This work sets out 'future possibilities' for feminist film studies that would address feminist and female directors, stars, agency, audiences, viewing and state actions such as censorship, regionalism and the womens' movement. The 'paucity of serious feminist film criticism' (Niranjana 1999: 91) remains to confront this wish list, and the works of Madhuja Chatterjee, Raminder Kaur, Anandi Ramamurthy, Anjali Gera Roy and Rosie Thomas would only be the beginning of a need to talk of democracy in media scholarship. Citation alone will not repair the imbalance; recall that Spivak refers to the performative failure of one person one vote as it is unable to ensure equal value in an uneven field. The performative politics of festivals of global munificence, aspirational staging, comes close to the danger of unmatched arrogance:

> The spectacle of India's 'rise' as a global player – mediated via branding campaigns, beauty pageants, massive infrastructure projects, sports extravaganzas, mass political movements that help showcase the 'world's largest democracy' in action – is predicated not only upon its capacity to attract attention but also on crafting appearances that can attract the global gaze. (Kaur and Hansen 2015: 290).

If it were possible to count the votes…

Whatever there is still to say about them, the old debates between Jameson and Ahmad matter less than the possibility of opening up an archive of educational film in that third cinema tradition. Cinema that documents events are far too easily erased from global memory, crushed under the formulaic of entertainment and trend. Of course the marketplace of ideas has its own trends and fashions, and Sen, like Ray, perhaps looks dated – whereas the films of Ghatak fare better through time because of a singular brilliance. There are many others to be recommended if the heritage of film were realigned to match Global South Asia to a place in a non-hierarchical parallel of globals.

If Rajagopal can point to socialization through film, then the theme of social reproduction and intentional construction of viewing schedules can become a thing for Left culture:

> As a medium, television's work is parallel to and interlinked with that of the economy. Both disseminate information to help circulate goods as well as to socialize members of society. Television is thus active in the material and symbolic reproduction of capitalist relations. Todd Gitlin has pointed out that just as, under capitalism, the surplus value accumulated in social labor is privately appropriated, men and women are estranged from the meanings they produce socially; these are privately appropriated by mass media and returned to them in alienated forms. (2009: 4)

What this means is that the efforts of film connoisseurship are not wasted when used as political education and community of resistance – 'I have a use for you' says Delaney in *Taboo* – with a socializing purpose that counters the hegemony of those that would block migration, block redistribution and block reparations. There are good reasons to become a militant for this kind of viewing. That social reproduction can include the labour, unpaid like much of such socializing effort, of constructing playlists of films from the old boxes of videos and DVDs that uncles and aunties too quickly stored in attics and forgot. This work is surely to be welcomed. The new Global South Asian film and television studies could find impetus in revival of the didactic films, delegating to the youth the work of going back to ask those uncles and aunties for the stash. What did you do in the migration wars uncle? Were you in the Asian Youth Movements? Did you go to the film clubs? To Blackpool? Were there zines on film in those days, and where is the box of them that you must surely have kept?

It might be necessary to adapt, but the issue is not to jettison the projects of different traditions. Rajagopal warns that 'critical analysis of the work of television ... entails sifting through historical assumptions that may carry over when transposing a theory from one society to another' (2009: 6). He recognizes the stakes: 'Whether politics pertains to the realm of civil order or to that of the state, it exists to a great extent through the means of communication' (Rajagopal 2009: 6). The point is that Global South Asia is carrying the theory, and practical movement, across any number of borders and communication channels that open onto possibility. At the same time as the imperial media cracks down and endlessly simplifies the demonization, a new Asian Youth Movement rises up looking for inspiration from an older generation. The Tandana project of Ramamurthy is exemplary in this regard, collecting community posters and zines of anti-racist and anti-imperialist struggle in a heritage project of renewal. It recovers the 'styles and phrasings of all those left-wing uncles and radical aunts who hoarded boxes of leaflets and pamphlets in back rooms and in attics so they could one day be retrieved as testimony to a difficult settlement in multi-racial Britain' (2013: backcover). It would have been tragic if the boxes of old zines and videos were lost. These means of communication constitute, in and connectivity of here and there, another global civil order, and the struggle over the sites of this 'order' becomes paramount.

In a more conceptual mode that has the merit of also starting with the Global South, Nikos Papastergiadis writes in favour of conceiving of many public spheres:

> So while the South is a big and spherical concept, it is nevertheless a useful heading for understanding a certain set of relationships within the global network of little public spheres. In the recent past it has been revived as a possible frame for representing the cultural context of not just regions that are geographically located in the South, but also those that share a common post-colonial heritage. (2011)

Perhaps Global South Asia is a minoritarian discourse, yet global, the question of where it places among these spheres becomes pertinent. It makes sense that there should be many globals in a diverse world, and perhaps it is useful to start here for a change. Relegation to secondary or minority really misses the point when a sixth of the world population is the base.

In this framing the nation does not dominate discussion, and if the reference is South Asia and its diasporas and influences, there are unavoidably several 'nationals' in the global, but even this nation as region cannot dominate as 'national cinemas' might in Europe or Africa. Regionalism is as much a focus and beyond of diaspora as the influence and fashions of other engagements that whole continents have with the images of Global South Asia. The regional here would be bigger than any nation and in this sense is also not a regionalism of a co-prosperity sphere or a geographical land and sea territory mode, but a time slot and theme preference, even a star system of fan zone. The inclusion of diaspora and other interests, and the Global South as a political rather than topological descriptor, displays other possibilities and welcome disorientations of the dominant.

Global trinketization

There are other works that explore material that could become significant in the conversation around a post-national conception of global cultural diversity but at the level of orientation often fall down on some point, aspect or fundamental difference. In media industry studies, what would perhaps seem like a parallel conception as that offered here might in the end expose a frivolous imposture. For example, Aswin Punathambekar's nevertheless excellent volume at one point refers to 'a widely circulated article titled "Bollystan: The Global India," in which the author Parag Khanna [2004] reflected on how processes of globalization had reframed relations between India and the vast Indian diaspora' (2013: 148). Well and good so far, but if we rehearse only the expected bits and bobs of global South Asian visibility, just one step away from representations that foreground national cultural industry exports, what is the advance? Following Khanna, Punathambekar presented 'Bollystan' as a way 'to refer to a vast space of transnational cultural production that included everything from henna tattoos and remix music to literature and films, Khanna and other writers sought to map how rapid flows of people, culture, and capital across national borders have rendered difficult any easy separation between nation and diaspora' (2013: 149)

A more satisfying yet ethnographic and American offering promises some unsettlement of the India-centric standard of discussion of Global South Asian diasporas. Purnima Mankekar writes perceptively of the proliferation, either in Delhi or San Francisco, of 'discourses of a Global India that proudly assumes its place on the global stage because of its economic and technological progress'. At 'a critical juncture in postcolonial India' (Mankekar 2015: 39), the discourses coincide with the construction of 'moral subjects with varying affiliations with Global India' through the circulation of affective transnational 'discourses of morality' (Mankekar 2015: 144). Mankekar's book tracks these moral discourses around attachments like nuclear weapons, financial investments, record-breaking films – for example, *Dilwale Dulhania Le Jayenge* (1995, dir. Chopra) as a film that emerged in field conversations irrespective of context or topic (Mankekar 2015: 41). It is disturbing but also honest to note that alongside nuclear tests and NRI investments, a shared diasporic identification which affiliates explicitly with global Hindutva is 'hatred of Muslims' (Mankekar 2015: 186). As a balance to the unsettling conservative boosterisms of this series, Mankekar also found informants who could express sentiments such as 'one can be a Global Indian without being from India' (2015: 187). In cases where neo-liberal and national conceptions of entrepreneurship coincided, such aspirations were 'allegorical of the (re)constitution of the Indian nation as it seeks to position itself in the global economy' (Mankekar 2015: 190). It is here that the potential of this analysis is brought to fruition, exposing the reification and fetishization of 'sedimented traditions' and concepts (Mankekar 2015: 227) and doing so in ways not different to the distorted economism of some other portrayals of emerging economies construed somehow as Global South (Arrighi 2007). In Mankekar's project on unsettling the nation, such emergent individualist, neo-liberal aspirations are roundly critiqued, even as the ethnographic is not as yet more than description. The welcome last words of the book, just before a short coda dedicated to the attack on the world trade towers, propose a future ambitious plan to 'unsettle the U.S. nation state' (Mankekar 2015: 228)

The emerging powers discourse has its counterpoint in the moral attachments Mankekar identifies. But it is deeply unfortunate that Arrighi transposes discussion of Global South from a political project with a longer heritage to a narrative of economic growth, which in itself is part admiration and part fear of a strong Asia. Of course there are adherents of the economic enthusiasm on all sides – shining India is the Hindutva version, muscular Buddhism in Sri Lanka – and it would not do to gainsay actual developments of capital in Asia if this is not also predicated upon a critique of US and European capital. And even with such a critique, the subject to be put to critique here is convolutedly joint capital anyway; the elites on all sides contrive to invest collectively. Smaller national capitals join with other national capitals to invest together in the name of the latest corporate shell company in pursuit of the latest site of super profit. So-called foreign capital is combined with local capital and much of it is enthusiastically involved in Asia already. The designation Global South Asia is cut through with divisions and internal demarcations that are also sites of conflict with flow on resonance in the diasporas. Hindutva and a strange historical revisioning, Islam devalued here, overbearing there, conjured by geopolitical as well as literary manoeuvres, used as a blanket term for demonization and demons while Jainism or Zoroastrianism trade as exotica in some markets, and while Hindu godmen preach tantric moves in California, Buddhists wield machine guns in Sri Lanka. The versions of Global South that turn towards boosterism are, I'd wager, imbricated in an economic but contrapuntal embrace where financial scheming, investment, industry and ownership forces irruptions into ideological extremism in crypto national-fascist forms. What however matters more is that the collapse of Left critique in the West or North should not become a template for narratives of the Global South.

Conflict and renewal

This book has not been about South Asian cinema and media effects, but about Global South Asia as it exists as a political and conceptual plane of activity with world significance. Within this, the book recognizes different approaches to the place of film and television in South Asia and its diasporas. These approaches can be grouped together variously, for convenience, in clusters of shared interests, but such demarcations should be held to be usefully porous. Among these clusters, there is a historical approach recently deepened by Thomas and Gera Roy; the Marxist inspired ideology critique that held sway for many years was thoroughly reworked and given a new theoretical impetus by Madhava Prasad's introduction of subsumption theory to discuss melodrama, which in turn makes possible further speculations about the ways we might break with a merely descriptive response to film appreciation. While this does more than any hitherto film studies schema that addresses the component parts of production, as if excised and separated all the better to manage control. Nationalism is excoriated in Rajadhyaksha's ever-important interventions and attention to codes and intellectual circles, movements, fandom and other pleasures as labour and making, while Sundaram offers an ethnographically literate coverage of similar terrain, electronically updated with a pirate tech fit out appropriate to transnational times and a global readership. Religious intolerance in Rajagopal and Bharucha, Nandy's incomparable psycho-social interventions add psychological and semantic precision to the discussion, and more ontological and cultural studies approaches, be it ethnographic work on screen events, assemblage, or liveness in Rai and Roy's work respectively, unfolds the discussion with power. Diasporic media scholarship is diverse as well, with major themes brought out by Niranjana, Kaur and Dudrah, where there are tendencies for and against hybridity, more or less numerate approaches working with screen numbers or trade figures, and a kind of local ethnographic regionalisms – with work in Fiji, Nigeria, Australia, Guyana, Senegal, Sweden and so on. The star system and regional, even sub-regional variations, audience studies, and persona, performance perspectives thrive. There is much to learn not only from viewing the films, but also within the enfolding sophistications of media genre and interpretive debates.

Global South Asia is at first a diagnosis of attacks that come through the media, that demonize and stereotype in the register of representation that foregrounds and reifies South Asia, Islam, Hindu, Muslim, Tamil, Bengali, Pakistani, Naxal or Gurkha, and so on. The point of this critique of attacks, and the only slightly better orientalism of a defence that frames exotica, is one of recognition, including of complicity, and the uses of terror in the entire public space, unevenly of course, but with deadly consequences everywhere. As a dialectical counterpoint to the terror, a possibility explored that comes from the films and media tradition to undo the power plays and military games that divide. A possibility and a hope that the hard fought for message and potential of revolutionary struggles did not fade forever, that the archive of those struggles lives on and is restored anew in the many and varied projects of younger generations who struggle not to fall for the trap of fear and anxiety. An accumulation of insights gathered together in whatever way to challenge the accumulation of power and profit that destroys. A stand-off. Global South Asia, diaspora and subcontinent, is presently the main theatre of a conflict and contest over meaning that shapes the world.

Is it plausible to rethink the global of Global South Asia that will both refuse the strawman commercialized homogeneity of globalization and at the same time extend the global beyond the vernacular and universal opposition so as to always interpret as global difference, a universe of alternatives in conversation? A transnationality which cannot be uniform even when it aspires to universal coverage, universal access. Alongside many languages, fluency in more than the dominant is a marker of cosmopolitanism – transposed to film traditions, support for other film languages can perhaps illustrate a worth while start.

But the ethical political anti-colonialism that gave shape to the Global South has been eroded by forgetfulness and censorship. Deep searchable tracts of archival memory can show the way, but what there is to learn is immense and discouragement for the learning holds sway. The Left, as it is, seems to prefer faster moves, let alone the identifications and formulas of Merchant Irony, tamed Viceroy's lunch chat, avoidance of any sense that hard won concessions through struggle are the only way Empires are undone.

This old and half-forgotten rhetoric of Global South in the tradition of Bandung, pan Africanism, the Comintern and the internationals for too many seems like an out of fashion and even repressed memory. Global South in the hands even of comrades has become merely a geographical reference in a series of guilty displacements effecting to find better words for Centre/Periphery, West/East, developed/underdeveloped and ultimately the racist throwbacks of civilized/primitive and Christian/heathen. In the metropolitan theory circuits, the political version of Global South seems out of favour, even as thinkers across Asia, including South Asia, are reinvigorated by Inter-Asian connectivity especially and examples such as CODESRIA or InterAsia are small bulwarks against the reaction.

Movies as mobilization?

Who offers political leadership for Global South Asia today? The non-aligned moves on the world stage by Nehru epitomized by Bandung – the city in Indonesia which hosted the 1955 meeting of the 'Konferensi Asia-Afrika' – are not delivered by current 'statesmen' and the national figure-head positions of the present powers do not promise much outside of the neo-liberal compact. Compared to the early independence period, prospects are not promising anywhere, given global diasporic attachments, opportunistic identitarian investment and strategic commercial realignments. Who then among the writers, filmmakers, theorists and commentators might give intellectual if not actual political leadership when anything other than brand ego promotion will get you a visit from a drone strike force or other assassination hit. Is Global South Asian leadership a viable construct in the post-identitarian era? Spivak, Bhabha, Nandy and the like belong to an effervescence established in the 1970s and 1980s. A newer generation including Prashad, Madhava Prasad, Kaur and Roy, and several others not yet as well known in the 1990s and 2000s, will in time also be noted for their scholarship, but in the political domain, adequate to an opposition to global terror, these newer writers will most likely not be not known enough to influence. The managerialist defanging of the university and the controlled apparatus of ideology – aka the press – works hard to undermine any hint of a Global South Asian moment along the lines of Chavez.

Maybe the question of leadership in any case is so problematic, and the flatter structure of the youth so important, that anonymity and vanguardism of the party can prevail. Arundhati Roy cannot enter the parliament and is unlikely to ever be a delegate to the United States, but the possibility of collective pressure through migration and settlement already has its impact. On the other hand, conservative Hindutva and remissions home have supported a mobilization of long-dormant fascist elements alongside or in parallel to the United States, administrations covert, and increasingly overt, sponsorship of death squads, assassinations and chaos strategy in the Muslim homelands such that diaspora seems too easily manipulated and arraigned against the Left.

Global South Asia also has its frozen moments, or rather, moments of global exposure that congeal onto an occluding permanence or allegorically ambiguous settlement. For example, in the category of world cinema, the films of Satyajit Ray, primarily, but also Mrinal Sen and Ritwik Ghatak, enjoyed film festival and then World Cinema popularity for several decades. No doubt deserved, the films are profound, varied, and they are contributions of unmatched scope. Subsequently, however, it has become difficult to add to the global list except in a few bespoke and unthreatening instances – some of the Bollywood superhits and middle road works by the likes of Mira Nair and the diasporic crossover success of Gurinder Chadha. What this means is that the classic period is fixed fast in a global sepia frame, with nothing added to upset the Gandhi-Nehru idyll, subsequently ruined by Maoists, commercialism, Shilpa Shetty and the BJP. Even as Nair produces ever-more eloquent expressions of her art – for example the film of Jhumpa Lahiri's (2003) book *The Namesake*, a Global South Asian family drama replete with syncopated New York to Calcutta transition shots, of Howrah and Brooklyn Bridge, and airport departure and arrival halls, at one point with Nitin Sawhney including State of Bengal's track 'IC408' as not quite background music. Partha Chatterjee has a cameo as a New York based Bengali intellectual raconteur, clearly method acting. But the film, with points to make about naming and expectations, has not ignited controversy or debate, despite hitting all the undoubted appeal buttons with its arranged marriage versus love match, sexual betrayal, minor drug use, and soft furnishings, fabrics and cushions (*The Namesake* (2006, dir. Nair)).

In this cine-tele-visual commercial domain, individual political credentials might champion the staging of progressive debate, but it also comes alongside a resurgent Hindutva nationalism, even an immaculate revivalism, which rewrites history with fanatical consequences and out of incredulity invents alternative facts and fake truths to land a Hindu on the moon and split the atom under the wheels of a chariot. Milk flows from the screens as Narendra Modi talks. The rise of the nationalist cult figure, it should not really surprise anyone, has a close parallel in the cinema, so much so that a certain film critic from the RSS weekly *Organiser* was one L. K. Advani. His move from cinema hall towards the Babri Masjid (see Rajagopal 2001: 63) parallels the trajectory of the BJP rise in ways that should be a warning. The international and specifically North American relations to power for Far Right Hindu groups is made by Rajagopal specifically in connection with a conference held in Washington just nine months after the Masjid demolition. Called 'Global Vision 2020' the destruction of the Babri Masjid is lauded as 'the most memorable day' by then BJP President Murli Manohar Joshi (Rajagopal 2001: 238). Shashi Tharoor called it fanaticism, but in 1992 this still did not seem something that would move to any long-term consequence. In what Rajagopal analyses as a 'mirror image' critique, Tharoor likened the kar-sevak RSS activists to 'Muslim fundamentalists trying to blow up New York (the first World Trade Centre bomb attempt). This 'liberal' mirroring (Rajagopal 2001: 239) indicates again the narrow repertoire of representation generally available for South Asian's acting politically. The go-to characterizations, even as affirmative action and critique of fascism is ostensibly claimed, are only able to reproduce the pantomime villain clichés and actively erase another possible history of the South Asian presence in America, not only temple building and 'fund-raising' religious events (Rajagopal 2001: 245).

What Rajagopal usefully points to is the 'anomalous' character of expatriate support for Far Right Hindu nationalism (Rajagopal 2001: 247). Tracking earlier diasporic investments in the radical Left Gadar Party, now well-educated and high earning Indians resident in the United States promote extremism in a model minority mode that Rajagopal diagnoses as 'guilt, frustration and political irresponsibility' (2001: 248). Prashad's critique of god men and other guru types in California would be relevant here (2012) as again would Bald's studies of early arrivals in *Bengali Harlem* (2013). What can also be anticipated are calls which suggest only the party discipline of Leninism could build a counter to the Right. Rajagopal cites Ahmad's critique again where he advises 'that the "refounding" of the Communist movement would help "the liberal centre in reconstructing those premises of Nehruvian social democracy and independent national development which is [*sic*] so much a target of the fascist attacks today"' (Rajagopal 2001: 299n54, Ahmad 1993: 66). Along with Rajagopal it might be necessary to say this mix of Nehru and communism might not be 'sufficient', though it remains to be seen if it is 'nostalgic' (Rajagopal 2001: 299n54). It is not without awareness of the need for substantial promotional and archival work that I say the record of Global South Asian media provides both a material and sonorous aesthetic audio-visual basis for this effort.

In this always lyrical space, the spiral of Jameson's dialectic would not look strange, nor would the howl of Kureishi's anti-Thatcherism; the Naxalites would 'counter and although it is not necessary', those in the West who look to Mao for inspiration in this case, might recognise with Badiou that 'any mass movement is obviously an urgent demand for liberation' ([2011] 2012: 49). The protesters who met the police killing of Mark Duggan with an anger that shook the whole of London in 2011 also channelled some of that spirit, and it was sustained even at the interstices of the heaviest logistical security effort yet seen for a sporting event, in 2012, and which coincided with the ongoing crackdown on dissent across North Africa, the Middle East and Asia. The Arab Spring turned into the Arab Sting (Chandan 2015) via the Libyan winter and the complexities of Muammar Gaddafi's links with 'friends in the Atlantic capitals' (Prashad 2012: 7), but there are still meetings and organizing as well as critical engaged thinkers working to expose the scandals and lies of state terror. Against those backed by exoticist forked-tongue apologetics, the challenge is building a Global South Asia that will not settle for exoticism, demonization of comprador compliance.

Close attention to the ways the other is othered, the masks of racism and skin prejudice, the silencing of subalterneity, the citation of canonical patriarchy and its internal castle consort critics, the malignancy of colonial bureaucracy and the hypocrisy of development make possible the necessarily long programme of restitution and reconstruction that is needed.

There is a sense in which these texts are the necessary or unavoidable portals through which a Global South Asian media studies must negotiate its orientation. Every reader has to construct his or her own library but for me; this is a work of solidarity. This book is written with a view to working out political and social reproduction and care for revolutionary politics in a diverse world confronted by racism and economic militarist ideological war.

Spivak and surplus

Despite a harsh, deserved, critique of the comprador migrant class and a warm but not overly enthusiastic embrace of Rosie, Spivak still has something worth saying which is relevant to both settled communities and migrations, indeed for all. We might start (to end) by noting that the West has nothing to lose by embracing settler migrant communities as a positive cultural horizon. Only then might some resolution of the colonial history – that British history happened 'overseas' – be possible. In substantive terms this is of course already long underway – Balti, rhythm and blues, chinoiserie, hip hop and so many other examples – but ideologically a strange resistance and a misrecognition makes it still necessary to ask if migrant settler communities can be the example of using surplus for social reproduction, for the upkeep of children, elders, family, community and for training? Of course this is rhetorical, since such ideas are necessary for survival for all communities; they work both to sustain those not able to work and to reproduce the group as community and thus be a model of social transformation. From there though, the transformation of the world contra to colonial accumulation is still a task of enormous scale.

Global South Asian politics largely remains, in both the geographic and conceptual South, a matter of elite educational and institutional possibilities, just as much as in other access points. Education, debate, political groups, party organization and political experience are required also, but even as economic opportunism means such possibilities are beleaguered, also under attack are all articulations of a political or politicized Global South since the university worldwide is increasingly privatized and subject to take over by the self-reproducing bureaucratic managerialist class. Despite this global onslaught, or rather decay, there is also well-meaning cultural appreciation supplemented by benevolent third world solidarity activism which, at least, offers the possibility of learning just how far and much distance and effort is necessary.

In this schematic, as Spivak might say – and as she demonstrates in her tireless effort – global education needs you to take the trouble to move around, to do fieldwork on the flexible imagination of other lives and ways of being. This is not 'alternative epistemologies', but expansive conversations with others who also move, with everyone doing this 'research' this impactful knowledge creation and democratization of what it is to learn, so as to learn different perspectives, to work towards the possibility of and to understand the contingency of your epistemological position so that you can indeed be engaged in a global education that does not remain ignorant of the needs of 'the largest sector of the electorate' (Spivak, Presidency College, December 2016). This also means that instead of liberal rights discourse and unexamined democracy talk, the alert critic cannot 'remain happy talking about democracy in a hierarchical state where simply the structure of democracy, which is body count – one equals one – does not produce a democratic society. A performative contradiction' (Spivak, Presidency College, December 2016). One vote per person does not prevail where groups can be demonized en block, allegiances can be bought, deceptions perpetrated, media outlets dominated, television channels become brand platforms, news becomes 24-hour social media and informed debate too smooth for anything but entertainment. The convivial festival of so-called democracy is also a threatening and malevolent force that removed the democratic impulse and sequesters it in a few hands. The vote like the open road does not signal a guaranteed future.

In the interest of making this thought accessible, Spivak insists on the importance of learning how teaching the humanities as imaginative activism can work at the transformation of the interests of both elites and masses. A programme that may take time to unfold. But might this then, also in Europe and the Americas, mean film and other media could become the focus of a critical humanities education that leads all in a migration to a genuinely global education where even those who are elites will know 'the importance of the flexibility of imagination' (Spivak, Presidency College, December 2016)? If it is migration as Global South Asian settlement in Europe and America that pushes towards a more universal solidarity, despite appearances thus far, then the films of new wave, masala, international South Asian and diasporic cinema, the television, talk-show and citizen journalism, the handheld screens and movie-cams, the home production kits, the in-camera edits, uploads to the cloud and the unending exchange of images understood critically, might it also mean a push back. These materials would then be construed as a push back against the poisonous demonization of Islam and of all migrants, against the horrors of poverty, exploitation and accumulation, against national allegory as some flippant third world exoticism and where the warmongers that bring closer the apocalypse of nuclear, environmental or other opportunistic destruction are challenged and defeated. The national security war crimes division – CIA, MI6 – poisons Islam by creating head-chopper death squads as models for disaffected youth, but this is only the publicity end of a more insidious media-arms trade. Seeing how these extremes are created as alibi for not showing the other 'stark' extremes of accumulation can only then be unsettled if the two sides of an assault on media – as rethinking knowledge and rethinking representation – become the most important parts of a Global South Asian film and television studies.

Here immigration activism that breaks with border anxiety and insists on both settlement and global belonging – perhaps citizenship, though the passports remain national – offers the chance to learn something from those who travel too. That said, the conditions in which to say even this are narrowed daily. To the degree that critical media, film or cultural studies had an academic base in some universities, the possibility of left reproduction has been undermined by at least three concurrent developments.

1 First, a perceived and actual decline of Left culture both within and without the university in conformity with job anxiety and requirements to toe the line under austerity and managerialism.

2 Second, careerism and identitarianism of an also parasitic fake Left, Eurocentric and Uncle Tom in the extreme, despite protestations of multiculturalism, by which they really mean exoticism.

3 Finally, though not exhaustively, the capture of what passes for theory by digital and ontological spruikers for the social media corporations, even in their professing of piracy a virulent free market and individualist survivalism prevails over genuine Leninist organising.

S. V. Srinivas may not have had exactly this in mind when presenting his views on teaching Asian cinema, but the points he makes are worth taking to heart as an opening towards further necessary consideration. Film analysis too often 'restages the obvious as a major discovery' (2012: 79). It talks itself into wanting to 'pass' in all contexts, then complains when this succeeds all too well, and hence benefits are withdrawn, and 'sometimes, you can't understand what's happening textually unless you are aware of the economic forces at work' (Srinivas 2012: 78). What Srinivas does say raises deep problems for this text and for future work in a reconfigured film studies generally. The different levels of attention, interpretation, fidelity to truth and fidelity to film, its excessive enjoyment, the pleasures of going to the cinema hall to sit in the dark awash with colour, to sit with others, on couches at home or virtually, bypasses the problem of distribution as a politics *with* economics – all demand attention. The grand claims of those who sit in the dark and proclaim themselves radical, subversive, pirates, revolutionaries and so on as if watching Jackie Chan in itself were progressive (see Srinivas 2012: 79) gives the lie to the obvious where if piracy can be reread and celebrated as theft and free content then that analysis has misunderstood both piracy and freedom (Srinivas 2012: 81).

View again, view better

It may be that the expectation that all cinema should be open to a more or less discernable political analysis, if not already interpreted into the content, is also no more than an exoticist imposition, even as allegory. A good thing that anyone with YouTube access can potentially make this decision themselves, and availability of interpretive autonomy must be welcome. It is also not a matter of pointing it out, but of pointing towards resources to facilitate, and felicitate, this development. For example, the collection of Bengali art film at https://indiancine.ma. All films are open to interpretive study, even if relaxed viewing in the comfort of your own home is not in itself the high point of solidarity. The setting of approved acts and expectations would also be restrictive even if it would be good to welcome some or all of the non-exclusive list of reproductive effects that open interpretation might deliver: contribution to public education, polemical maturity and fearless honesty, shared viewing and community reproduction, diversity and critique of fake diversity, democratizing, non-normative, provocative, self-representing, always causing dismay to the nationalists, pro-situ, picked up by international art festivals and spilling over to the mainstream, able to find an audience and survive without begging for funding and so on.

What if Global South Asia could also be considered a small step in a long process that undoes the often-rehearsed teleological contact stories of Western theoretical, cultural and technological dominance? The Euro-American representation machinery has circulated versions of culture that are medieval in provenance and have the character of plunder and siege. Years of privileged interpretation as if by rote place Hollywood before Bollywood, and challenges to this must still battle an entrenched order. Critique of Eurocentrism and ethnocentrism perhaps have a longer track record, but still too few consequences that are not merely critique, which fail to impact either the culture industry – Disney, Universal, Miramax – or the arms trade – Lockheed Martin, BAE, Boeing. A newly opened politics of knowledge awaits, otherwise burnt books and a world of ashes. We must work together to see that Jaidev will be able to tell his tales to the children.

Notes

Introduction

1 'Asia' is a problematic referent – as ever Spivak is my guide here when she questions its reach (Spivak 2008). How anyway did *west* Asia become the *middle* East when it is still also the Global *south*, but *north* of the equator? Desai justifiably complains that 'discussions of India dominate the study and meaning of South Asia in most (inter)disciplinary scholarship and (identity) politics' and 'the framework of "South Asian" can reflect a liberal Euro-American discourse that views the region as a homogenous monocultural area in which an orientalized version of India represents South Asia' (Desai 2004: 5). I am also taken by Madhava Prasad's (2014b) discussion of the 'India' that struggled for independence as being a creation of an English trained elite. I adapt Desai to warrant that Global South Asia is used 'not to suggest a coherency or uniformity in discussing a singular diaspora but rather heterogeneous and multiple diasporas' (2004: 5).

1 From *Viceroy's House* to the Situation Room

1 Global South Asia should be a pro-immigrant solidarity position that endorses a subcontinental infiltration of the globe for civilizational, anti-racist, anti-imperialist and reparative reasons. Any adequate mode of reparation will not be delivered by the politicians we currently have since they, along with the majority of cultural commentators, historians, scholars and the public in general cannot conceive of their full responsibility for hundreds of years of colonial extraction. The necessary process of a defective reparation by means of migration and settlement only makes sense in this larger frame – a dedicated and near sacrificial movement since who would endure the lousy weather otherwise? That this demographically distributed civilizational dividend for all is only slowly being acknowledged – cinema, food, national allegories – is a happy consequence.

2 That the general demonization is of Muslims, as in Trump's Muslim immigration ban 2017, or 'targets' as in Obama's drone strikes in Pakistan 2011, or against the 'enemy combatants' of the Taliban and Iraq in Bush's war on terror from 2001, does not in each case mean that other Asians are not at risk, and by extension, associates of all kinds, diaspora and citizens of cities that prepare attacks, and are attacked. Paris, London, Brussels and New York

are all on high alert at times because of a generalized anxiety that is at root racist and inflamed by sentiments that construe the enemy as a certain type, rather than seeing how the head-choppers and death squads are trained and equipped by the West's own security services. In this rather more bleak context the question of who has an interest in seeing the world differently implicates us all.

3 For an interesting survey of White House information, telecommunications and computing security protocols, see Laprise (2009).

4 See for example the comparison of a 2008 image and the 2011 image here: http://todaysnewsnj.blogspot.com/2011/05/osama-bin-laden-corpse-photo-is-fake.html (accessed 25 July 2011). In 2012 Judge James Boasberg ruled that the defence department was within its rights to refuse freedom of information requests to see whatever images there were (Judicial Watch 2012).

5 See http://youtu.be/ctepAW35O9Q for AC/DC and http: //youtu.be/bOWmTyrz1RA for Manson (accessed 25 July 2014).

6 For a development of this, showing that '(negative) leftist vernacular propaganda in the countryside against globalisation, warning people that soon cheap mass-consumption goods of everyday use would flood the Indian market' is not the only game in town, see Bhaskar Mukhopadhyay's nuanced ethnographic investigations of food, film and filth in *The Rumour of Globalisation: Desecrating the Global from Vernacular Margins* (2012: 53).

7 Here perhaps it is useful to remember – what Adorno says apropos of Hegel: 'nothing can be understood in isolation, everything is to be understood only in the context of the whole, with the awkward qualification that the whole in turn lives only in the individual moments. In actuality, however, this kind of doubleness of the dialectic eludes literary presentation' (Adorno [1963] 1993: 91).

8 Though it was significant that there were such films on British screens at all. Desai contextualizes the importance of an 'influx of new migrants and new technology [which] reshaped older communities, formed new diasporas, and created new cultural processes and flows of cultural products. For example, with the growth of cable, then the VCR, and now satellite television, South Asian diasporans initiated the showing of Hindi, Telugu, Bangla, and other vernacular language films on television and in movie theaters to wide audiences' (2004: vi)

9 It should perhaps be explained that I continue to single out these proper names as foundational because of something Madhava Prasad wrote in the preface of his magnificent *Ideology of the Hindi Film* (1998) – a book widely accepted as 'canonical' (Rajadhyaksha 2012b: 95) – where film studies in India [I will say globally] began to take on an 'institutional specificity' as a 'field' or 'discipline' of serious 'cultural significance' in the 1990s. Madhava Prasad's invocation of the names Rajadhyaksha, Vasudevan and others, even while recognizing earlier forays into cinema by 'anthropologists, sociologists, psychologists and indologists' was a powerful declaration of renewal (1998: vii). Since then, a radical effervescence of film studies joined hands perhaps with new studies of television and now extends to other formats and devices to explore the 'overflow of value, memory [and] intensity' (Rai 2009: 218) in the 'confluence of technologies, affects, rhythms, intensities, spaces, bodies, becomings and temporalities' (Rai 2009: 168) of Global South Asian film and television. This in turn 'stretches and fragments across multiple digital media' (Mazzarella 2013: 220), even if for the purposes of the exploration in this book I will disagree that it is 'hybridized' (Vasudevan 2010: 357) nor do I think much of the cannon metaphor in canonical – slightly inappropriate given the rank being pulled via military parlance, still...

2 Sammy and Rosie – and Salman – Get Laid

The initial ideas for this chapter were first presented as a provocation at the 2004 workshop on television at the Films Studies Department of Jadavpur University, Kolkata. It has been rewritten substantially in 2011 and 2015, with thanks to Abhijit Roy, Moinak Biswas and Atticus Che Narain.

1 Less famously, the book is reported to have been first burnt in Bolton on 2 December 1988 (Ventura 2014: 42). For more on chronology, see the later footnote on *Index on Censorship*.

2 Another antecedent may have been the less well-remembered burning of H. G. Wells's 1922 book *Short History of the World*, which was incinerated after objections were raised against the great Fabianists' challenge to the divine authority of the *Qur'an* first in Calcutta and then at a meeting at the Kings Hall in London (Burke 2016: 114, *Guardian*, 13 August 1938).

3 The fatwah was declared on the 14 February 1989, perhaps a mischievous Valentine's Day card, initially perceived as a bit of Khomeini theatrics ten years after the Iranian hostage drama, which in turn had its part to play in the US change of president – enter Ronald Reagan, former film actor: grim chuckle. Khomeini had been voted *Time Magazine* Man of the Year in 1979.

4 The Rajiv Gandhi government banned import of the book in 1988 after author Kushwant Singh advised Penguin India that a local edition 'might offend the religious sensibilities of Muslims' (Mitta 2012). Vaz was a long-serving Labour MP and may or may not be the basis of characters in Kureishi's novels.

5 Thirty-seven Alevi poets, artists and supporters died in a hotel fire in Turkey after a mob attacked the presumed location of Rushdie's Turkish publisher. Also a large number of persons died in protests against the book, though these are harder to document: for example, six in Pakistan on 12 February 1989 and twelve shot by police at a protest in Bombay on 25 January 1989 (Amir Hussein in Campo 2009: 595).

6 A chronology prepared by *Index on Censorship* in 2008 names Syed Shahabuddin as the instigator of the first campaigns against the book in India in mid-September 1988, while Faiyazuddin Ahmad of the Islamic Foundation of Leicester is credited with contacting British Muslim Organisations in October of 1988, and soon after the Islamic Conference Organisation (ICO) in Saudi Arabia (Index on Censorship 2008: 144).

7 There are immense problems with the terms here, but it is useful to keep them difficult. I favour the uncomfortable and slightly awkward neologism 'Br-Asian' (Kaur and Kalra 1996) used in *Dis-Orienting Rhythms* (Sharma et al. 1996) and *A Postcolonial People* (Ali et al. 2006). I don't use it in this particular chapter because the commentary is about the projection of allegedly 'not-quite' Britishness, and the 'it' and the 'ish' is erased in Br-Asian (though of course on purpose). As already noted, I refer to Global South Asia and Global South Asian, and do so as a problematically wide specificity that could include any and all the geographic and diasporic spaces of Afghanistan, Pakistan, India, Bangladesh, Nepal, Sri Lanka and the diasporized South Asians in Mauritius, Guyana, Britain, United States, Canada, Fiji, Malaysia, Japan Brazil and so on, discussed as 'Br-Asian' in the aforementioned volumes. Consider also there are many other Asias: East, South East, Austral- and Middle. For further discussion, see Spivak (2008).

8 For the Br-Asian section of Global South Asian film and television studies I am keen on Kureishi, the pre-*Bhaji* work of Gurinder Chadha – who also has made some surprisingly snarky assertions about Kureishi's introspection being a consequence of his British-Asian 'mix' – the excellent *Wild West* (1992, dir. Attwood), written by Harwant Bains, and critiques like that of *East Is East* by Sharma in his book *Multicultural Encounters* (2006). The primer on this cinema is still in draft form but will surely include Madhava Prasad's insightful comments on the 'a little bit desperate to say the least' influence of Baz Luhrmann's Bollywood-inspired flick *Moulin Rouge!* (2001). Madhava Prasad is correct to comment that such films and their reception 'should be located in a larger trend of commodification of film styles in a postmodern world where a new logic of commodification is in operation' (2008: 48). Yet the influence of Luhrmann's film on the subsequent Bollywoodization of Western Cinema – meaning the return of the musical – can also be stressed.

9 *Injustice* deals with the stories of families and friends fighting for justice in the cases of police custody deaths in the United Kingdom. A report on this film, and the controversy surrounding its screening, can be found in Imogen Bunting's 2003 article, 'Rationality, Legitimacy and the "Folk Devils" of May'.)

10 Hobson-Jobson was, or is, the dictionary of Anglo-English colonial slang and colloquial loan words, like umbrella, thug, pajama, bungalow, and other pukka formulations.

11 I found Harveen Sachdeva Mann's essay too late for it to influence this chapter in its original form, which was mostly written in 2012, revised 2014, but her comments are a confirmation – with much well-observed detail, for example noticing the developer forcing through the evictions of the squatter troupe's caravans is Alice's son – 'A pivotal scene in Sammy and Rosie Get Laid, three quarters of the way through the film, is the horizontal, triple split screen shot of the three couples – Sammy and Anna, Rosie and Danny, and Rafi and Alice – having sex' (2014: 491). Useful also for this chapter would have been Mann's documentation of the link between *Sammy and Rosie* and *Satanic Verses*: 'In this the screenplay anticipates by little more than a year the end of Salman Rushdie's *The Satanic Verses*, in which the Indian Gibreel Farishta proposes a "metamorphosis of London into a tropical city"' (2014: 492). Also too late to comment on Mann's noticing of the musical score, but my earlier footnote did try to put some specificity on the Asian sounds – as opposed to Wagnerian ones – when I noted in passing that although it is not necessarily Kureishi's 'Rafi' that is named on the album *Rafi's Revenge* (2006), Asian Dub Foundation also talk about the old 'we are here because you were there' slogan of anti-racist, anti-imperialist politics. A slogan not simply something to chant at a demonstration. A demonstration is nothing if it is merely a masquerade drama festival or carnival.

12 Comment by Spivak in discussion of this text with the author in a 1995 workshop at Keele University.

13 The street protests in the north of England during the summer of 2001 were not unanticipated, and in some quarters were quite a conflagration. That mosque leaders and families subsequently 'shopped' wayward sons to the police was problematic enough, but that the lag between these events and the court cases for these youth meant that 11 September 2001 became a back-story and the sentences handed down for minor misdemeanours and first offences were unconscionably severe. This was replicated again with the 2010 London student protests and more severely in the 2011 London 'riots' aka 'uprising'.

3 The Electronic Palanquin

The initial ideas for this chapter were first presented as a provocation at the 2004 workshop on television at the Films Studies Department of Jadavpur University, Kolkata. It has been rewritten substantially in 2011 and 2015, with thanks to Abhijit Roy, Moinak Biswas and Atticus Che Narain.

1 The link between Bombay, the East India Company and film for me is made all the more interesting by the place of Wadia's wife, Mary Evans, who hailed from Australia and featured first as a stuntwoman and then heroine in a number of films as 'Fearless Nadia' and on marriage to Homi became Nadia Wadia. Thomas describes her film roles in appropriately flamboyant terms: 'a swashbuckling princess in disguise, she roamed the countryside on horseback sporting hot pants, big bosom and bare white thighs and, when she wasn't swinging from chandeliers, kicking or whipping men, she was righting wrongs with her bare fists and an imperious scowl' (2014: 92). 'Righting wrongs' is of course the title of an important Spivak essay (2008), but here the gender of the usual do-gooder is reversed; it is not the white man saving brown women from brown men, and yet. Homi Wadia's brother, also a filmmaker, later teamed up with M. N. Roy, an important early Indian Communist fighter, and founder of the University of the Toiling Masses in Tashkent, who had returned to India by the 1930s.

2 Renamed the Aurora Cinema Company in 1911, it was initially based at 41 Kashi Mitter Ghat St Bagbazar, now Kashi Mitra Ghat St off Strand Rd, north of Beniatola Ghat. The company at first screened films with the help of Hiralal Sen and Anadinath Bose at village melas, at zamindar's houses and in the city in North Calcutta. This is evidenced through documents meticulously photographed and shown in the film as stills, possibly in homage to style of Mrinal Sen. Sen's friend Ghatak also 'started his film career as a documentary filmmaker of Aurora Film Corporation. His two documentary films for the state of Bihar were 1) *Ghar Ghar mein Bijli* (Electricity in every house) and 2) *Adivasi o ka Jiban Katha* (The Life of tribal people in Bihar). Then Aurora distributed his first feature film *Ajantrik*' (Anjan Bose, personal communication). Researched both in Europe and in the Aurora and other archives in India, significant and rich details are shown of the early film houses of Calcutta, while also offering footage of Rabindranath Tagore reciting a Bengali nationalist poem, of Subhas Chandra Bose calling for unity of the progressive and anti-imperialist forces, and of the funerals of both Chitaranjan Das and of Gandhi. A claim is made that Aurora's feature length film *Ratnakar* (1921, dir. Roy) was the first Bengali language feature film and made before *Bilet Ferot* (1921, dir. Lahiri) although under pressure from Madan company, *Ratnakar* was only screened first at the Rasa Theatre in Bhawanipore in 1921.

3 I once included a footnote in an article suggesting root and branch transformation of anthropology. Soon made uncomfortable in that department, I moved to cultural studies, but since I had at one point planned to include the article as a chapter in this book, I at least bring forward the footnote here unchanged. Hic Salta. 'A test to gauge the elimination of racism from British Anthropology might be to ask this hypothetical and fantasy question: What if, in just one department anywhere in the system, or a newly formed department, exactly no Anglo-Saxon, white, anthropologists were involved in any way with the teaching of the discipline, yet all the tasks of teaching anthropology were performed by fully accredited and qualified British Anthropologists, i.e., by black or Asian British anthropologists? Can such a scenario be imagined and would this department still be considered to teach 'British' Social Anthropology? Would it be considered a British department? People will dismiss this as impossible, impracticable, and unworkable – they might say there is not the staff, no new departments are planned, it would be a ghetto, it would cause 'imbalances', separatism, etc. But the abstract absurdity of even suggesting a black Anthropology Department indicates that white supremacy prevails as normalcy, as a never challenged standard and essential core. Race is the criteria for ensuring a 'proper' representation among the teaching staff – which is to say, race is used as criteria for exclusion of at least one possibility – an all black, all British department – and at best a tolerant tokenistic mix might be approved. Why would it be so unimaginable to appoint ten black Britons to one anthropology department in Britain? For those who think critically about knowledge and politics, the impossibility of a Black Anthropology means only that the entire system, disciplinary forms and protocols, appointments, teaching programs and curricula, must be done away with – anything less maintains an unexamined white supremacy that will never relinquish its presumptuous right to rule' (Hutnyk 2005b: 359–360).

4 Biren Das Sharma's commentary on dress codes, facial hair and turbans in colonial India, their part in subjugation, authority and hierarchy, and the history of Delhi's Durbar's – 1877, 1903, 1911 – should not be hidden away in the last paper of the second edition of *Journal of the Moving Image* (2001: 144), especially given the dramatic narration of the Gaekwad of Baroda's allegedly unintended 'disloyal', 'misconduct' and insult to the colonial power of 2011 (2001: 144).

5 Here I am again building on the work of a group of scholars who have, over more than twenty years, interrogated the representation of Global South Asians as exotic, trendy, in fashion, at a time that coincides with increasing racism, attack and murder – the first of these texts was *Dis-Orienting Rhythms: The Politics of the New Asian Dance Music* (edited by Sharma, Hutnyk and Sharma 1996; see also: Kalra and Hutnyk 1998, Sharma and Housee 1999, Kaur and Hutnyk 1999, Kalra 2000, Hutnyk 2000, Kaur 2003, Kalra, Kaur and Hutnyk 2005 , Ali, Kalra and Sayyid 2006, Kaur and Sinha 2005, Sharma 2006, Kalra , Kaur 2013, Hutnyk 2014a.

6 Documentaries about Nepal most often focus upon trekking and the Sherpas, or the trafficking of Nepalese girls for the sex trade in Mumbai, with obligatory section on the girl-god of Kathmandu. For text on the Sherpas, see Fisher (1990). Also see Campbell (1997) for discussion of the Tamang peoples.

7 A decade and a half after this, Dixit was in exile and his brother had been jailed, with both in difficulty facing questions about property and assets. *Himal's* access to donor funding was frozen by the current government.

8 I have attempted a biographical essay on these figures in a text mentioned in a previous footnote, which starts: 'All through the commentary on politics and diaspora in Britain there seems to have by and large been a tendency for critics to ignore left wing political activity among South Asian settlers. This in itself is a part of a double repetition; a two-ply silencing of agency for an agency that poses no threat. Comics not communists. The lustrous career of South Asian communists active in the UK is however not to be romanticised and of course there were many more people not involved in class politics than can be registered in the annals of communist champions. But it is clear that the groundwork for many of the kinds of political positions taken for granted today were forged in adversity and struggle under scarlet flags. That this again means that not everyone is involved in left wing groups and causes today goes without saying, and again it should not need to be pointed out that an overly rosy view of the inheritance of South Asian politicals would be inappropriate and misguided (but all those slightly strange left wing uncles and aunties do have an influence). The point is that given the really existing conditions into which most South Asian youth are born in multi-racist Britain, and given the heritage to which they can, if they wish, lay claim, it should be no surprise that comprehension of the struggle is "imbibed as if with mother's milk", as one informant described it to me' (Hutnyk 2005b: 345).

9 Well, I thought this was a little joke until I discovered a US television station website page calling itself 'The Public Kitchen: Discover Himalayan Food with Michael Palin' (KCET 2015).

10 I am necessarily avoiding some significant audience studies of television here. As ever, I have learnt much from David Morley's sustained work from *The Nationwide Audience: Structure and Decoding* (1980) through to *Home Territories: Media, Mobility and Identity* (2002). In the latter book especially there is a discussion of television and distance, encompassing exposure of French government restrictions on North African immigrant viewing habits and anxieties about national integrity in the face of global media (Morley 2000: 103) through to the anxieties of shoppers purchasing exotic consumer products in purpose-built shopping malls (Morley 2000: 237). Though it is difficult to see how the celebration of border crossing, which is then rightly followed up by critiques of the erasure of 'ethnic' peoples at the very moment of cultural and gastronomic celebration, can also ignore the necessity of a concomitant political and economic readjustment in favour of the Global South and the necessary but difficult political mobilization it will take to get there. Morley's condemnation of any pandering to those who would prefer to stay home and 'cultivate new arts of reading existing travellers' tales' (2002: 235) might line Palin's project up while a redistributive politics must necessarily go along with 'talk' about the reconfigured nation.

11 Of course, let us not neglect the micro corners of the Global South Asian story cycle where, for those who have the interest, a series of reports from the participants and critical commentary is available in the theoretical journal of the Maoist International Movement, *MIM Theory*, available at: http://www.etext.org/Politics/MIM, and see also *A World to Win* at http://www.awtw.org for an alternate Maoist angle. Also, bless Arundhati Roy for *Walking with the Comrades* (2011).

12 Prometheus angers the titan Zeus by dividing a sacrificed bull unfavourably to the gods – meat for man, bones for the deity – and in response Zeus withholds fire for cooking from mankind. Prometheus goes to Olympus and steals some embers of fire, hiding them inside fennel, and gives them along with arts and science to humanity. In retaliation Zeus creates Pandora who has a box – television perhaps – that should not be opened lest all manner of problems escape, as they of course do. Bernard Stiegler has more on the Prometheus metaphor, see his book with Derrida (Derrida and Stiegler 2002).

4 The Hanging Channel: For Mohammad Afzal Guru

1 The ideas behind this chapter were first presented as the keynote of the Sacred Media Cow 'Indian Mass Media and the Politics of Change' conference at SOAS in October 2007, and appeared in the proceedings of that conference in due course. They were subsequently refined for the Shimla workshop, '50 Years of Indian Television: Contemporary Issues' held in July 2009 and benefited immensely from the discussion there and became a different version yet again as I rewrote for this book.

2 Abhijit Roy's PhD thesis from Jadavpur will appear as a book in the next year or so. It is a detailed piece of scholarship on how media render democracy and public opinion visible as constructed. Covering the range of media studies literature within India and beyond, it is a spirited and controlled critique of media/television studies' Euro-American biases. The text discusses broadcast regulatory frameworks, the popular telenovella format, newscasting, public opinion, participation and liveness. Flow, democracy, communicative architecture, trial media and cinematic influences progressively build up an argument about public participation, its consequences and significance.

3 It would no doubt be possible to say something here about the 2016 JNU demonstrations and arrests which only started with the 'pretext' of an Afzal Guru commemoration, but Afzal's 'case' was soon drowned out by more 'national' concerns and the celebrity status of the speechifying of Kanhaiya Kumar. Readers will already have joined the dots.

5 *Mela*

1 If male desire (*naagor* is male lover) and back and forth movement (*dola*) are resonant in the meaning of the Bangla word for Ferris wheel (*nagardola*, hat tip Abhijit Roy) then this film has an appropriate symbolic icon for a story so poignantly delaying gratification.

2 This is the theme of a future book and an initial effort to map the concerns is forthcoming in the chapter 'Marx Reading India Sources' in Niranjana Goswami's *Desiring India: Representations through British and French Eyes (1584–1857)* (Kolkata: Jadavpur University Press).

3 The film is also a 'remake' of sorts, and was originally going to be called *Calcutta 90* (Mukhopadhyay 2009: 200) as a follow-up to the documentary-like film about the violent death of a Naxalite in *Calcutta 71*. The latter film was plundered for the newsreel footage shown in *Mahaprithidi.*

4 This again raises the ongoing cultural importance of Pakistan for Bollywood, since it cannot be disregarded that the economic interests of distributors can trump the ideological agendas of governments. Despite banning films, border controls, restrictions and so forth, Bollywood and especially the music of Bollywood, owes much to Lahore and Karachi from its earliest years, and beyond. Certainly the name Shah Rukh Khan might not have the same resonance if, as noted by Gera Roy (2015: 1), so many families hailing from Peshawar or Faisalabad – for example those of Dilip Kumar, Raj Kapoor, Dev Anand, the Bachchans – had not entered the movies.

5 Teaching Marx's *Capital* every year, so far in seven different countries, in the first lecture I talk about all the prefaces, by Marx and Engels, all the introductions, commentaries and summarizing works by other readers of Marx, the interpretations and the rumours of Marx, the ideological weight, pro and con, that is always-already there in our heads before we can sit down to read Marx. We can never read him 'as new' – yet it is worth the try, each time – and it does seem like we get a new Marx every decade (see Hutnyk 2014b). Perhaps there is also something similar to be taken into account when thinking about all the guidebooks, films, anecdotes and rumours heard about Calcutta, now Kolkata, before ever visiting that place (Hutnyk 1996). A 'shared' perspective then, that was first expressed in Jameson's book *The Political Unconscious*, where he writes: 'texts come before us as the always-already-read; we apprehend them through sedimented layers of previous interpretations, or – if the text is brand-new – through the sedimented reading habits and categories developed by those inherited interpretive traditions' (1981: 9). The always-already describes Heidegger's idea in *Being and Time*, where Dasein 'is always already given over to a world', it is 'In-der-Welt-Sein' ([1927] 2006): ch. 5, §29) and I read this when writing *The Rumour of Calcutta* (1996). But it is also in Derrida ([1967] 1998: 215), which I came to of course through Spivak (Spivak intro to Derrida [1967] 1998: xvii).

6 I wrote this sentence on the day that Chris Bayly passed away (1945–2015) and in a strange and sad coincidence had been rereading his book on bazaars over the previous week (1983).

7 It is here that we might more readily be able to unpack Spivak's challenging style where she writes as if summarizing the core idea for a book on Global South Asia: 'If we as a group are in the grip of a dream of reparation by our culturalism, our negotiable nationalism can, through teaching and learning of rational transnational awareness, come to realise that in the current post-Soviet conjuncture, to work at the *différance* of capitalism and socialism in the heart of dominant capital may be more reparatory toward the places we left behind than the culturalism that feeds, financially or otherwise, the various fanaticisms that lodge in the fault line between nation and state opened by that very conjuncture' (2012: 187).

8 It is possible nevertheless to agree with Prashad that 'the only way for the transition to multipolar regionalism to occur is if the old elites are dethroned from political power by social movements that now take political power' (2012: 289).

6 Conclusions and Further Viewing

1 In 1970 Ghatak made a short for the West Bengal Government called *Amar Lenin*, translated *My Lenin*, making considerable effort to comply with the Board of Censors; it had been shown in the USSR but banned in India. I have not been able to find a copy, and would welcome word from anyone who has.

Filmography

10 Days in Kolkata (1984), [Film] Dir. Reinhard Hauff, Germany: Bioskop.
1971 (2011), [Documentary] Dir. Tanvir Mokammel, Bangladesh: Kino-Eye Films.
A Passage to India (1984), [Film] Dir. David Lean, UK/USA: EMI Films, Home Box Office.
Ajantrik (1958), [Film] Dir. Ritwik Ghatak, India: L.B. Films International.
Akash Kusum (1965), [Film] Dir. Mrinal Sen, India: Purbachal Film Promotions.
Ali Baba (1903), [Lost Film] Dir. Hiralal Sen.
Apocalypse Now (1979), [Film] Dir. Francis Ford Coppola, USA: Zoetrope Studios.
Aranyer Din Ratri (*Days and Nights in the Forest*) (1970), [Film] Dir. Satyajit Ray, India: Priya Films.
Aurora Bioscope (2017), [Documentary Film] Dir. Anjan Bose, India: Film Division, Ministry of Information and Broadcasting.
Baishey Shravana (1960), [Film] Dir. Mrinal Sen, India: Kollai.
Battle of Algiers (1966), [Film] Dir. Gillo Pontecorvo, Italy/Algeria: Igor Film, Casbah Films.
Battlestar Galactica (2004), [Series] David Eick Productions, USA: NBC Universal Television.
Begum Jaan (2017), [Film] Dir. Srijit Mukherji, India: Vishesh Films.
Bend It Like Beckham (2002), [Film] Dir. Gurinder Chadha, UK: Kintop Pictures.
Bhaji on the Beach (1993), [Film] Dir. Gurinder Chadha, UK: Channel Four Films.
Bhariya Mela (1966), [Film] Dir. Aslam Irani, Pakistan: Lovely Pictures.
Bhuvan Shome (1969), [Film] Dir. Mrinal Sen, India: Mrinal Sen Productions.
Bilet Firot (1921), [Film] Dir. N. C. Lahiri, India: Dhirendra Nath Ganguly.
Bombay (1995), [Film] Dir. Mani Ratnam, India: A.B.C.D. Jhamu Sughand Productions, Madras Talkies.
Born Free (2010), [Music Video] Dir. Romain Gavras, USA: MIA, XL Recordings.
Bride and Prejudice (2004), [Film] Dir. Gurinder Chadha, UK/USA/India: Pathé/UK Film Council/Kintop Pictures/Bend It Films.
Calcutta 71 (1971), [Film] Dir. Mrinal Sen, India: DS Pictures.
Chiranjeevulu (1956), [Film] Dir. Vedantam Raghavaiah, India: Vinoda Pictures.
Cinema Paradiso (1988), [Film] Dir. Giuseppe Tornatore, Italy/ France: Christaldifilm, Les Films Ariane, Rai Films.
Citizen Kane (1941), [Film], Dir. Orsen Welles, USA: Mercury Theatre.
City of Joy (1992), [Film] Dir. Roland Joffé, France/UK: Allied Filmmakers, Lightmotif.
Dil Se (1998), [Film] Dir. Mani Ratnam, India: India Talkies.
Dilwale Dulhania Le Jayenge (1995), [Film] Dir. Aditya Chopra, India: Yash Raj Films.
East is East (1999), [Film] Dir. Damien O'Donnell, UK: FilmFour, BBC.

Ek Din Achanak (1989), [Film] Dir. Mrinal Sen, India: National Film Development Corporation.
Ek Din Pratidin (1979), [Film] Dir. Mrinal Sen, India: Mrinal Sen Productions.
Exotic India (2000), [Film] Dir. Rebecca Graversen, UK: MA Visual Anthropology, Goldsmiths College.
Fire (1996), [Film] Dir. Deepa Mehta, Canada/India: Trial by Fire Media, Kaleidoscope Entertainment.
Four Lions (2010), [Film] Dir. Christopher Morris, UK/France: Film 4, Warp Films.
Four Weddings and a Funeral (1994), [Film] Dir. Mike Newell, UK: PolyGram Filmed Entertainment, Channel Four Films.
Full Metal Jacket (1987), [Film] Dir. Stanley Kubrick, UK/USA: Natant, Stanley Kubrick Productions, Warner Bros.
Gandhi, (1982), [Film] Dir. Richard Attenborough, UK/India/USA: Columbia Pictures.
Gandu (2010), [Film] Dir. Qaushik Mukherjee, India: Overdose Joint.
Good Morning Vietnam (1987), [Film] Dir. Levinson, USA: Touchstone Pictures.
Goodness Gracious Me (1998), [Series] BBC2, UK: BBC.
Guerrilla (2011), [Film] Dir. Nasiruddin Yousuff, Bangladesh: Impress Telefilm.
Heat and Dust (1983), [Film] Dir. James Ivory, London: Merchant Ivory.
Histoire(s) du cinema: Toutes les histories (1989), [Series] Dir. Jean Luc Godard, France: Canal +.
I'm British, But... (1990), [Film] Dir. Gurinder Chadha, UK: BFI, FilmFour.
Indian Summers (2015), [Series] Dir. Anand Tucker, Jamie Payne, and David Moore, UK: Channel 4.
Injustice (2001), [Documentary Film] Dir. Ken Fero and Tariq Mehmood, UK: Migrant Media.
In Which Annie Gives It Those Ones (1989), [Film] Dir. Pradip Krishen, India: Grapevine Media.
It Ain't Half Hot Mum (1974–1981), [Series] Dir. David Croft, UK: BBC.
Jewel in the Crown (1984), [Series] Dir. Christopher Morahan, Jim O'Brian, Ken Taylor, and Irene Shubik, UK: ITV Granada.
Jinnah (1998), [Film] Dir. Jamil Dehlavi, UK/Pakistan: Dehlavi Films, Petra Films, The Quaid Project.
Khalaghar (2006), [Film] Dir. Morshedul Islam, Bangladesh: Monom Chalachitra.
Komal Gandhar (1961), [Film] Dir. Ritwik Ghatak, India: Chitrakalpa.
Lagaan: Once Upon a Time in India (2001), [Film] Dir. Ashutosh Gowariker, India: Aamir Khan Productions.
Maa Tujhhe Salaam (2002), [Film] Dir. Tinnu Verma, India: Indian Movies.
Mahabharat (1988), [Series] Dir. Ravi Chopra, India: DD National.
Mahaprithibi (1991), [Film] Dir. Mrinal Sen, India: Government of India.
Mangal Pandey (2005), [Film] Dir. Ketan Mehta, India: Kaleidoscope Entertainment.
*M*A*S*H* (1970), [Film] Dir. Robert Altman, USA: Aspen productions.
Meghe Dhaka Tara (1960), [Film] Dir. Ritwik Ghatak, India: Chitrakalpa.
Mela (1948), [Film] Dir. S. U. Sunny, India: Wadia Films.
Mela (1971), [Film] Dir. Prakash Mehra, India: A.A. Nadiadwalia, A.G.Films.
Mela (1980), [Film] Dir. K. G. George, India: Visal Movies.
Mela (1986), [Film] Dir. Asakari, Hassan, Pakistan: Nadia Production.

Mela (2000), [Film] Dir. Dhiamesh Darshan, India: Venus Records and Tapes.
Mela (2010), [Film] Dir. Dhananjay Mondal, India: no details.
Mera Gaon Mera Desh (1971), [Film] Dir. Raj Khosia. India: Khosia Productions.
Mission Kashmir (2000), [Film] Dir. Vidhu Vinod Chopra, India: Destination Films.
Monsoon Wedding (2001), [Film] Dir. Mira Nair, India/USA/Italy/Germany/France/UK: IFC Productions, Mirabai Films.
Mother of 1084/Hazaar Chaurasi Ki Maa (1999), [Film] Dir. Govind Nihalani, India: Udbhav Productions.
Moulin Rouge! (2001), [Film] Dir. Baz Luhrmann, Australia/USA: Twentieth Century Fox, Bazmark Films.
My Beautiful Laundrette (1985), [Film] Dir. Stephen Frears, UK: Working Title Films.
My Name Is Khan (2010), [Film] Dir. Karan Johar, India: Dharma Films, Fox Searchlight Pictures.
Neel Akasher Niche, (1959), [Film] Dir. Mrinal Sen, India: Hemanta Bela Productions.
Ontorjatra (2006), [Film] Dir. Tareque Masud and Catherine Masud, Bangladesh: Audiovision Maasranga.
Pardes (1997), [Film] Dir. Subhash Ghai, India: Mukta Arts.
Partition, (2007), [Film] Dir. Vic Sarin, Canada: Partition Films, Astral Media, Khussro Films.
Pather Panchali (1955), [Film] Dir. Satyajit Ray, India: Government of West Bengal.
Phir Bhi Dil Hai Hindustani (2000), [Film] Dir. Mizra, India: Dreams Unlimited.
Pinjar (2003), [Film] Dir. Chandra Prakash Dwivedi, India: Lucky Star Entertainment.
Raja Harishchandra (1913), [Film] Dir. Dadahseheb Phalke, India: Phalke Films.
Rajkahini (2015), [Film] Dir. Srijit Mukherji, India: SVF Entertainment.
Ramayana (1987), [Series] Dir. Ramanand Sagar, India: Doordarshan.
Ramayana (2008), [Series] Dir. Anand Sagar, India: NDTV Imagine.
Ratnakar (1921), [Film] Dir. Roy, India: Aurora Cinema Company.
Roja (1992), [Film] Dir. Mani Ratnam, India: Madras Talkies, Hansa Pictures, Kavithalayaa Productions.
Sammy and Rosie Get Laid (1987), [Film] Dir. Stephen Frears, UK: Channel Four Films, Working Title Films.
Sholay (1975), [Film] Dir. Ramesh Sippy, India: United producers, Sippy Films, Sholay Media and Entertainment.
Shree 420 (1955), [Film] Dir. Raj Kapoor, India: R.K. Films Ltd.
Shyambol Chhaya (2004), [Film] Dir. Humayan Ahmed, Bangladesh: Impress Telefilm.
Stop Genocide (1971), [Film] Dir. Zahir Raihan, Bangladesh: Chalachitra.
Subarnarekha (1962), [Film] Dir. Ritwik Ghatak, India: Chitrakalpa.
Taboo (2017), [Series] Dir. Kristoffer Nyholm and Anders Engström, UK: BBC.
The 100 (2000), [Series] Dir. Jason Rothenberg, USA: Bonanza Productions.
The Best Exotic Marigold Hotel (2011), [Film] Dir. John Madden, UK/USA/UAE: Blueprint Pictures.
The Bitter Tea of General Yen (1933), [Film] Dir. Frank Capra, USA: Columbia Pictures Corporation.
The Buddha of Suburbia (1993), [Series] Dir. Roger Mitchell, UK: BBC.

The Day After Tomorrow (2004), [Film] Dir. Roland Emmerich, USA: Twentieth Century Fox.
The Guide (1965), [Film] Dir. Vijay Anand, India: Navketan Films.
The Hero: Love Story of a Spy, (2003), [Film] Dir. Anil Sharma, India: Time Movies.
The Japanese Wife (2010), [Film] Dir. Aparna Sen, India: Saregama Films.
The Kumars at Number 42 (2005), [Series] BBC2, UK: Hatrick Productions.
The Living Daylights (1987), [Film] Dir. John Glen, UK: Eon Productions.
The Namesake (2006), [Film] Dir. Mira Nair, USA/India: Mirabai Films, UTV Motion Pictures.
The Razor's Edge (1946), [Film] Dir. Edmund Golding, USA: Twentieth Century Fox.
The Razor's Edge (1984), [Film] Dir. John Byrum, USA/UK: Columbia Pictures Corporation.
The Thief of Baghdad (1924), [Film] Dir. Raoul Walsh.
The Year of Living Dangerously (1982), [Film] Dir. Peter Weir, Australia/USA: McElroy & McElroy, MGM.
Time Bomb 9/11 (2005), [Serial] Dir. Ketan Mehta, India: Zee TV.
True Lies (1994), [Film] Dir. James Cameron, USA: 20th Century Fox.
Viceroy's House (2017), [Film] Dir. Gurinder Chadha, UK/India/Sweden: Pathe International.
War and Peace (2002), [Film] Dir. Anand Patwardhan, India: Anand Patwardhan.
Wild West (1992), [Film] Dir. David Attwood, UK: British Screen productions, Channel Four Films.
Zakhm (1998), [Film] Dir. Mahesh Bhatt, India: Pooja Bhatt Productions, Vishesh Films.

Bibliography

Adorno, Theodor W. ([1963]1993) *Hegel: Three Studies*, Cambridge, MA: MIT Press.

Adorno, Theodor W. ([1970] 1997) *Aesthetic Theory*, Minneapolis, University of Minnesota Press.

Adorno, Theodor W. ([1978] 1999) *Sound Figures*, Stanford, CA: Stanford University Press (translated from the German, *Musikalische Schriften* 1–3, *Gesammelte Schriften*, vol. 16, 1978, Frankfurt: Suhrkamp Verlag).

Ahmad, Aijaz (1987) 'Jameson's Rhetoric of Otherness and the "National Allegory"', *Social Text*, 17(Autumn): 3–25.

Ahmad, Aijaz (1993) 'Fascism and National Culture: Reading Gramsci in the Days of Hindutva', *Social Scientist*, 3–4: 32–68.

Ahmad, Ali Nobil (2016) 'Explorations into Pakistani Cinema: Introduction' *Screen*, 57(4): 468–479.

Ali, Nasreen, Kalra, Virinder S., and Sayyid, Salman (2006) *A Postcolonial People: South Asians in Britain*, London: Hurst.

Amin, Samir (2005) 'China, Market Socialism, and U.S. Hegemony', *Review*, 28(3): 274–275.

Amin, Samir (2010) *Eurocentrism*, 2nd Edition, New York: Monthly Review Press.

Anon. (1948) 'Mela Should Be Re-censored', *Film India*, 12: 55–57.

Appadurai, Arjun (1996) *Modernity at Large: Cultural Dimensions of Globalisation*, Minneapolis: University of Minnesota Press.

Arrighi, Giovanni (2007) *Adam Smith in Beijing: Lineages of the Twenty-first Century*, London: Verso.

Bachelard, Gaston ([1938] 1987) *The Psychoanalysis of Fire*, London: Quartet Books.

Badiou, Alain ([2011] 2012) *The Rebirth of History: Times of Riots and Uprisings*, New York: Verso.

Báez, Fernando ([2004] 2008) *A Universal History of the Destruction of Books*, New York: Atlas & Co. Publishers.

Bald, Vivek (2007) '"Lost" in the City. Spaces and Stories of South Asian New York, 1917–1965', *South Asian Popular Culture*, 5(1): 59–76.

Bald, Vivek (2013) *Bengali Harlem and the Lost Histories of South Asian America*, Cambridge, MA: Harvard University Press. Balibar Étienne and Wallerstein, Immanuel (1991) *Race, Nation, Class: Ambiguous Identities*, London: Verso.

Banaji, Shakuntala (2006) *Reading Bollywood: The Young Audience and Hindi Films*, London: Palgrave Macmillan.

Bataille, Georges ([1957] 1985) *Literature and Evil*, London: Calder and Boyars.

Bayly, Christopher A. (1983) *Rulers, Townsmen and Bazaars. North Indian Society in the Age of British Expansion, 1780–1870*, Cambridge: Cambridge University Press.

Beller, Jonathan (2006) *The Cinematic Mode of Production: Attention Economy and the Society of the Spectacle*, New Haven, CT: University Press of New England.

Benjamin, Walter ([1940] 1968) *Illuminations*, trans. Hanna Arendt, New York: Schocken Books.

Bharucha, Rustom (1998) *In the Name of the Secular: Contemporary Cultural Activism in India*, New Delhi: Oxford University Press.

Bhatia, Arjun (2017) 'Partition Museum Project: creating a refuge for the memories of Partition', *South Asia @ LSE*, 10 Mar, http://blogs.lse.ac.uk/southasia/2017/03/10/partition-museum-project-creating-a-refuge-for-the-memories-of-partition/ [Accessed 24 January 2018].

Bhattacharyya, Gargi (2008) *Dangerous Brown Men: Exploiting Sex, Violence and Feminism in the War on Terror*, London: Zed Books.

Bhutto, Fatima (2017) 'Fatima Bhutto on Indian Partition film Viceroy's House: "I Watched This Servile Pantomime and Wept" ', *The Guardian*, 3 March, https://www.theguardian.com/film/2017/mar/03/fatima-bhutto-viceroys-house-watched-servile-pantomime-and-wept [Accessed 16 March 2017].

Biswas, Moinak (1999) 'Bengali Film Debates: The Literary Liaison Revisited', *Journal of the Moving Image*, 1: 1–13.

Biswas, Moinak (2000) 'The Couple and Their Spaces: Harano Sur as Melodrama Now', in Ravi Vasudevan (ed.), *Making Meaning in Indian Cinema*, New Delhi: Oxford University Press, pp. 122–142

Biswas, Moinak (2006) 'Early Films: The Novel and Other Horizons', in Moinak Biswas (ed.), *Apu and After: Revisiting Ray's Cinema*, Calcutta: Seagull, pp. 42–43.

Bradbury, Ray (1953) *Fahrenheit 451*, New York: Ballantine Books.

Bronte, Charlotte (1947) *Jane Eyre*, London: Smith, Elder and Co.

Buck-Morss, Susan (1979) *Origin of Negative Dialectics*, New York: Simon and Schuster.

Bunting, Imogen (2003) 'Rationality, Legitimacy and the "Folk Devils" of May', *Left Curve*, 27, http://www.leftcurve.org/LC27WebPages/ FolkDevils.html [Accessed 29 March 2014].

Burgin, Victor (2004) *The Remembered Film*, London: Reaktion Books.

Burke, Kenneth (2016) *On the Burning of Books*, London: Unicorn.

Butalia, Urvashi (2000) *The Other Side of Silence: Voices from the Partition of India*, Durham, NC: Duke University Press.

Callaghan, John (1993). *Rajani Palme Dutt: A Study in British Stalinism*, London: Lawrence & Wishart.

Campbell, B. (1997) 'The Heavy Loads of Tamang Identity', in David Gellner, Joanna Pfaff-Czarnecka and John Whelpton (eds), *Nationalism and Ethnicity in a Hindu Kingdom: The Politics of Culture in Contemporary Nepal*. Amsterdam: Harwood Academic.

Campo, Juan Eduardo (2009) *Encyclopedia of Islam*, New York: Facts on File Inc.

Caton, Steve (1999) *Lawrence of Arabia: A Film's Anthropology*, Berkeley: University of California Press.

Chadha, Gurinder (2017) 'My Film Has Been Wilfully Misrepresented as Anti-Muslim', *The Guardian,* 3 March, https://www.theguardian.com/film/filmblog/2017/mar/03/gurinder-chadha-defends-viceroys-house-film-fatima-bhutto [Accessed 16 March 2017].

Chakrabarty, Dipesh (2000) *Provincializing Europe: Postcolonial Thought and Historical Difference*, New Jersey: Princeton University Press.

Chakravorty, Sumita S. (1993) *Indian Popular Cinema 1947–1987*, Austin: University of Texas Press.

Chandan, Sukant (2015) 'Address' to 'Libya: NATO's Untold Story', Conference at the Committee Rooms, Houses of Parliament, London, 12 January.

Chen, Kuan-Ksing (2010) *Asia as Method: Toward Deimperialization*, Durham, NC: Duke University Press.

Chow, Rey (2002) *The Protestant Ethnic and the Spirit of Capitalism,* New York: Columbia University Press.

Chun, Allen (2012) 'The Americanization of Pop Culture in Asia?', *Inter-Asia Cultural Studies*, 13(4): 495–506.

Dadi, Iftikhar (2016) 'Lineages of Pakistan's "Urdu" Cinema: Mode, Mood and Genre in *Zehr-e Ishq/Poison of Love* (1958)', *Screen*, 57(4): 480–487.

Dalrymple, William (1998) *The Age of Kali: Indian Travels and Encounters*, New Delhi: Penguin.

Das Sharma, Biren (2001) 'Beyond the Visual: The Case of the Delhi Durbar Films', *Journal of the Moving Image*, 2: 140–149.

De, Aparajita, ed. (2016) *South Asian Racialization and Belonging after 9/11: Masks of Threat*, Lanham, MD: Lexington Books.

Delueze, Gilles (1995) *Negotiations*, New York: Columbia University Press.

Deleuze, Gilles and Guattari, Felix ([1972] 1983) *Anti-Oedipus: Capitalism and Schizophrenia*, trans. R. Hurley et al., Minneapolis: University of Minneapolis Press.

Derrida, Jacques ([1967] 1998) *Of Grammatology*, trans. Gayatri Chakravorty Spivak, Baltimore, MD: Johns Hopkins University Press.

Derrida, Jacques, and Stiegler, Bernard (2002) *Echographies of Television: Filmed Interviews*, trans. Jennifer Bajorek, Cambridge: Polity Press.

Desai, Jigna (2004) *Beyond Bollywood: The Cultural Politics of South Asian Diasporic Film*, New York: Routledge.

Desai, Jigna and Dudrah, Rajinder, eds (2008) *The Bollywood Reader*, Maidenhead, UK: Open University Press.

Deshishku, Stacia and Yellin, Jessica (2011) 'Even More Details on the OBL Photos', CNN, 3 May, http://whitehouse.blogs.cnn.com/2011/05/03/even-more-on-the-photos/ [Accessed 13 June 2015].

Desiblitz (2017) 'In Conversation with Gurinder Chadha', *Desiblitz,* https://youtu.be/xTO7vQiXHDg [Accessed 4 April 2017].

Dirks, Nicholas B. (2001) 'The Home and the Nation: Consuming Culture and Politics in "Roja"', in Rachel Dwyer and Chris Pinney (eds), *Pleasure and the Nation: Politics and Consumption of Public Culture in India*, New Delhi: Oxford University Press, pp. 161–185.

Dissanayake, Wimal (2003) 'Rethinking Indian Popular Cinema: Towards Newer Frames of Understanding Cinema', in Anthony R. Guneratne and Wimal Dissanayake (eds), *Rethinking 'Third Cinema'*, London: Routledge, pp. 202–225.

Douglas, Mick, ed. (2005) *Tramjatra: Imagining Melbourne and Kolkata by Tramways*, Melbourne: RMIT University Press.

Du Bois, W. E. B. ([1935] 1992) *Black Reconstruction in America 1860–1880*, New York: Free Press.

Dudrah, Rajinder (2002) 'Vilayati Bollywood: Popular Hindi Cinema-going and Diasporic South Asian Identity in Birmingham (UK)', *Javnost*, 9(1): 19–36.

Dudrah, Rajinder (2006) *Bollywood: Sociology Goes to the Movies*, London: Sage.

Dudrah, Rajinder (2012) *Bollywood Travels: Culture, Diaspora and Border Crossings in Popular Hindi Cinema*, London: Routledge.

Dudrah, Rajinder, Mader, Elke and Fuchs, Bernhard (2015) *SRK and Global Bollywod*, Oxford: Oxford University Press.

Dutta, Anshuman G. (2010) 'My Hanging Won't Create Any Problem: Afzal Guru', mid-day.com, http://www.mid-day.com/articles/my-hanging-wont-create-any-problem-afzal-guru/83341 [Accessed 28 May 2010].

Dwyer, Rachel (2006) *Filming the Gods: Religion and Indian Cinema*, Abingdon: Taylor and Francis.

Dwyer, Rachel and J. Pinto, eds (2011) *Beyond the Boundaries of Bollywood: The Many Forms of Hindi Cinema*, New Delhi: Oxford University Press.

Dye, Dale and Dale, Julia (2011) 'An American Celebration', Interview with *The Associated Press*, reported in *The Guardian*, 24 June, http://www.guardian.co.uk/world/feedarticle/9710347 [Accessed 24 July 2011].

Dye, Dale and Dale, Julia (2011a) *Code Word: Geronimo*, San Diego: IDW.

Eco, Umberto (1983) *The Name of the Rose*, London: Harcourt.

EDL, (2011) 'EDL Please Don't Burn the Koran', *EDL*, http://englishdefenceleague.org/content.php?311-EDL-Leadership-Please-Don-t-Burn-The-Koran [Accessed 9 December 2011]

Fabian, Johannes (1990) *Time and the Other: How Anthropology Makes Its Object* New York: Columbia University Press.

Fisher, James F. (1990) *Sherpas: Reflections on Change in Himalayan Nepal*. Berkeley: University of California Press.

Fried, Richard (1990) *Nightmare in Red: The McCarthy Era in Perspective*, Oxford: Oxford University Press.

Gaur, Meenu (2011) 'The *Roja* Debate and the Limits of Secular Nationalism', in Somnath Batabayal, Agnad Chowdhry, Meenu Gaur and Matti Pohjonen (eds), *Indian Mass Media and the Politics of Change*, London: Routledge, pp. 68–91.

Geelani, Syed Bismilah (2006) *Manufacturing Terrorism: Kashmiri Encounters with Media and the Law*, New Delhi: Promila & Co.

Gehlawat, Ajay (2010) *Reframing Bollywood: Themes of Popular Hindi Cinema*, New Delhi: Sage.

Gehlawat, Ajay (2015) *Twenty-First Century Bollywood*, London: Routledge.

George, Rosemary Marangoly (2013) *Indian English and the Fiction of National Literature*, Cambridge: Cambridge University Press.

Gera Roy, Anjali (2010) '"Global Flows": Ethnographic Studies of the Hindi Movie in Africa', *Journal of African Literature and Culture*, 7(8): 33–48.

Gera Roy, Anjali, ed. (2012) *The Magic of Bollywood: At Home and Abroad*, New Delhi: Sage.

Gera Roy, Anjali (2015) *Cinema of Enchantment: Perso-Arabic Genealogies of the Hindi Masala Film*, Hyderabad: Orient Blackswan.

Gilroy, Paul (1993) *The Black Atlantic: Modernity and Double Consciousness*, London: Verso.

Gilroy, Paul (2004) *After Empire: Melancholia or Convivial Culture?* Abingdon: Routledge.

Gokulsing, K. Moti and Dissanayake, Wimal (2013) *Routledge Handbook of Indian Cinemas*, London: Routledge.

Gooptu, Sharmistha (2010) *Bengali Cinema: An Other Nation*, London: Routledge.

Gopal, Sangita and Morrti, Sujata, eds (2008) *Global Bollywood: Travels in Hindi Song and Dance*, Minneapolis: Minnesota University Press.

Gopinath, Gayatri (2005) *Impossible Desires: Queer Diasporas and South Asian Public Cultures*, Durham, NC: Duke University Press.

Guha, Ranajit (1968) *Elementary Aspects of Peasant Insurgency in Colonial India*, Oxford: Oxford University Press.

Guneratne, Anthony R. (2003) 'Introduction: Rethinking Third Cinema', in Anthony R. Guneratne and Wimal Dissanayake (eds), *Rethinking 'Third Cinema'*, London: Routledge, pp. 1–28.

Gupta, Nilanjana (1998) *Switching Channels: Ideologies of Television in India*, New Delhi: Oxford University Press.

Habib, Irfan (1997) 'Civil Disobedience 1930–31', *Social Scientist*, 25(9/10): 43–66.

Hammond, Andrew (2007) 'The Hybrid State: Hanif Kureishi and Thatcher's Britain', in Joel Kuortti and Jopi Nyman (eds), *Reconstructing Hybridity: Post-Colonial Studies in Transition*, Amsterdam: Editions Rodopi, pp. 221–240.

Hannerz, Ulf (2004) *Foreign News*, Chicago: Chicago University Press.

Hansen, Kathryn (2003) 'Languages on Stage: Linguistic Pluralism in Community Formation in the Nineteenth Century Parsi Theatre', *Modern Asian Studies*, 37(2): 381–405.

Hassam, Andrew (2009) 'Melbourne, Indian Popular Cinema and the Marketing of "An Enviable Cosmopolitan Lifestyle" ', *South Asian Film and Media*, 1(1): 45–64.

Heidegger, Martin ([1927] 2006) *Sein und Zeit*, Tübingen: Max Niemeyer Verlag.

Hersch, Seymour M. (2015) 'The Killing of Osama bin Laden' *London Review of Books*, 37(10): 3–12.

Himal Association (2010) 'Kathmandu International Mountain Film Festival', http://www.himalassociation.org/ [Accessed June 10, 2010].

Hitchins, Christopher (2007) *God Is Not Great: The Case Against Religion*, London: Atlantic Books.

Hoek, Lotte (2014) *Cut-Pieces: Celluloid Obscenity and Popular Cinema in Bangladesh*, New York: Columbia University Press.

Hood, John (2015) *The Bleeding Lotus: Notions of Nation in Bangladeshi Cinema* New Delhi: Palimpsest.

Horkheimer, Max und Adorno, Theodor (1947) *Dialektik der Aufklärung*, Amsterdam: Querido.

Hoskins, Andrew (2004) *Televising War: From Vietnam to Iraq*, London: Continuum.

Hutnyk, John (1996) *The Rumour of Calcutta: Tourism, Charity and the Poverty of Representation*, London: Zed Books.

Hutnyk, John (2000) *Critique of Exotica: Music, Politics and the Culture Industry* London: Pluto Press.

Hutnyk, John (2005a) 'Hybridity', *Ethnic and Racial Studies,* 29(1): 79–102.

Hutnyk, John (2005b) 'The Dialectic of Here and There: Anthropology 'at Home' and British Asian Communism', *Social Identities,* 11(4): 345–361

Hutnyk, John (2014a) *Pantomime Terror: Music and Politics,* London: Zero Books.

Hutnyk, John (2014b) 'Citizen Marx/Kane', in Ewa Mazierska and Lars Kristensen (eds), *Marx at the Movies: Revisiting History, Theory and Practice,* London: Palgrave Macmillan.

Index on Censorship (2008) 'The Satanic Verses: A Chronology', *Index on Censorship,* 37(4): 144–147.

Jameson, Fredric (1981) *The Political Unconscious: Narrative as a Socially Symbolic Act,* New York: Cornell University Press.

Jameson, Fredric (1986) 'Third World Literature in the Era of Multinational Capitalism', *Social Text,* 15: 65–88.

John, Mary E. and Niranjana, Tejaswini (1999) 'Mirror Politics: Fire, Hindutva and Indian Culture', *Economic and Political Weekly* (6–13 March): 581–584.

John, Mary E. and Niranjana, Tejaswini (2000) 'The Controversy over "Fire": A Select Dossier (Part I), Introduction', *Inter-Asia Cultural Studies,* 1(2): 371–374.

Joshi, Priya (2010) 'Bollylite in America', *South Asian Popular Culture,* 8(3): 245–259.

Judicial Watch (2012) 'Judicial Watch, inc., Plaintiff, v. Civil Action No. 11–890 (JEB) U.S. Department of Defence, et al., Defendants', United Stated Judicial Court for the District of Columbia, Civil Action No. 11–890 (JEB), http://legaltimes.typepad.com/files/obl.pdf [Accessed 13 June 2015].

Kabir, Ananya Jahanara (2003) 'Allegories of Alienation and Politics of Bargaining: Minority Subjectivities in Mani Ratnam's *Dil Se*', *South Asian Popular Culture,* 1(2): 141–159.

Kalra, Virinder (2000) *From Textile Mills to Taxi Ranks: Experiences of Migration, Labour and Social Change,* Aldershot: Ashgate.

Kalra, Virinder (2014) *Sacred and Secular Musics: A Postcolonial Approach,* London: Bloomsbury Academic.

Kalra, Virinder and Hutnyk, John (1998) 'Brimful of Agitation, Authenticity and Appropriation: Madonna's "Asian Kool"', *Postcolonial Studies,* 1(3): 339–356.

Kalra, Virinder, Kaur, Raminder and Hutnyk, John (2005) *Diaspora and Hybridity,* London: Sage.

Kamath, Sudhish (2010) 'A Telling Tale', *The Hindu,* 30 December, http://www.thehindu.com/todays-paper/tp-features/tp-metroplus/A-telling-tale/article12718028.ece [Accessed 27 March 2017].

Karki, Arjun and Seddon, David, eds (2003) *The People's War in Nepal: Left Perspective.* Delhi: Adroit Publishers.

Katyal, Anjum (2015) *Badal Sircar: Towards a Theatre of Conscience,* New Delhi: Sage.

Kaur, Raminder (2003) *Performative Politics and the Cultures of Hinduism: Public Uses of Religion in Western India,* New Delhi: Permanent Black.

Kaur, Raminder (2013) *Atomic Mumbai: Living with the Radiance of a Thousand Suns.* India: Routledge.

Kaur, Raminder and Sinha, Ajay J. (2005) *Bollyworld: Popular Cinema Through a Transnational Lens,* New Delhi: Sage.

Kaur, Raminder and Hutnyk, John (1999) *Travel Worlds: Journeys in Contemporary Cultural Politics.* London Zed Books.

Kaur, Raminder and Kalra, Virinder S. (1996) 'New Paths for South Asian Identity and Musical Creativity', in Sanjay Sharma, John Hutnyk and Ash Sharma (eds), *Dis-Orienting Rhythms: The Politics of the New Asian Dance Music* London: Zed Books, pp. 217–231.

Kaur, Raminder, Virinder, Karla and Hutnyk, John (2005) *Diaspora and Hybridity*, London: Sage.

Kaur, Ravinder and Hansen, Thomas Blom (2015) 'Aesthetics of Arrival: Spectacle, Capital, Novelty in Post-Reform India', *Identities: Global Studies in Culture and Power*, 23(3): 265–275

Kay, Jeanne (2016) '*Suis-je Chalie*. A Postcolonial Genealogy of the French Response to the Charlie Hebdo Attack', in Šarūnas Paunksnis (ed.), *Dislocating Modernity: Deterritorialization, Difference and Resistance*, Leiden: Koninklidjke Brill, pp. 29–45.

KCET (2015) 'The Public Kitchen: Discover Himalayan Food with Michael Palin', *KCET* 28 Los Angeles, http://www.kcet.org/living/food/the-public-kitchen/discover-himalayan-food-with-michael-palin.html[Accessed 14 June 2015].

Kesavan, Mukul (1994) 'Urdu, Awadh and the Tawaif: The Islamicate Roots of Hindi Cinema', in Zoya Hasan (ed.), *Forging Identities: Gender, Communities and the State*, New Delhi: Kali.

Khanna, Parag (2004) 'Bollystan – The Global India', *Globalist*, 3 December.

Kishore, Vikrant, Sarwal, Amit and Patra, Parichay (2014) *Bollywood and Its Other(s): Towards New Configurations*, Basingstoke: Palgrave Macmillan.

Kumar, Amitava (2000) *Passport Photos*, Berkeley: University of California Press.

Kumar, Amitava (2002) *Bombay London New York*, New York: Routledge.

Kumar, Shanti (2013) 'Unimaginable Communities: Television, Globalization and National Identities in Postcolonial India', in Ravi Sundaram (ed.), *No Limits: Media Studies from India*, New Delhi: Oxford University Press, pp. 256–276.

Kureishi, Hanif (1988) *Sammy and Rosie Get Laid*, London: Faber and Faber.

Kureishi, Hanif (1990) *The Buddha of Suburbia*, London: Faber and Faber.

Kureishi, Hanif (1995) *The Black Album*, London: Faber and Faber.

Kureishi, Hanif (1996) *My Beautiful Laundrette and Other Writings*, London: Faber and Faber.

Kureishi, Hanif (2005) *The Word and the Bomb*, London: Faber and Faber.

Kureishi, Hanif (2008) *Something to Tell You*, London: Faber and Faber.

Kureishi, Hanif (2014) *The Last Word*, London: Faber and Faber.

Lallmahomed-Aumeerally, Naseem (2014) 'A Reading of Bollywood Cinema as a Site of Melancholia for Indo-Mauritian Muslim Female Youth', *South Asian Popular Culture*, 12S(3): 149–162.

Lahiri, Jhumpa (2003) *The Namesake*, Boston: Houghton Mifflin Harcourt.

Lapierre, Dominique and Collins, Larry (1975) *Freedom at Midnight*, New Delhi: Vikas.

Lapierre, Dominique and Collins, Larry (1983) *Mountbatten and the Partition of India*, New Delhi: Tarang Publishers, Vikas.

Laprise, John Paul (2009) 'White House Computer Adoption and Information Policy', PhD Thesis, Northwestern University, Evanston, Illinois.

Lévi-Strauss, Claude ([1955]1974) *Tristes Tropiques*, New York: Athenaeum.

Lutgendorf, Philip (2006) 'Is There an Indian Way of Filmmaking?', *International Journal of Hindu Studies*, 10(3): 227–256.

Madhava Prasad, M. (1998) *Ideology of the Hindi Film: A Historical Construction* Delhi: Oxford University Press.

Madhava Prasad, M. (1999) 'On the Political Significance of Cinema in South India', *Journal of the Moving Image*, 1: 37–52.

Madhava Prasad, M. (2000) 'Signs of Ideological Re-form in Two Recent Films: Towards Real Subsumption', in Ravi Vasudevan (ed.), *Making Meaning in Indian Cinema*, New Delhi: Oxford University Press, pp. 145–167.

Madhava Prasad, M. (2008) 'Surviving Bollywood', in Anandam P. Kavoori and Aswin Punathambekar (eds), *Global Bollywood*, New York: University Press, pp. 41–51.

Madhava Prasad, M. (2014a) *Cine-Politics: Film Stars and Political Existence in South India*, Delhi: Orient Blackswan.

Madhava Prasad, M. (2014b) *Thoughts of Freedom: India's 20th Century*, Lecture Course, National Chiao Tung University, Taiwan.

Madhava Prasad, M. (2014c) 'Emergence: Stuart Hall and Cultural Studies Across the World', *InterAsia Cultural Studies*, 15(2): 191–3.

Maharghya (2015) 'Comment on *Baishey Shravana*', Indiacine.ma archive, Jadavpur University Media Lab, Kolkata: Jadavpur University.

Maira, Sunaina (2000) 'Henna and Hip Hop: The Politics of Cultural Production and the Work of Cultural Studies', *Journal of Asian American Studies*, 3(3): 329–369.

Maira, Sunaina (2008) 'B-Boys and Bass Girls: Sex, Style and Mobility in American Youth Culture', in Ajay Nair and Murali Balaji (eds), *Desi Rap: Hip-Hop and South Asian America*, Lanham, MD: Lexington Books, pp. 41–70.

Majumdar, Neepa (2007), 'Film Fragments, Documentary History, and Colonial Indian Cinema', *The Canadian Journal of Film Studies* 16(1): 63–79.

Malik, Kenan (2008) 'The Rushdie Affair Twenty Years On', *Battle of Ideas Conference*, http://www.kenanmalik.com/lectures/rushdie_boi.html [Accessed 6 June 2009].

Malik, Kenan (2009) *From Fatwa to Jihad: The Rushdie Affair and Its Legacy*, London: Atlantic Books.

Mankekar, Purnima (1993) 'Television Tales and a Woman's Rage: A Nationalist Recasting of Draupadi's "Dis-robing"', *Public Culture*, 5(3): 469–492.

Mankekar, Purnima (1999) *Screening Culture, Viewing Politics: An Ethnography of Television, Womanhood, and Nation in Postcolonial India*, Durham, NC: Duke University Press.

Mankekar, Purnima (2015) *Unsettling India: Affect, Temporality, Transnationality*, Durham, NC: Duke University Press

Mann, Harveen Sachdeva (2014) 'Cultural Representations of London in British-Asian and Bollywood Films', *Quartely Review of Film and Video*, 31(5): 486–507.

Marantidou, Virginia (2014) 'Revisiting China's "String of Pearls" Strategy', *Issues and Insights*, 14(7), https://www.csis.org/analysis/issues-insights-vol-14-no-7-revisiting-chinas-string-pearls-strategy [Accessed 24 June 2014].

Marx, Karl (1843) 'Marx to Ruge', *Deutsch-Französische Jahrbücher*, https://www.marxists.org/archive/marx/works/1843/letters/43_09.htm [Accessed 5 April 2010].

Marx, Karl ([1852] 2000) 'The 18th Brumaire of Louis Boneparte', in Mark Cowling and James Martin (eds), *Marx's Eighteenth Brumàire: (Post) Modern Interpretations*, London: Pluto Press, pp. 19–109

Marx, Karl ([1867] 1967) *Capital, A Critique of Political Economy: Volume one*, Harmondsworth: Penguin.

Mathew, Biju (2005) *Taxi! Cabs and Capitalism in New York City*, New York: New Press.

Mathur, Shubh (2013) 'The Perfect Enemy: Maps, Laws and Sacrifice in the Making of Borders', *Critique of Anthropology*, 34(4): 429–446.

Maugham, W. Somerset (1944) *The Razor's Edge*, London: Heinemann.

Mazzarella, William (2013) *Censorium: Cinema and the Open Edge of Mass Publicity*, Durham, NC: Duke University Press.

McQuire, Scott (1986) 'It Is Believed There Was Once a Time When Television didn't Exist', *Melbourne Journal of Politics*, 17: 18–34.

McQuire, Scott (2008) *The Media City: Media, Architecture and Urban Space*, London: Sage.

Mehta, Nalin (2008) *Indian Television: How Satellite News Channels Have Changed the Way We Think and Act*, New Delhi: Harper Collins.

Mendes, Anna Cristina (2007) 'The Empire on Film: Recasting India from the Raj Revival to Lagaan', in J. Carlos Viana Ferreira and Theresa de Ataída Malafaia (eds), *A Tangled Web: Ideas, Images, Symbols*, Lisbon: Colibro, pp. 65–80.

Mercer, Kobena (1990) 'Black Art and the Burden of Representation', *Third Text*, 4(10): 61–78.

Mikuriya, Junko Theresa (2017) *A History of Light: The Idea of Photography*, London: Bloomsbury Academic.

Miller, Don (2015) 'Charlie Hebdo', Unpublished Manuscript. Available from author.

Miller, Toby, ed. (2002) *Television Studies*, London: BFI Publishing.

Mishra, Vijay (2002) *Bollywood Cinema: Temples of Desire*, New York: Routledge.

Mitra, Royona (2015) *Akram Khan: Dancing New Interculturalism*, London: Palgrave Macmillan.

Mitta, Manoj (2012) *Reading 'Satanic Verses' Legal* in The Times of India, 25 January, http://timesofindia.indiatimes.com/india/Reading-Satanic-Verses-legal/articleshow/11622048.cms?referral=PM [Accessed 23 June 2015].

Moore-Gilbert, Bart (2001) *Hanif Kureishi (Contemporary World Writers)* Manchester: Manchester University Press.

Moore, Rachel (2000) *Savage Theory: Cinema as Modern Magic*, Durham, NC: Duke University Press.

Morcom, Anna (2009) 'Bollywood, Tibet, and the Spatial and Temporal Dimensions of Global Modernity', *South Asian Film and Media*, 1(1): 145–172.

Morcom, Anna (2011) 'Film Songs and the Cultural Synergies of Bollywood and South Asia', in Rachel Dwyer and J. Pinto (eds), *Beyond the Boundaries of Bollywood: The Many Forms of Hindi Cinema*, New Delhi: Oxford University Press, pp.156–187.

Morley, David (1980) *The Nationwide Audience: Structure and Decoding*, London: BFI Publishing.

Morley, David (2002) *Home Territories: Media, Mobility and Identity*, London: Routledge.

Moten, Fred (2003) *Into the Break: The Aesthetics of the Black Radical Tradition*, Minneapolis: University of Minnesota Press.

Mukhopadhyay, Bhaskar (2012) *The Rumour of Globalization: Desecrating the Global from Vernacular Margins*, London: Hurst & Company.

Mukhopadhyay, Dipankar (2009) *Mrinal Sen: Sixty Years in Search of Cinema*, Delhi: Harper Collins Publishers.

Nandy, Ashis (1983) *The Intimate Enemy: Loss and Recovery of Self Under Colonialism*, Oxford: Oxford University Press.

Nandy, Ashis (1990) 'The Discrete Charm of Indian Terrorism', *Journal of Commonwealth and Comparative Politics*, March: 25–43.

Nandy, Ashis (1998) *The Secret Politics of Our Desires. Innocence, Culpability, and Indian Popular Cinema*, London: Zed Books.

Nandy, Ashis ([1989] 2000) The *Tao of Cricket: On Games of Destiny and the Destiny of Games*, New Delhi: Oxford University Press.

Narain, Atticus Che (2008) '"Bring Back the Old Films, Our Culture is in Disrepute": Hindi Film and the Construction of Femininity in Guyana', in Anandam P. Kavoori and Aswin Punathambekar (eds), *Global Bollywood*, New York: New York University Press, pp. 164–179.

Nawaz, Aki (2009) 'What Happened to the Book Burners?', *BBC News Magazine*, 13 February, http://news.bbc.co.uk/2/hi/uk_news/magazine/7883308.stm [Accessed 23 June 2015].

Negt, Oskar (1978) 'Mass Media: Tools of Domination and Instruments of Liberation: Aspects of the Frankfurt School's Communication Analysis', *New German Critique*, 14 (March): 61–80.

Nilanjana Roy, S. (2014) 'Speaking Volumes: Where They Burn Books', *Business Standard* , 13 October, https://nilanjanaroy.com/2014/12/21/speaking-volumes-where-they-burn-books/ [Accessed 20 March 2017].

Niranjana, Tejaswini (1994) 'Interrogating Whose Nation? Tourists and Terrorists in "Roja" ', *Economic and Political Weekly*, 15 January, pp. 79–82.

Niranjana, Tejaswini (1999) 'Questions for Feminist Film Studies', *Journal of the Moving Image*, 1: 91–101.

Niranjana, Tejaswini (2006) *Mobilizing India: Women, Music, and Migration between India and Trinidad*, Durham, NC: Duke University Press.

Orwell, George (1944) 'As I Please', *The Tribune*, 4 February, http://alexpeak.com/twr/hiwbtw/ [Accessed 16 March 2017].

Pandey, Gyanendra (2002) *Remembering Partition: Violence, Nationalism and History in India*, Cambridge: Cambridge University Press.

Pao, Basin (2004) *Inside Himalaya*, London: Weidenfeld and Nicolson.

Papastergiadis, Nikos (1993) *Modernity in Exile: The Stranger in John Berger's Writing*, Manchester: Manchester University Press.

Papastergiadis, Nikos (2011) 'South Remembers: What Is the South?', *South As a State of Mind*, http://southasastateofmind.com/south-remembers-south-nikos-papastergiadis/ [Accessed 22 March 2017].

Pape, Stefan (2017) 'Huma Qureshi and Manish Dayal on Viceroy's House', *HeyUGuys*, http://www.heyuguys.com/huma-qureshi-manish-dayal-interview-viceroys-house/ [Accessed 16 March 2017].

Parmar, Chandrika (2003) 'State Violence and Migration: Indo-Pak Partition Community and Violence', Presentation at 'Sustainable Development: Bridging the Research/Policy Gaps in Southern Contexts', Islamabad.

Patel, Aakar (2015) 'The Jawaharlal Nehru today's India does not know', *Quartz India*, https://qz.com/463197/the-jawaharlal-nehru-todays-india-does-not-know/ [Accessed 25 January 2018].

Phipps, Peter (1999) 'Tourists, Terrorists, Death and Value', in Raminder Kaur and John Hutnyk (eds), *Travel Worlds: Journeys in Contemporary Cultural Politics*, London: Zed Books, pp.74–93.

Pinney, Chris (2001) 'Piercing the Skin of the Idol', in Christopher Pinney and Rosie Thomas (eds), *Beyond Aesthetics: Art and the Technologies of Enchantment*, Oxford: Berg, pp.157–180.

Pinney, Christopher (1995) 'Hindi Cinema and Half-forgotten Dialects: An Interview with Ashis Nandy', *Visual Anthropology Review*, 11(2): 7–16.

Prashad, Vijay (2000) *The Karma of Brown Folk*, Minneapolis: University of Minnesota Press.

Prashad, Vijay (2001) *Everybody Was Kung Fu Fighting: Afro-Asian Connections and the Myth of Cultural Purity*, Boston: Beacon Press.

Prashad, Vijay (2007) *The Darker Nations: A People's History of the Third World*, New York: New Press.

Prashad, Vijay (2008) 'My Hip-Hop Life', in Ajay Nairand Murali Belaji (eds), *Desi Rap: Hip-Hop and South Asian America*, Lanham, MD: Lexington Books, pp. 3–16.

Prashad, Vijay (2012) *Uncle Swami: South Asians in America Today*, Minneapolis: University of Minnesota Press.

Press Association (2012) 'David Cameron: School Sports Targets Result in "Indian Dance" Classes', *The Guardian*, 10 August, http://www.theguardian.com/education/2012/aug/10/david-cameron-school-sports-targets [Accessed 12 December 2012].

Pritchett, Frances (1985) *Marvellous Encounters: Folk Romance in Hindi and Urdu*, New Delhi: Manohar.

PTI (2006) 'Nepal Maoists Bomb TV Station', *India As It Happens*, http://www.rediff.com/news/2005/feb/26nepal.htm [Accessed 12 June 2016].

Punathambekar, Aswin (2013) *From Bombay to Bollywood: The Making of a Global Media Industry*, New York: New York University Press.

Ragavendra, M. K. (2012) 'Mainstream Hindi Cinema and Brand Bollywood: The Transformation of a Cultural Artefact', in Anjali Gera Roy (ed.), *The Magic of Bollywood: At Home and Abroad*, Delhi: Sage, pp. 27–41.

Rai, Amit (2006) '"Every Citizen Is a Cop Without the Uniform": The Populist Outsider in Bollywood's New Angry Young Man Genre', *Interventions: International Journal of Postcolonial Studies*, 8(2): 193–227.

Rai, Amit, S. (2009) *Untimely Bollywood: Globalization and India's New Media Assemblage*, Durham, NC: Duke University Press.

Rajadhyaksha, Ashish (1999) '"You Can See Without Looking": Reconsidering Freedom of Expression in the Cinema', *Journal of the Moving Image*, 1: 68–90.

Rajadhyaksha, Ashish (2004) 'Rethinking the State after Bollywood', *Journal of the Moving Image* 3: 47–90.

Rajadhyaksha, Ashish (2008) 'The "Bollywoodization" of the Indian Cinema: Cultural Nationalism in a Global Arena', in Anandam P. Kavoori and Aswin Punathambekar (eds), *Global Bollywood*, New York: New York University Press, pp. 17–40.

Rajadhyaksha, Ashish (2009) *India in the Time of Celluloid: From Bollywood to the Emergency*, Delhi: Tulika Books.

Rajadhyaksha, Ashish (2012a) 'Teaching Film Theory?', *Journal of the Moving Image*, 11: 40–65.
Rajadhyaksha, Ashish (2012b) 'Roundtable', *Journal of the Moving Image*, 11: 94–98.
Rajadhyaksha, Ashish (2012c) 'A Theory of Cinema that Can Account for Indian Cinema', in Lucia Nagib, Chris Perriam and Rajinder Dudrah (eds), *Theorizing World Cinema*, London: I.B. Tauris, pp. 45–59.
Rajadhyaksha, Ashish (2013) 'Plenary Talk', [Talk] Inter Asian Cultural Studies Graduate Conference, Singapore, July 1–2.
Rajadhyaksha, Ashish (2015) 'Indian New Wave Cinema Revisited', [Talk] 'Indian New Wave Cinema Workshop, Chicago: University of Chicago.
Rajagopal, Arvind (2001) *Politics After Television: Hindu Nationalism and the Reshaping of the Public in India*, Cambridge: Cambridge University Press.
Rajagopal, Arvind (2009) 'Comment Response to John Hutnyk, 6 August, Violence, Publicity, and Sovereignty', *The Immanent Frame*, 29 November 2008, http://blogs.ssrc.org/tif/2008/12/15/violence-publicity-and-sovereignty/ [Accessed 16 June 2015].
Rajagopal, Arvind (2015) 'Media and Utopia', *Comparative Studies of South Asia, Africa and the Middle-East*, 35(1): 1–7.
Ramamurthy, Anandi (2013) *Black Star: Britain's Asian Youth Movements*, London: Pluto Press.
Rao, Ursula (2005) 'News from the Field', in Ursula Rao and John Hutnyk (eds), *Celebrating Transgression*, London: Berghahn Books.
Robins, Neil (2012) *The Corporation That Changed the World: How the East India Company Shaped the Modern Multinational*, London: Pluto Press.
Ronell, Avital (2010) *Fighting Theory*, Urbana: University of Illinois Press.
Roy, Abhijit (2012) 'A Reflexive Turn in Television Studies: Conjecture from South Asia', *South Asian History and Culture*, 3(4): 636–648.
Roy, Abhijit (2014) 'Television, Consumerism and the Emergent Forms of Publicness in Post-liberalization India', PhD dissertation, Jadavpur University.
Roy, Arundhati (1997) *The God of Small Things*, London: Fourth Estate.
Roy, Arundhati, ed. (2006) *The December 13 Reader: The Strange Case of the Attack on the Indian Parliament*, Delhi: Penguin Books.
Roy, Arundhati (2011) *Walking with the Comrades*, New Delhi: Penguin.
Rushdie, Salman (1981) *Midnight's Children*, London: Jonathan Cape.
Rushdie, Salman (1983) *Shame*, London: Jonathan Capa.
Rushdie, Salman (1988) *The Satanic Verses*, London: Random House.
Rushdie, Salman (2009) 'A Response', in Daniel Herwitz and Ashutosh Varshney (eds), *Midnight's Diaspora*, Delhi: Penguin, pp. 136–140.
Rushdie, Salman (2012a) 'Christopher Hitchens' *Vanity Fair*, February, http://salmanrushdie1.tumblr.com/post/15369634397/christopher-hitchens-vanity-fair-feb-2012 [Accessed 12 December 2012].
Rushdie, Salman (2012b) *Joseph Anton*, London: Random House.
Said, Edward (1978) *Orientalism*, New York: Vintage.
Sarila, Narendra Singh (2005) *The Shadow of the Great Game*, New Delhi: Harper Collins.
Sarkar, Sumit (2002) *Beyond Nationalist Frames: Relocating Postmodernism, Hindutva, History*, Delhi: Permanent Black.

Schivelbusch, Wolfgang (1988) *Disenchanted Night*, Berkeley: University of California Press.

Sharma, Sanjay (2006) *Multicultural Encounters*, London: Palgrave Macmillan.

Sharma, Sanjay (2009) 'Teaching British South Asian Cinema – Towards a "Materialist" Reading Practice', *South Asian Popular Culture*, 7(1): 21–35

Sharma, Sanjay and Housee, Shirin (1999) '"Too Black Too Strong"? Anti-racism and the making of South Asian political identities in Britain', in Tim Jordon and Adam Lent (eds), *Storming the Millennium: The Politics of Change*, London: Lawrence and Wishart.

Sharma, Sanjay and Sharma, Ash (2003) 'White Paranoia: Orientalism in the Age of Empire', *Fashion Theory*, 7(3–4): 1–18.

Sharma, Sanjay, Hutnyk, John and Sharma, Ash, eds (1996) *Dis-Orienting Rhythms: The Politics of the New Asian Dance Music*, London: Zed Books.

Sharma, Shalini and Kalra, Virinder S. (2013) 'State of Subversion: Aspects of Radical Politics in Twentieth Century Punjab', *South Asian History and Culture*, 4(4): 435–442.

Sloterdijk, Peter ([1983] 1987) *Critique of Cynical Reason*, Minneapolis: University of Minnesota Press.

Solanis, Fernando and Getino, Octavio (1969) 'Toward a Third Cinema', *Tricontinental*, 14: 107–132.

Sontag, Susan (1977) *On Photography*, New York: Farrar, Straus and Giroux.

Spigel, Lynn and Jan Olsson, eds (2004) *Television after TV: Essays on a Medium in Transition*, Durham, NC: Duke University Press.

Spivak, Gayatri Chakravorty (1988) 'Can the Subaltern Speak', in Cary Nelson and Lawrence Grossberg (eds), *Marxism and the Interpretation of Culture*, Illinois: University of Illinois Press, pp. 271–313.

Spivak, Gayatri Chakravorty (1993) *Outside in the Teaching Machine*, New York and London: Routledge.

Spivak, Gayatri Chakravorty (1996) *The Spivak Reader: Selected Works of Gayatri Chakravorty Spivak*, ed. Donna Landry and Gerald MacLean, London: Routledge.

Spivak, Gayatri Chakravorty (1999) *Critique of Postcolonial Reason: Towards a History of the Vanishing Present*, Cambridge, MA: Harvard University Press.

Spivak, Gayatri Chakravorty (2000) 'Discussion: An Afterword on the New Subaltern', in Partha Chateterjee and Pradeep Jeganathan (eds), *Subaltern Studies X1: Community, Gender and Violence*, New York: Columbia University Press.

Spivak, Gayatri Chakravorty (2003) *Death of a Discipline*, New York: Columbia University Press.

Spivak, Gayatri Chakravorty (2004) 'Terror: A Speech after 9–11' *Boundary*, 2, (Summer): 80–111.

Spivak, Gayatri Chakravorty (2008) *Other Asias*, Oxford: Blackwell Publishing.

Spivak, Gayatri Chakravorty (2012) *An Aesthetic Education in the Era of Globalization*, Cambridge, MA: Harvard University Press.

Srinivas, S. V. (2012) 'Teaching India/Asian Cinema', *Journal of the Moving Image*, 11: 78–84.

Stiegler, Bernard ([1996] 2009) *Technics and Time, 2: Disorientation*, trans. Stephen Barker, Stanford: Stanford University Press.

Sundaram, Ravi (2009) *Pirate Modernity: Media Urbanism in Delhi*, Delhi: Routledge.

Sundaram, Ravi (2011a) 'Postcolonial Media after the Informal' YouTube lecture, 31 October, Melbourne, https://youtu.be/CUtLDhyl2tQ [Accessed 19 December 2016].

Sundaram, Ravi (2011b) 'The Post-Colonial New Media Event: The Secret and the Transparent in Contemporary India', Presentation to the Moving Images Research Group, 28 April, Seattle: University of Washington.

Sundaram, Ravi, ed. (2013) *No Limits: Media Studies from India*, New Delhi: Oxford University Press.

Tagg, John (1984) 'The Burden of Representation: Photography and the Growth of the State', *Ten*, 8(14):10–12.

Tagg, John (1988) *The Burden of Representation: Essays and Photographies and Histories*, Amherst: University of Massachusetts Press.

Tanbunan, Shuri Mariasah Gierry (2012) 'Bollywood Film Culture in Indonesia's Mediascapes', in Gera Roy (ed.), *The Magic of Bollywood: At Home and Abroad*, New Delhi: Sage.

Thomas, Rosie (2014) *Bombay before Bollywood: film city fantasies*, New Delhi: India Orient BlackSwan.

Thorpe, Vanessa (2017) 'A British Film with a Punjabi Heart: Director's Personal Take on Partition' *The Guardian*, 16 January, https://www.theguardian.com/film/2017/jan/16/viceroys-house-tells-bloody-truth-of-partition [Accessed 16 March 2017].

Thussu, Daya Kishan (2007) *News as Entertainment: The Rise of Global Infotainment*, London: Sage.

Thussu, Daya Kishan (2014) 'Internationalising Media Studies', *World Financial Review*, July 28, http://www.worldfinancialreview.com/?p=2573 [Accessed 18 October 2014].

Ulmer, Gregory (1989) *Teletheory: Grammatology in the Age of Video*, New York: Routledge.

Vasudevan, Ravi (2001) 'Nationhood, Authenticity and Realism in Indian Cinema: The Double-Take of Modernism in the Work of Satyajit Ray', *Journal of the Moving Image*, 2: 52–76.

Vasudevan, Ravi (2010) *The Melodramatic Public: Film Form and Spectatorship in Indian Cinema*, New Delhi: Permanent Black.

Vasudevan, Ravi (2011) 'The Meanings of "Bollywood"', in Rachel Dwyer and Jerry Pinto (eds), *Beyond the Boundaries of Bollywood: The Many Forms of Hindi Cinema*, New Delhi: Oxford University Press.

Vasudevan, Ravi (2013) 'Notes on Contermporary Film Experience: "Bollywood", Genre Diversity, and Video Circuits', in Ravi Sundaram (ed.), *No Limits: Media Studies from India*, New Delhi: Oxford University Press, pp. 199–223.

Ventura, Marco (2014) *From Your Gods to Our Gods: A History of Religion in Indian, South African, and British Courts*, Eugene, OR: Cascade Books.

Verma, Rahul (2015) '*Sholay*: The *Star Wars* of Bollywood?', *BBC Culture*, 14 August, http://www.bbc.com/culture/story/20150813-sholay-the-star-wars-of-bollywood [Accessed 31 March 2017].

Vidal, Gore (2000) *The Golden Age*, London: Little Brown.

Virdi, Jyotika (2003) *The Cinematic ImagiNation: Indian Popular Films as Social History*, Delhi: Permanent Black.
Visvanathan, Shiv and Sethi, Harsh (1989) 'Bhopal: A Report from the Future', *Lokayan Bulletin*, 7(3): 47–67.
Vitali, Valentine (2010) *Hindi Action Cinema: Industries, Narratives, Bodies*, Bloomington: Indiana University Press.
Wadsworth, Marc (1998) *Comrade Sak: Shapurji Saklatvala MP, A Political Biography*, Leeds: Peepal Tree Press.
Wayne, Mike (2003) *Marxism and Media Studies*, London: Pluto Press.
Wells, H. G. (1922) *A Short History of the World*, New York: Macmillan.
Widmark, Anders (2011) 'Voices at the Borders, Prose on the Margins: Exploring the Contemporary Pashto Short Story in a Context of War and Crisis', PhD dissertation, Uppsala University, Sweden.
Williams, Raymond (1975) *Television: Technology and Cultural Form*, New York: Schocken.
Wilson, Amrit (2006) *Finding a Voice: Asian Women in Britain*, London: Vintage.
Zimmerman, Patricia R. (2000) *States of Emergency: Documentaries, Wars, Democracies*, Minneapolis: University of Minnesota Press.

Index